Zeppelin: Rigid Airships

LZ130 Graf Zeppelin II, *built at Friedrichshafen and first flown in September 1938, was the last of the line. Rigid airships were vast structures, LZ130 having a length of 245m (nearly 804ft) and a maximum diameter of 41.2m (135ft). By comparison, the liner* Queen Elizabeth 2 *had a length of 963ft and a breadth of 105ft*
(Lufthansa)

Zeppelin: Rigid Airships 1893–1940

Peter W Brooks

PUTNAM

ALSO BY PETER W BROOKS

The Modern Airliner
The World's Airliners
Cierva Autogiros

In memory of Patricia Stroud,
who, with her husband John, contributed so much
to the Putnam series of aviation books
over the past thirty years

© Peter Brooks 1992

First published in Great Britain in 1992 by
Putnam Aeronautical Books, an imprint of
Conway Maritime Press Ltd,
101 Fleet Street
London EC4Y 1DE

British Library Cataloguing-in Publication Data
Brooks, Peter
Zeppelin: rigid airships 1893–1940
1.   Airships, history
I.   Title
629.1332409

ISBN 0 85177 845 3

Designed by Tony Garrett
Typeset by Inforum Typesetting, Portsmouth
Printed and bound in Great Britain by
Butler & Tanner Ltd, Frome

Contents

Count Ferdinand von Zeppelin.

Introduction and Acknowledgments

Zeppelin: Rigid Airships 1893–1940 sets out to cover as concisely as possible the entire story of those mammoth aircraft which had such an irresistible appeal to both the general public and the technically-informed. Moreover, for a brief period in the 1920s and 1930s the rigid airships looked as if they might assume the long-distance transport task which has since been so decisively taken over by today's large jet aircraft. Every one of the 163 rigid airships, of about fifty different types built, is described in detail. Included are the Schwarz, Upson and Slate metalclads, not because they are necessarily regarded as rigids but because they form part of the rigid airship story.

A compact and self-contained episode in the history of human transport, this is a story that spans almost exactly forty years,

providing an unusual 'case history' in the evolution of technology. Rigids are close relations of pressure-airships which have outlived them and are still to be seen in small numbers, but they do not have more in common than working principles. Pressure-airships have never been able to offer a serious method of transport although they are in limited use as flying platforms for sightseeing, radar antennae, sky signs and television cameras. The rigid, on the other hand, most certainly tried to be – and for a while looked as though it might become – a great new system of transport.

It failed for two reasons which were to some extent related. First, to carry a useful load, both as payload and as fuel for range, the rigid had to be impractically large; indeed, the larger the better. Second, it failed because

of its timing. Its development depended on a light prime-mover so that, although in all other respects it might have been invented 120 years earlier, it did not appear until the internal combustion engine made aeroplanes and helicopters practical propositions.

Excessive size was the fundamental weakness of the rigid. Even a test vehicle had to be enormous and therefore wildly expensive as well as extraordinarily difficult to handle, particularly until its pilot could gain experience. This could only be done the hard way, incurring even more expense. One can argue with some justification that there would have been no rigid airships but for that extraordinary man, Count Ferdinand von Zeppelin. He was imaginative enough, sufficiently eccentric and obstinate, with enough wealth

Zeppelin progress. The photograph (left) of the Schaffhausen Falls on the Rhine was taken on 4 August, 1908, from LZ4 during the attempt to achieve a 24hr flight. The LZ4 reached Mannheim but had to make two forced landings and was wrecked at Echterdingen near Stuttgart on the following day. By contrast the LZ127 Graf Zeppelin (right) successfully operated scheduled services between Germany and Brazil, only being withdrawn after the loss of the Hindenburg.

and influence and with the necessary talents and skills at hand, just to get the thing started. Even he succeeded by only the narrowest of margins; the rigid was nearly killed in infancy half a dozen times.

The rigid airships's large size was due to inescapable physical laws; not so much because hydrogen, and later helium, were not light enough (even a gas of zero weight would have been only marginally better) but because the atmosphere itself is not dense enough. Large size and associated high costs meant that only relatively small numbers were built with a resulting slow accumulation of manufacturing and operating experience. Large size also meant that the airship was slow, clumsy and extremely vulnerable to mistakes in handling. With hindsight, it is now possible to see that it had no chance of keeping pace, in almost any sense, with its far more competitive contemporaries, the aeroplane and the helicopter. Finally, its large size was a dreadful handicap in the unruly, unpredictable and often hostile element in which all aircraft have to live. On or near the ground, the large airship was always a handful, and if one were looking for a single reason for its failure, that would be it.

This book attempts to provide a short, non-technical history of the rigid airship. The emphasis is on its development and on some of the factors which influenced that development, rather than on the operational history of airships which has been most effectively covered in many previous books on the subject. Because its story cannot be properly understood without a background of some general history of lighter-than-air flight, and particularly of the pressure-airship, this has been summarised in the first four chapters, which conclude with a passing reference to more recent LTA activities.

Those interested in the operational history of the airship, a fascinating story in itself, are referred to the bibliography. Particularly recommended are Dr Douglas H Robinson's *The Zeppelin in Combat, 1912–18* and *Giants in the Sky*, Capt J A Sinclair's *Airships in Peace and War*, Capt Ernst Lehmann's *Zeppelin* and Sir Peter Masefield's *To Ride the Storm*. Available quantitive and statistical information on rigid airship operations is summarised in the Appendices.

A few words of explanation are required about weights and measures, and money values quoted. The former are in metric units because the story of the rigid airship is largely one of technical development in – or initiated by – Germany. Metric units are therefore the natural language of the subject; pound/feet units are given in brackets where appropriate and first in the case of British and US ships. The 'hp' abbreviation is used loosely for the metric 'pferde starke' or 'cheval vapeur'. For computation of 'typical gross lift' (*See* Note 1A). So far as money values are concerned, these are always quoted first in contemporary values in the appropriate local currency with a computed, approximate present-day equivalent in sterling, in brackets. (*See* Note 1)

The author would like to acknowledge much help in his historical research over the years from Peter Amesbury, Wing Cdr R S Booth, Air Marshal Sir Victor Goddard, Thurstan James, Alec Lumsden, Sir Peter Masefield, Arnold Nayler, John Provan, David Sawers, Beverley Shenstone, Peter Spiro, John Stroud, Maj P L Teed, J E Temple, Lord Ventry, Sir Barnes Wallis, Alex Wright and H B Wyn Evans. Although they, and a few others, have provided previously unpublished information, my main sources have been published ones, chiefly those listed in the bibliography. David Sawers and the late Thurstan James were good enough to read the orig-

inal manuscript and made a number of helpful suggestions. I am also most grateful to my wife who has done all the typing, much of the editing and is largely responsible for the index.

The line drawings are the work of Carl G Ahremark. John Provan has been extremely helpful in providing information for the drawings. The illustrations on pages 178–181 are reproduced by kind permission of *Flight International*. The photographic illustrations are from many sources acknowledged in the captions. Others are from the author's collection or from slides which belonged to the late Maj J E M Pritchard, the first man to arrive in the United States by air from another continent. (Few of the millions who have flown there since can have heard his name.) Maj Pritchard, who was one of Britain's airship pioneers, parachuted from R34 to supervise her mooring when she reached New York at the end of her historic first transatlantic flight in 1919. He lost his life two years later in the R38 disaster. Dugald Cameron and the Glasgow School of Art were most helpful in copying photographs.

PETER W BROOKS

The Pightle, Ford
June 1992

Origins of Buoyant Flight

Long before recorded history man must have thought about flying. His earliest ideas on the subject were probably in imitation of the birds, but smoke and clouds must also have suggested the idea of floating in the air, rather like a boat on water.

There have been suggestions that the flying dove of Archytas of Tarentum (fifth century BC) may have been some kind of model balloon. However, there is no evidence to support this; indeed, the basic idea of static lift was not adumbrated until about 250BC in the Law of Archimedes: 'When a gas less dense than air is enclosed in a container, the difference between the density of the gas and the air it replaces causes the container to rise.'

Perhaps the first lighter-than-air device contrived by man was the Chinese flying egg trick, which is said to date from 200–100BC. In this trick, an empty egg-shell is made to rise briefly into the air by strongly heating it. A similar trick, but using steam instead of hot air in the egg-shell, is said to have been popular in Europe during the Seventeenth Century.

Miniature hot-air balloons, in the form of large globular paper lanterns, are believed to have been popular during the Han Dynasty in China, the period from 202BC to AD220. The fact that similar model balloons, made of oiled paper spread over a light bamboo framework, were apparently flown in Cambodia and in northwest Yunnan Province (Western China) until recent times suggests that the technique of manufacturing such toys may, indeed, have been handed down over something like two thousand years.

The only other report of balloons in ancient China is a curious reference in a book by Amadée de Bast to a letter dated 5 September, 1694, from a missionary in Canton, Father Vassou. This refers to a balloon

The start of the first aerial voyage by human beings. Pilâtre de Rozier and the Marquis d'Arlandes leaving the Bois de Boulogne in a Montgolfier hot-air balloon on 21 November, 1783. They flew for 25 minutes and travelled about 5 1/2 miles.
(James Gardner for Shell)

which ascended at the coronation of the Emperor Fo-Kian in Peking in 1306. The ascent is said to have been recorded in authentic official documents.

There are undatable traditions of hot-air flight ('travelling on smoke') in the Carolina Islands in the Pacific and by the Mysians in Asia Minor. According to some authorities, small hot-air balloons were used for military signalling in Europe from the ninth century. This view is based on several surviving illustrations of tethered, dragon-like objects flown by soldiers but these were more likely to have been kites or windsocks than balloons.

In the thirteenth century, Albertus Magnus seems to have speculated about a bladder's tendency to rise when filled with warm air. In the fifteenth century, a manuscript attributed to Giovanni de Fontana, refers to unsuccessful experiments with a full-size parachute-like device which may have been a crude form of hot-air balloon.

Leonardo da Vinci (1452–1519), who illustrated and discussed most potential methods of flying in his notebooks, left no record of interest in the lighter-than-air principle. However, according to his contemporary, the art historian Giorgio Vasari, in 1513 Leonardo inflated with his mouth wafer-thin wax figures which floated in the air. At about the same time J C Scaliger (1484–1558) suggested the use of goldbeaters' skin in *volant automata* but whether he had in mind some kind of balloon is not clear. In 1658 a Jesuit, Gaspar Schott (1608–66) wrote of the possibility of aerostatic flight and, in 1670, another Jesuit, Francesco de Lana-Terzi (1631–87), proposed a 'flying ship' to be supported in the air by four evacuated copper or iron globes. Evacuation of the globes had been suggested by the invention of the vacuum pump by Otto von Guericke twenty years earlier. This is the first known design of a lighter-than-air flying machine, although the idea of evacuating lightweight and, therefore, inevitably thin-skinned metal globes was obviously impractical. A third Jesuit, Honorat Fabri (d.1688), made experiments to reproduce Archytas's 'dove' which may have been based on aerostatic principles.

It is probable that the model flying machine successfully demonstrated before King John V of Portugal on 8 August, 1709, by a Brazilian priest, Fr Bartholomeu Laurenço de Gusmão (1685–1724), was a small hot-air balloon. The details which survive are sketchy; nor is there any adequate record of the possibly related experiments of Gusman, also in Lisbon, in 1736. There is an unconfirmed story that de Gusmão attempted a manned hot-air balloon flight and there is a tradition that N Kriakoutnoi

Model in the Science Museum of Francesco Lana's aerial carriage of 1670. Air was to have been exhausted from the copper spheres and the sail was for steering.
(Science Museum)

made a short flight in a hot-air balloon at Nerekhta near Yaroslavl' in Russia in 1731. However, it was not until more than fifty years later that the first authenticated balloon flights were made, in France.

Despite its earlier tentative appearance, the practical balloon was in fact (as Professor J Needham has pointed out) essentially a product of advances in 'pneumatic chemistry' in Europe in the eighteenth century. That is to say, it resulted from work during that period on the identification of gases and their properties. In contrast, the glider, as ancestor of the aeroplane, derived from equivalent increased understanding of fluid mechanics in the nineteenth century.

In 1766 in Britain, Henry Cavendish (1731–1810) had discovered hydrogen and established its low density, and Joseph Black (1728–99) had pointed out its resulting lifting properties in the following year. In 1781, Tiberius Cavallo (1749–1809) made successful demonstrations with hydrogen-filled soap bubbles as well as unsuccessful experiments with

too-heavy animal bladders and too-porous paper envelopes. The following year, in a paper read to the Royal Society on 20 July, he suggested a hydrogen balloon. However, all experiments in Britain at the time were frustrated by the failure to find a sufficiently light and impermeable envelope material.

In 1774, Joseph Priestley (1733–1804) discovered oxygen and shortly afterwards published details of his researches in *Experiments and Observations on Different Kinds of Air*. This was published in France in 1776 and helped to stimulate practical aeronautical developments in that country. It was Priestley's book which is said to have inspired the first experiments by the inventors of the hot-air balloon. They may also have read another book, *L'Art de Navigeur dans les Airs* by Joseph Galien (1699–1762), first published in Avignon in 1755, which referred to rarified-air aerostats.

In November 1782, four months after Cavallo had suggested a hydrogen balloon to the Royal Society, the first fully-authenticated successful experiments with model hot-air balloons were made in France, first by Joseph Montgolfier (1740–1810) in Avignon and then, a month later, in Annonay with his brother, Etienne (1745–99). The Montgolfiers progressed from relatively small models to full-scale tests with large, paper-lined, linen, hot-air balloons. Their first public demonstration was made at Annonay on 4 June, 1783. Within six months, on 21 November, 1783, they achieved the first manned free flight with one of these in Paris. The pilots on this historic occasion were Jean Francois Pilâtre de Rozier (1754–85) and Francois Laurent, Marquis d'Arlandes (1742–1809). (*See* Note 2).

The Montgolfier hot-air experiments immediately revived interest in the hydrogen balloon. Indeed, it was probably because members of the Academie Française in Paris thought that the

First Balloon Flights

Date	Hot-Air or H₂	See below	Place	Main Motivator	Crew	Balloon Capacity	Remarks
25.11.82	H	UF	Avignon	Joseph Montgolfier	none	1cu m (35cu ft)	Preliminary test with small box balloon
Early 12.82	H	UF	Vidalon	Joseph Montgolfier	none	1cu m (35cu ft)	Test repeated at Annonay
14.12.82	H	UF	Vidalon	Joseph Montgolfier	none	3cu m (106cu ft)	
3.4.83	H	UC	Vidalon	Joseph Montgolfier	none	300cu m (10,594cu ft)	Globe balloon. Wind too strong to fly
25.4.83	H	UF	Vidalon	Joseph Montgolfier	none	800cu m (28,250cu ft)	Flew ¾ mile
Early 5.83	H	UC	Vidalon	Joseph Montgolfier	none	800cu m (28,250cu ft)	
4.6.83	H	UF	Annonay	Joseph Montgolfier	none	800cu m (28,250cu ft)	First public demonstration
25.8.83 (Two ascents)	Hy	UC	Place des Victoires	J A C Charles	none	26cu m (920cu ft)	First hydrogen balloon. Flew 1½ miles
26.8.83	Hy	UC	Place des Victoires	J A C Charles	none	26cu m (920cu ft)	
27.8.83	Hy	UF	Champ de Mars	J A C Charles	none	33cu m (1,165cu ft)	Destroyed on landing at Gonesse. Flew 15 miles
14.9.83	H	UC	Reveillon Gardens	Etienne Montgolfier	none	1,000cu m (35,300cu ft)	Destroyed in storm during trial inflation
18.9.83	H	MC	Reveillon Gardens	Etienne Montgolfier	none	1,400cu m (49,400cu ft)	Replacement balloon
19.9.83	H	UF	Versailles	Etienne Montgolfier	none duck, cock and sheep	1,400cu m (49,400cu ft)	Animals carried on flight before King and Queen. Flew two miles
12.10.83 (Several ascents)	H	MC	Reveillon Gardens	Etienne Montgolfier	Etienne Montgolfier	2,200cu m (77.700cu ft)	First manned captive flights
15.10.83 (Several ascents)	H	MC	Reveillon Gardens	Etienne Montgolfier	Pilâtre de Rozier	2,200cu m (77,700cu ft)	
17.10.83	H	MC	Reveillon Gardens	Etienne Montgolfier	Pilâtre de Rozier	2,200cu m (77,700cu ft)	
19.10.83 (Four ascents)	H	MC	Reveillon Gardens	Etienne Montgolfier	P de Rozier G de Villette	2,200cu m (77,700cu ft)	Captive flight, first to carry two people
21.11.83	H	MC	La Muette	Etienne Montgolfier	P de Rozier F d'Arlandes	2,200cu m (77,700cu ft)	Damaged, then repaired
21.11.83	H	MF	La Muette	Etienne Montgolfier	P de Rozier F d'Arlandes	2,200cu m (77,700cu ft)	First manned free flight
1.12.83	Hy	MF	Tuileries	J A C Charles	J A C Charles and M-N Robert	260cu m (9,200cu ft)	First manned free flight by hydrogen balloon. Flew 27 miles

Note: H = Hot-Air, Hy = Hydrogen, C = Captive, F = Free, M = Manned, U = Unmanned

Chronology of Lighter-than-Air Development

Year	Mainstream of Lighter-than-Air Development	Evolution of Rigid Airship Concept
1790	First balloon flights Meusnier designs airship First cross-Channel balloon flight Baron Scott designs airship	Kramp proposes cars rigid to envelope
1800	Military captive balloon at Mauberge	
1810	Cayley proposes trout-shaped airship	
1820	Pauly and Egg build goldbeaters' skin airship	Leppich builds semi-rigid airship
1830	Green introduces coal gas balloon Green introduces trail rope	Aluminium isolated as rare metal
1840	Lennox and Le Berrier test airship Lauriat builds goldbeaters' skin balloons Lennox airship built Wise introduces ripping panel	Marey Monge proposes metal balloon Cayley proposes sectional airship envelope
1850	Monck Mason flies clockwork model airship Le Berrier flies steam model airship Bell builds man-powered airship	Dupuis Delcourt builds copper balloon
1860	Giffard flies steam-powered airship Lenoir gas engine runs	Prosper Meller proposes iron rigid airship
1870	Balloons in American Civil War Delamarine and Yon fly man-powered airship Balloons in siege of Paris	Vannaisse builds multi gas cells model airship Yon designs propellers on sides of hull Boyman patents steel rigid airship
1880	Haenlein flies gas engine airship Otto petrol engine runs Baumgartner and Wölfert build petrol engine airship	Spiess patents rigid airship Zeppelin starts thinking about airships Stedman proposes aluminium airship
1890	Tissandier flies electric engine airship Renard and Krebs *La France* flies Wölfert flies petrol engine airship	Ganswindt proposes rigid airship Schwarz proposes aluminium airship Aluminium production starts
1900	Wölfert II flies Santos Dumont I flies	Zeppelin designs "airship-train" rigid Schwarz No.1 built Schwarz No.2 flies Zeppelin LZ1 flies

first reported Montgolfier experiments in distant Annonay employed hydrogen that tests using the gas were started in the capital. As a result, a distinguished physicist, Jacques-Alexandre-Cesar Charles (1746–1823), not only designed the fully-practical gas balloon in 1783, in a form that was to remain largely unchanged for the next 200 years, but also hit upon the essential light envelope material that was sufficiently impermeable to hydrogen gas. Construction of a hydrogen balloon was made possible by a public subscription of 10,000 livres (£180,000 in today's values) which was launched for the purpose by Faujas de Saint-Fond (1741–1819).

Suppliers of the envelope material and builders of the first hydrogen balloon were the brothers Robert (*See* Note 3.)

The first unmanned, free flight of a hydrogen balloon took place in Paris on 27 August, 1783. On 1 December of the same year, J A C Charles and Marie-Noel the younger Robert, made the first manned free flight, only ten days after de Rozier's and d'Arlandes's first ascent in a hot-air balloon.

First Balloons

Enthusiasm about the balloon in the years following its invention led to a number of spectacular flights being attempted, such as the first air crossing of the English Channel in 1785 by Jean-Pierre Blanchard (1753–1809) and John Jefferies (1744–1819). During this period the spherical balloon was adopted, in captive form, for military reconnaissance. The French first used it for this purpose at Maubeuge in 1794, the year they set up their first military air establishment at Chalais-Meudon. (It was closed, however, before the end of the century). The earliest scientific observations from a balloon had

The first air crossing of the English Channel. Jean-Pierre Blanchard and Dr John Jeffries floated from Dover to the forest of Guînes near Calais in a hydrogen balloon on 7 January, 1785.
(James Gardner for Shell)

been made by Jefferies ten years before, in 1784, while the first ascent made expressly for scientific purposes was by Etienne Gaspard Robertson (1763–1837) from Hamburg in 1803. Germany was also to see the first showmen aeronauts, men like Sickman, Drechster and Bittorf who used the balloon for entertainment purposes in the years 1803 to 1810.

Inevitably there were accidents. The first fatality occurred in 1785 when Pilâtre de Rozier (the pioneer balloon pilot) and Jules Romain died in an attempt to cross the English Channel in a balloon which combined the hot-air and hydrogen principles. In general, however, ballooning did not prove as dangerous as might have been expected. It is a matter of record that there were only 16 fatalities in the first 87 years of human flight in balloons, perhaps equivalent to one in about every 233 ascents, or one in every 300 hours flown.

Although the hot-air balloon survived in limited use for many years, the disadvantages and dangers in its original form were such that its eclipse by the gas

balloon was inevitable. The latter remained largely as first designed by Charles, with an open neck at the bottom of the envelope and a controllable valve at the top. A net covered the balloon and supported a hoop to which the basket was attached. The valve remained unchanged until 1875 when a safer design was introduced. The Roberts' rubberised silk was sometimes replaced by cheaper cotton cloth and there were variations in the type of elastomer used to render the material impervious. The most important design improvement was the lowering of the hoop at the bottom of the net which enclosed the envelope. Charles had positioned his hoop near the balloon's equator and had attached the lines which supported the wicker-basket car directly to it so that they stretched over and therefore were liable to chafe the lower half of the envelope. Blanchard improved on this design in 1784 by lowering the hoop to a position well below the envelope and reducing it considerably in diameter. The net now ended in 'crow's feet' and lead-lines to the hoop and this supported the car close below it. The new arrangement became standard practice.

The only other major advance in balloon design was the addition of the ripping panel by the American aeronaut, John Wise (1808–79), in 1839. This enabled the gas to be released rapidly on landing so reducing dangerous dragging over the ground after touching down. Landing thus became safer, particularly in a high wind.

A new, although more expensive, envelope material was introduced in the first half of the nineteenth century. This was goldbeaters' skin, made from the large intestine of the ox. It derived its name from the fact that goldleaf was produced from mediaeval times by beating the gold between these skins. (*See* Note 4). The skins were first used for aeronautical purposes in toy balloons by Baron de Beaumanoir soon after the invention

British Army balloon with goldbeaters' skin envelope. (Pritchard collection)

A gas-filled balloon ascending from the Royal Aeronautical Society's garden party at White Waltham in 1949.

A modern hot-air balloon.

A German kite balloon of the 1914–18 War.
(Pritchard collection)

of the manned balloon. In 1816–17 goldbeaters' skin appears to have been applied to the manufacture of a full-sized envelope, that of the unsuccessful *Dolphin*. This was a man-powered, fish-shaped airship, built at Knightsbridge in London by Samuel J Pauly and Durs Egg. The envelope consisted of seven layers of skin on top and six at the sides formed over a wooden mould. In 1834 a well-known American balloonist, Louis A Lauriat (1785–1858), manufactured a full-size free balloon envelope in goldbeaters' skin and thereafter the material seems to have been used occasionally until, at the instigation of James L B Templer, it was adopted by the British Army for military balloons in 1883. (*See* Note 5). This material, usually multi-ply and stuck to cotton cloth, was later to be widely used for the gas cells of rigid airships.

Towards the end of the nineteenth century, the British Army achieved a significant technical ascendancy over other nations with its ballooning equipment. In addition to the superior goldbeaters' skin envelopes, the British went over to hydrogen stored under pressure in steel cylinders, thus avoiding the need to generate new gas every time it was required in the field. Italian hemp was adopted for nets and rigging at this time. The British superiority ended in 1896 with the appearance in Germany of the first kite-balloons which were far superior to captive spherical balloons.

The other most important technical development in ballooning during the nineteenth century was the substitution of domestic coal-gas for hydrogen as the usual lifting agent. First suggested by the Belgian scientist J P Minielers, in 1784, it was not until commercial production and distribution of coal-gas for domestic and industrial purposes started to become general, after about 1820, that the advantages of its use became obvious. In 1821 the English aeronaut, Charles Green (1785–1870), was the first to use coal-gas in a balloon. Thereafter it was generally adopted in place of hydrogen despite its much lower lifting power. Its cheapness, general availability, lower diffusion rate through envelope materials, and higher specific heat which made it less susceptible to changes in temperature, were overriding advantages. Green was responsible in 1828 for another technical advance. This was the introduction of the trail rope, a heavy line lowered from the balloon before landing or used as an aid to low flying. Its function was to act as variable ballast: as the balloon dropped lower, more and more of the heavy rope rested on the ground thus unloading the balloon and slowing its descent.

The free balloon, filled with hydrogen or coal-gas, remains technically pretty well unaltered to this day except that progressively improved envelope materials have come into use over the years. Cotton treated with natural rubber remained the most common material into the 1920s although, as already mentioned, rubberised silk or the more expensive goldbeaters' skin was used for some military balloons. In the 1930s neoprene began to replace natural rubber as the elastomer; since the 1950s envelopes have often been made of nylon or Dacron treated with chemigum vinyl, butyl or polyurethane.

At intervals during the first half of the twentieth century attempts were made to revive the hot-air balloon which had never, in fact, completely disappeared. It was tried several times over the years with various types of heat generator and it remained popular with the professional showmen who preferred its simplicity and cheapness. Today hot-air balloons with propane burners have been revived on a considerable scale for sporting purposes, particularly in the United States. They are, in fact, much more widely used now for manned ascents than gas balloons.

The 200-year history of practical ballooning can be summarised as follows. First there was the initial phase of experimentation which lasted for a few years after 1783. This was followed by a period of over 100 years during which the free balloon became primarily a source of public entertainment in the hands of a long series of professional aeronaut showmen. Interest fluctuated considerably throughout this period: it waned in the late 1780s, revived in the early 1820s, waned again in the later 1830s, picked up during the middle of the 1800s and then gradually expanded in the second half of that century, particularly after military interest was re-stimulated by the use of balloons in the American Civil War (1861–65) for observation and, later, during the Siege of Paris (1870–71) as a means of transport and communication.

Professional balloonists, who were numbered in hundreds, were primarily concerned with earning their living by turning

A Caquot observation balloon during the 1914–18 War.

their flights into exciting public spectacles. However, in the process these airmen accumulated the first substantial body of practical experience of the air. The more experienced of them made hundreds of ascents. Quite a few achieved 400 to 500 flights each, probably accounting for 500 to 600 hours of flying time in careers which extended over many years. The most experienced balloonist of all time seems to have been an Englishman, Henry T Coxwell (1819–1900), who made well over a thousand ascents, totalling perhaps 1,400 flying hours in a career which lasted for more than 40 years.

In addition to its use by these showmen, the balloon was also used occasionally for joy-riding, typically in very large captive form at some of the great exhibitions which first became popular during the nineteenth century. At other times during this period balloons were also applied to scientific purposes but these instances were relatively few and infrequent. However, ballons did contribute materially to mankind's advancing knowledge of the atmosphere, and in the present century they have played an important part in research to the

limits of the atmosphere, leading on to the exploration of space itself by other means. Since 1892, unmanned balloons have been the most important in the scientific role. They continue, particularly in radio-sonde form, to be of great importance, notably in meteorology.

Towards the end of the nineteenth century ballooning began to become popular as a sport for the well-to-do. Balloon competitions of various types and ascents for pleasure remained in vogue until 1914, and in fact survived to a limited degree between the wars and since. And as already noted, the reappearance of hot-air balloons in recent years has led to a tremendous expansion of the sport.

In parallel with these civil uses, balloons have also been employed more seriously by the military Services in many countries. Their main military application has been in captive flying for observation over the battlefield. This is how they were first used by the French and how they continued to be used during the Napoleonic Wars (until Napoleon became disillusioned with balloons and stopped their further use). They were employed in the American Civil War, in the Franco-Prussian War and in a whole series of colonial wars, particularly by the British in many parts of the world. The spherical balloon was used as a captive in all these cases, despite its instability in the lightest of winds. To overcome this difficulty, Transon suggested a form of kite-balloon in 1844 and so did Archibald Douglas about a year later. Alphonse Pénaud (1850–1880) designed another in 1874. However, it was not until 1896 that the first successful Drachen kite-balloon was developed in Berlin by Maj von Parceval and Capt von Sigsveld of the Prussian Balloon Detachment. This led to many types of kite-balloon, including the French Caquot in 1916 (*See* Note 6). Powered kite-balloon winches were also introduced at this time. Caquot balloons were used for

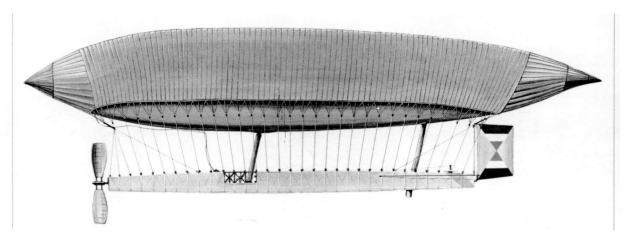

observation purposes during the First World War and as barrage ballons in both wars.

Other uses of the balloon in war included bomb-dropping, first demonstrated in Berlin by the English aeronaut, Henry Coxwell, in 1848. In 1849 the Austrians attempted, unsuccessfully, to use small unmanned hot-air balloons to bomb Venice. This technique has been attempted on a few occasions since, notably by the Japanese with the 'Fu-Go Weapons' during the Second World War. The Japanese despatched a total of over 9,300 paper balloons against Canada and the United States of which 235 caused incidents. During an eight-month period in 1944–45, the Americans found some 168 of these balloons which had been blown across the Pacific carrying anti-personnel and incendiary bombs. Only a few of them inflicted fatalities or damage – and these were negligible. After the Second World War and before the development of reconnaissance satellites, the Americans sent unmanned, camera-carrying balloons over the Soviet Union for strategic reconnaissance.

During the Siege of Paris in 1870–71 the free balloon was used for transport out of the beleaguered city. No less than sixty-six balloons carried 168 people out of Paris over the heads of the investing Prussian armies, undoubtedly giving an important stimulus to the development of the dirigible balloon.

Dirigible Balloons

Soon after the invention of the balloon it became apparent that it was useless as a serious means of transport: it could be tethered or allowed to drift with the wind but there was little the aeronaut could do about it. True, many of the pioneers believed at first, and some continued to claim for a time, that they could steer and propel their balloons by means of wings, oars or similar devices, but actual results soon exploded the myth. Some experienced balloonists were able to demonstrate in time that they could direct the paths of their craft to a limited extent by rising or descending into more favourable air currents. A theoretically possible scheme for propelling balloons was put forward by David Bourgeois in 1784 and was subsequently revived in various forms on a number of occasions by different inventors. This was for so-called glide-propulsion, whereby the balloon was to be made to travel in the required direction by ascending and descending rapidly so that the resulting vertical airflow would act on suitably disposed inclined planes. It appears, however, that nobody was ever able to make this scheme work. In 1846 Green suggested, with some justification, that a combination of trail rope and sails

Renard-Krebs' La France of 1884 was the first airship to fly a complete closed circuit. This was of 4.75 miles (7.6km) flown in 23 minutes at an average speed of nearly 15mph (6.5m/s). This pressure airship was powered by an 8.5hp electric motor supplied by a battery.
(Drawn by Peter W M Griffin. © 1973 Hugh Evelyn Ltd)

might be used to deflect a balloon slightly from its track straight down-wind and this scheme was tried a number of times with limited success. However, the practical fact remains that the free balloon is useless as a means of transport to a predetermined destination.

As a result, schemes for dirigible balloons were advanced from the earliest days. In 1784 Brisson proposed a dirigible before the Académie Française, and in the same year Jean B M Meusnier (1754–93) prepared detailed designs for a man-powered elongated balloon incorporating a number of features (including notably the ballonet to keep the envelope tight if the gas pressure fell) which were later important in the practical airship. Meusnier's design did not get off the drawing board but, still in 1784, the Robert brothers did build and fly an elongated hydrogen balloon, under the patronage of the Duc de Chartres, which was intended to be propelled manually by oars.

The Meusnier and Robert dirigible envelopes were ovoid in

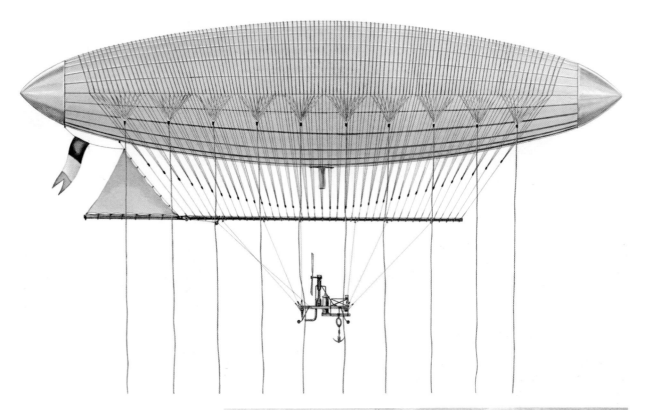

The Giffard steam dirigible of 1852 was the first airship to make a powered controlled flight. This was achieved at the Hippodrome in Paris when this pressure airship of 88,300cu ft (2,500 cu m) capacity achieved a measured speed of 6mph (2.7 m/s) in still air.
(Drawn by Peter W M Griffin.
© Hugh Evelyn Ltd)

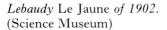

Lebaudy Le Jaune *of 1902.*
(Science Museum)

form with the object of reducing air resistance in the line of flight. This thinking was first carried a stage further by Patinho, who is said to have tested a fish-shaped balloon in Spain in 1784. The same envelope form was proposed by Dalberg in 1785, by Baron Scott in 1789 and by Sir George Cayley (1773–1857) in 1809. Soon after Cayley revived the idea, the Pauly and Egg *Dolphin* airship was built to this shape in London in 1816. However, a satisfactory envelope was not by itself enough. Even more important was a solution to the

propulsion problem. The *Dolphin* had completely ineffective man-powered oars but it did incorporate an ingenious method of control: a weight that was movable fore and aft for pitch control. It also had a ballonet to regulate the gas pressure in the envelope. This was followed in 1835 by Comte de Lennox's *L'Aigle* with more sophisticated, but equally ineffective, flapping surfaces. But Cayley had shown the way in 1816 when he had suggested propellers as an alternative. This idea was taken up by Hugh Bell in 1850 with his 'loco-

motive balloon' which had man-powered propellers. It was built and tested but, not surprisingly, proved unsuccessful. A more significant manual propeller-powered dirigible was built in 1872 at the expense of the French Government by S C H L Dupuy de Lôme (1816–85). This achieved a low speed and demonstrated limited control.

Well before this, mechanical power had been applied through propellers to balloon propulsion with some success. Model airships, clockwork or steam-powered, were flown successfully

The British Nulli Secundus *first flew on 10 September, 1907. It was 120ft long and had a gas capacity of 56,000cu ft (1,585cu m).* (Pritchard collection)

by Thomas Monck Mason (b.1803) and Dr Le Berrier in 1843 and by Pierre Jullien (1804–76) in 1850. The last directly inspired what may be described as the first partly successful dirigible. Henri Giffard (1825–82) built a steam-powered 2,500cu m (88,300cu ft) airship in Paris in 1852 which achieved a speed of 2.7m/s (6mph) and clearly demonstrated that such a craft could be controlled in still air.

The first airship to be fitted with an internal combustion engine was built in Vienna by Paul Haenlein (1835–1905) in 1872. The Frenchman, Etienne Lenoir, had invented the gas engine in 1860 and Haenlein adopted an engine of that type which used gas from the envelope as fuel. Although an advance on the steam engine because it saved the weight of firebox and boiler, the gas engine was little more efficient and Haenlein's airship was only partly successful, achieving a speed of 4m/s (9mph).

The use of balloons in the

Siege of Paris not only directly inspired the de Lôme man-powered airship, already mentioned, but also led in 1877 to the setting up by the French Government of the first official aeronautical research establishment in the world, at Chalais-Meudon near Paris. This was on the same site as the earlier military balloon centre which had been temporarily organised in 1794–99. Charles Renard (1847–1905) was the moving spirit at the new establishment and, in 1884, with the help of Arthur C Krebs (1847–1935) and with a subsidy of Frs 40,000 (£30,000 in present-day values) from Léon Gambetta (1838–82), he built an electric-powered 1,864cu m (66,000cu ft) airship called *La France*. This, for the first time, achieved fully-controlled powered flight and a speed of 6.5m/s (nearly 15mph). *La France* made a number of successful flights and clearly demonstrated that, with a lighter and more powerful engine, the airship could be made into a practical vehicle. Renard continued his experiments at Chalais-Meudon for many years; in 1903 he and a colleague, Henri Hervé (d.1922), conceived the idea of using stabilising planes attached to the aft end of the air-

ship hull, an arrangement which may have been originally suggested by Frederick Marriott (1805–84) in 1869.

From the appearance of the practical petrol engine in the 1880s, it became clear that this was the prime-mover for which the dirigible had been waiting. The first airship to fly with a petrol engine (a Daimler) was built by the German Dr Frederich Hermann Wölfert (1852–97) in 1888. This machine was only partly successful and, although Wölfert built two more petrol-powered airships before he was killed in the first fatal airship accident in 1897, he never really achieved success. However, there were others who soon followed his example. In particular, in the year after his death, the Brazilian, Alberto Santos Dumont (1873–1932) built his first airship in Paris. Over the next few years Santos Dumont built and flew a whole series of little airships of steadily increasing effectiveness. His No.6 of 1901 won the Deutsch de la Meurthe Prize for a flight of 11km (7 miles) from St Cloud to the Eiffel Tower and back within half-an-hour. Two fatal accidents to experimental airships near Paris within five months, in 1902 (*See* Note 7), did not stop Santos Dumont who continued his experiments until he turned to heavier-than-air machines some years later.

Santos Dumont's part in the history of airships was, however, more that of propagandist than of engineer. Technically, his airships showed little advance on *La France* which had flown fifteen years earlier. His success was due to the fact that he was able to use petrol engines, whose application to airships had been pioneered, fatally, by Wölfert.

Pressure-Airships

At the same time as Santos Dumont was publicising the possibilities of aircraft by demonstrating his little aerial runabouts over the Paris roof-tops, a technically more important airship was being developed at Moisson, near Mantes. This was the Lebaudy, designed by Henri Julliot (b.1855) and Don Simoni, and built by the sugar refiners, Lebaudy Frères; the airship, popularly known as *Le Jaune* from its yellow calico envelope, was first flown by Georges Juchmés (1874–1918) on 13 November, 1902. It was of the type which came to be known as semi-rigid. That is to say, although its gas was contained in a fabric envelope like a balloon, it also had a keel member beneath the envelope to distribute the weight of power-unit and car suspended from it.

Le Jaune marked the beginning of practical powered human flight which was to be confirmed in a totally different manner by the Wright brothers with their first successful aeroplane flights in the following year. The Lebaudy was powered by a 40hp Daimler petrol engine which gave it a speed of 11.2m/s (25mph), enough to make it a practical vehicle on calm days. After a series of highly successful flights, *Le Jaune* was flown, on 12 November, 1903, 52km ($32\frac{1}{2}$ miles) in one hour forty-one minutes, from Moisson to Paris where it was put on public display in the Galerie des Machines. Later, this airship was

Two S.S. pressure-airships, one British and one American, moored in a wood. (Pritchard collection)

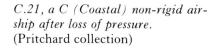

An Italian Nobile semi-rigid pressure-airship.
(Pritchard collection)

C.21, a C (Coastal) non-rigid airship after loss of pressure.
(Pritchard collection)

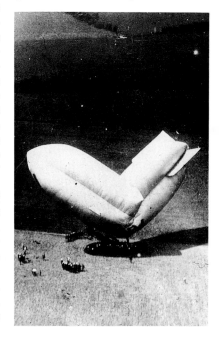

enlarged and modified, and finally handed over to the French Army. It remained in service until 1909.

With the Lebaudy, the practical pressure-airship can be said to have arrived. Ever since, pressure-airships have been operated in small numbers and have continued to be to this day. When the gas contracts, pressure is maintained by a ballonet, a bag within the main envelope which is inflated with air by an engine-driven fan or by air scooped from the slipstream of the main propulsive engine. An envelope, free to expand and contract with changes in the pressure of the contained gas, was tried as an alternative to a ballonet in a few early airships.

During the first 90 years of this century, something like 900 pressure-airships were built and it is estimated that they probably flew about 1.1 million hours. To put these numbers into perspective, they should be compared with an estimated total of well over 1.5 million aeroplanes built during the same period. These probably flew at least 1,200 million hours. It will be apparent from these figures that airships have played only a small part in the history of practical human flight; indeed, for the past 30 years their contribution has been negligible even though some of them incorporate elements of relatively advanced technology.

During the past 90 years, the pressure-airship has had three significant, though minor, practical roles. The first was its military use in the First World War. Early in that war, pressure-airships were used on a small scale by the French and Germans and, later, on a much larger scale by, notably, the British for anti-submarine patrol. Between the wars and since, the Goodyear Company in the United States (now part of the Loral Systems Group) has operated pressure-airships primarily for advertising purposes. In addition, well over a million passengers have been given local joy-rides in these 'craft. In the 1980s, a United

Kingdom company, Airship Industries, built and operated a modestly growing fleet of pressure-airships.

In the Second World War, pressure-airships were used by the US Navy for anti-submarine patrol out of range of hostile aircraft, very much on the pattern of the British in the First World War. The American operations continued on a more limited scale after the war until they were shut down in the early 1960s. The last US Navy blimp was dismantled in September 1962. Latterly, the airships were used primarily as radar pickets for early warning of the approach of potentially hostile aircraft and ships.

The Lebaudy originally had a gas capacity of 2,265cu m (80,000 cu ft). Most pressure-airships used in the First World War had capacities in the range, 1,700–10,200cu m (60,000–360,000cu ft). The civil blimps, operated by Goodyear, have been of 1,400–5,650cu m (50,000–200,000cu ft) capacity; the United States naval airships of the Second World War were mainly of about 12,000cu m (about 425,000cu ft), although a few, of up to 20,500cu m (725,000cu ft), were also used. After the war the US Navy used small numbers of pressure-airships of 14,150–28,300cu m (500,000–1 million cu ft) capacity and a few of up to 42,500cu m (1.5 million cu ft).

Thus, most pressure-airships have been small in modern aircraft terms. An airship of 4,250cu m (150,000cu ft), filled with helium, has a gross lift of about 4,000kg (9,000lb), and is thus only what would be called a light aircraft in today's terminology. Even the few 42,500cu m (1.5 million cu ft) giants of the US Navy, which were flown for only a short time in the late 1950s to early 1960s, were considerably lighter than the medium-capacity, short-haul airliners such as now carry holiday-makers, in their millions, from Northern Europe to the Mediterranean every summer.

In assessing the capabilities of

pressure-airships, one must take account of the fact that these aircraft are slow, with a cruising speed of, at most, 25m/s (56 mph) and often less. Current advertising blimps cruise at only about 15m/s (35mph). This speed is much too low for serious transport purposes. Average wind speeds (*See* Note 8) experienced at most times of the year, all over the world, are such that an air speed of 25m/s is too low for regular operations. Indeed, experience has shown that, in practice, the modern blimp is prevented from operating at all in winds of more than about 10m/s (23mph). Operations with aeroplanes established, from the 1930s, that cruising speeds of

Airship Industries Skyship 600, G-SKSC, which made its first flight, at Cardington, on 6 March, 1984. (Courtesy Airship Industries)

75m/s (167mph) are about the minimum at which regular, economic scheduled air transport becomes possible. There is no prospect, at present, of airships achieving such speeds. Even the helicopter has barely done so, as yet.

Aircraft not used for transport still need adequate speed and range to reach and return from their missions' objectives. Without this capability, airships are poorly qualified to tackle most tasks, military or civil.

Numbers of Pressure-Airships Built

Country	Pre-1914	1914–1920	1920–1945	From 1945	Totals
Austria	9	–	–	–	9
Belgium	4	–	–	–	4
France	60	67	7	3	137
Germany	40	5	3	6	54
Italy	15	16	6	–	37
Japan	5	1	5	1	12
Netherlands	1	–	–	–	1
Russia/USSR	18	–	19	4	41
Spain	2	1	3	1	7
United Kingdom	27	198	2	12	239
United States	25	46	218	68	357
Totals	206	334	263	95	898

Chronology of Lighter-than-Air Development

Mainstream of Lighter-than-Air Development

1780-89	1790-99	1800-09	1810-19	1820-29	1830-39
First balloon flights Meusnier designs airship First cross-Channel balloon flight Baron Scott designs airship	Military captive balloon at Maubeuge	Cayley proposes trout-shaped airship	Pauly and Egg build gold-beaters' skin airship	Green introduces coal gas balloon Green introduces trail rope	Lennox and Le Berrier test airship Lauriat builds gold beaters' skin balloons Lennox airship built Wise introduces ripping panel

1840-49	1850-59	1860-69	1870-79	1880-89	1890-1900
Monck Mason flies clockwork model airship Le Berrier flies steam model airship	Bell builds man-powered airship Giffard flies steam-powered airship	Lenoir gas engine runs Balloons in American Civil War Delamarine and Yon fly man-powered airship	Balloons in siege of Paris Haenlein flies gas engine airship Otto petrol engine runs	Baumgartner and Wölfert build petrol engine airship Tissandier flies electric engine airship Renard and Krebs *La France* flies Wölfert flies petrol engine airship	Wölfert II flies Santos Dumont I flies

Evolution of Rigid Airship Concept

1780-89	1790-99	1800-09	1810-19	1820-29	1830-39
Kramp proposes cars rigid to envelope			Leppich builds semi-rigid airship	Aluminium isolated as rare metal	Marey Monge proposes metal balloon Cayley proposes sectional airship envelope

1840-49	1850-59	1860-69	1870-79	1880-89	1890-1900
Depuis-Delcourt builds copper balloon	Prosper Meller proposes iron rigid airship	Vannaisse builds multi gas cells model airship Yon designs propellers on sides of hull Boyman patents steel rigid airship	Spiess patents rigid airship Zeppelin starts thinking about airships Stedman proposes aluminium airship	Ganswindt proposes rigid airship Schwarz proposes aluminium airship Aluminium production starts	Zeppelin designs airship – 'Train' rigid Schwarz No.1 built Schwarz No.2 flies Zeppelin LZ1 flies

Rigid Airship Concept

The idea of stiffening the main gas envelope of a pressure-airship with a structural keel (the so-called semi-rigid) was first put forward in an unsuccessful design built by the German Leppich for the Russian Government in 1812. As already mentioned, this principle was later used to good effect by Julliot in the first practical Lebaudy airship in 1902. Much earlier, in 1785, Professor Kramp had suggested that airship cars should be rigidly attached to the hull. In 1831, Edmond Marey Monge had proposed a metal vacuum balloon, harking back to the impractical design of de Lana and, in 1834–44, J F Dupuis-Delcourt (1802–64), built an unsuccessful copper spherical balloon. Although not flown, be-

cause of the difficulties of inflation, this metal envelope of Dupuis-Delcourt (who seems to have associated with Marey Monge in the enterprise) was a considerable technical achievement for its time. The copper sheet was an eighth of a millimetre thick (0.005in) and the envelope 10m (32.8ft) in diameter. It weighed 400kg (880lb) and would have had a gross lift, filled with hydrogen, of about 615kg (1,360lb).

These designs had metal envelopes because of the difficulty of finding a lighter, sufficiently impermeable material. However, other experimenters thought in terms of metal because they visualised airships with rigid hulls. In 1851, Prosper Meller proposed a large rigid in Bordeaux. His design was for a large cylindrical hull 200m (656ft) long and 40m (131ft) in diameter with conical ends. It was to be covered either in cloth or sheet iron and to incorporate a car movable fore and aft on cables for pitch control. In 1886, R B Boyman patented the

design of an even larger (403m or 1,322ft long) rigid airship to be made of steel. He improved his design two years later. The hull of the Boyman airship was to be built of internally-braced metal rings with covering of sheet metal. In 1873, the Alsatian, Joseph Spiess, patented in Paris a crude design for a rigid, incorporating a number of separate gas cells (*See* Note 9) an idea which had been advocated by Sir George Cayley in 1837 and adopted in model form by H Vannaisse in 1863. Spiess had taken out another patent, this time in Germany, in 1895.

The 1870s saw the setting-up of Government committees in several countries to study the military possibilities of aeronautics. This was followed, within a few years, by the creation of Government aeronautical research establishments in France, Britain, Germany and Russia. Official interest in aerostation stimulated the design of airships, particularly in France, as already recounted, and also in Germany.

In the latter country, this was to be important because of its influence on the development of the rigid airship.

An aristocratic and wealthy German cavalry general, Count Ferdinand Adolf August Heinrich von Zeppelin (1838–1917), who had been interested in ballooning since 1863 (*See* Note 10), began to think seriously about airships in 1874. His interest was

first aroused by reading a pamphlet by the German Postmaster-General, Heinrich von Stephan, entitled *International Post and Aviation* (published in Berlin in 1873).

Initially, Zeppelin was interested in airships for civil purposes but soon he began to think of them mainly in military terms. Strongly patriotic, he was convinced that Germany needed

Count Zeppelin's airship train proposal of 1895, with twin-engined power section and two trailers. (Pritchard collection)

rigid airships to hold her own against France whom he saw as a potential enemy. He may well have been inspired by Spiess's 1873 patent, already mentioned, and he is reported to have been influenced later by the thinking

The develop-
ment of the
rigid airship.

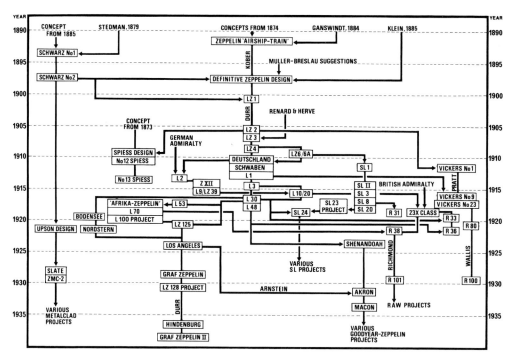

of another Alsatian, Klein, who proposed a rigid airship in 1885. A further influence must have been the German, H Ganswindt (1856–1934). He published a book in 1884 in which he described the design of a large airship with a cylindrical hull, 152m (500ft) long and 15m (49.2ft) in diameter, which he had patented the previous year.

Ganswindt also probably influenced David Schwarz (1845–97), a former Dalmatian timber merchant from Zagreb, then called Agram (in what is now Yugoslavia). He later worked in an aluminium factory and, in 1885, proposed a design of rigid airship to be built of this metal. Some years later he submitted his proposals to the Austro-Hungarian War Ministry in Vienna. Schwarz advocated the use of straight aluminium (not an alloy as later became common for aircraft) as his main structural material and would also use the same material for the covering of the gas container. An American, Edmund C Stedman, had first suggested aluminium for airships in 1879. There are, however, unconfirmed reports that Schwarz used a 'Viktoria' aluminium alloy of unknown composition.

Aluminium had been isolated

as a rare metal in 1827 but did not become commercially available until the late 1880s following discovery, simultaneously by Hall in the USA and by Héroult in France, of the electrolytic process for its manufacture. The Austro-Hungarian authorities took their time evaluating Schwarz's proposals but finally turned them down in 1890.

Meanwhile, Zeppelin had been developing his ideas. In 1877, he had proposed the use of airscrews on a vertical axis to control an airship in climb and descent, an idea which strangely enough was never to be used on a Zeppelin even though swivelling propellers were tried on several British airships and became a feature of the last two American rigids of the 1930s. Ten years later, in 1887, Zeppelin advocated the development of dirigibles to King Charles V of Württemberg. In 1890, at the age of 52, he retired from the army and hired an engineer, named Gross, to work with him full-time on his ideas. In June 1891, he put forward his first proposals for a rigid airship to the Prussian General Staff. At this stage, Zeppelin's design seems to have been a train of rigid airships consisting of a prime-mover powered by two 11

hp Daimler petrol engines flexibly coupled to two trailing sections, each capable of carrying a 500kg (1,100lb) useful load. The prime-mover could fly alone but would not normally do so. Each section consisted of a fabric-covered cylindrical rigid structure built of seamless aluminium tubes joining aluminium discs. The discs separated a number of bays, each of which contained a gas cell. The design speed was 20m/s (45mph). Zeppelin's proposals were studied by Capt Georg von Tschudi, the Commanding Officer of the Prussian Balloon Corps based at Tempelhof, but they were not taken up officially at this time.

Later, in 1891, Gross had a disagreement with his employer and left. He was succeeded in May 1892 by Dr Theodor Kober (1865–1930), an engineer from the Riedinger balloon firm in Augsburg. In the latter part of 1893, Zeppelin and Kober produced an improved version of the train design which was finally patented on 31 August, 1895. Well before this, in the latter part of 1893, the Prussian War Ministry agreed to Zeppelin's suggestion that these proposals should be evaluated by a German Government aeronautical commission.

Schwarz and Zeppelin

In 1892, following discussions with the Russian military attaché in Vienna, David Schwarz was engaged by the Russian Government to build his airship in a new hangar then under construction at Volkhov near St Petersburg (later Leningrad). The well-known Russian aeronautical and space pioneer, K E Ziolkovski (1857–1935), had himself proposed a metal-covered airship design in 1885 and had done wind-tunnel tests on a model in 1891. He published proposals in 1892 at about the time Schwarz came to Russia. It is not known to what extent, if at all, the work of the two men was connected. Ziolkovski visualised an expansible sausage-shaped envelope which would have been structurally difficult to build and make work but which would probably have coped satisfactorily with the problem of gas expansion and contraction with changes in height and temperature. Schwarz employed a rigid envelope which depended on an automatic valve to let out the gas as it expanded and, presumably, although no record of this has survived, some form of air ballonet or valve to provide for the admission of air into the hull to prevent its collapse when the gas contracted. It is just possible, however, that the Schwarz hulls were themselves intended to be expandible and that this was the reason for both being slightly oval, rather than circular, in cross-section. On 23 August, 1892, before leaving for Russia, Schwarz signed an agreement with Carl Berg, the aluminium manufacturer, for the design, manufacture and delivery to St Petersburg via Vienna, of the components and other materials required for the airship.

In appearance the Schwarz de-

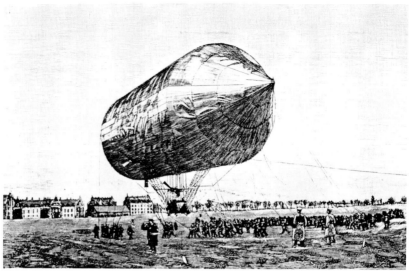

The Schwarz No.2 at Berlin.
(Popular Flying)

David Schwarz.
(Popular Flying)

sign was not greatly different from Zeppelin's prime-mover except that the wire-braced tubular lattice girder and tubular aluminium structure was covered with thin aluminium sheet instead of fabric. Capacity was 4,545cu m (160,590cu ft) and the gross lift 4,700kg (10,360lb). The power-unit was a single 12hp Daimler petrol engine. Because the gas was to be contained directly within the metal hull, it was obviously difficult to fill. When the airship was completed in 1893, it seems that this was done by having expendable bags in the hull which were filled with gas. When the bags were full, all air had been expelled from the hull. The bags were then pulled to pieces and removed. Unfortunately, during this process the internal bracing wires were damaged and the hull collapsed.

After this failure, Schwarz re-

turned to Vienna and submitted his design to the Prussian authorities. Thus it was that Schwarz's and Zeppelin's designs were evaluated side-by-side by the German Government's aeronautical commission in 1894. Under the chairmanship of the distinguished physicist, Professor Hermann L von Helmholtz (b.1821), who died in that year, the commission decided that Schwarz's design was the more promising and recommended that the German Government should sponsor its development at the aeronautical establishment at Tempelhof. If the design were successful, the Government agreed to buy it for 300,000 marks (about £260,000 in present-day values).

Work started in the balloon shed at Tempelhof late in 1895. The structure of this second Schwarz airship seems to have been a considerable advance on the first. It was about 20 per cent smaller, having a capacity of 3,700cu m (130,664cu ft), with a gross lift of 3,680kg (8,113lb). The design was apparently largely in the hands of two German engineers, Weisspfennig and von Watzesch-Walbach, and seems to have been mainly, or perhaps

Zeppelin LZ1 in its floating shed at Manzell on Bodensee.

Count Zeppelin in the control car of LZ1

inflated with air. Gas was then introduced between the outer skin and the bags thus expelling the air. The bags were then ripped and removed. The system seems to have worked surprisingly well because filling was completed in only three-and-a-half hours. Again no record survives of an air ballonet or of any arrangement for admitting air to the hull when the gas contracted. The hull was of the same oval section, 14m (45ft 11in) deep by 12m (39ft 4¹/₂in) wide, as the first airship. It, too, may have been intended to be free to expand or contract slightly under changes in gas pressure.

Other features of the Schwarz airships were significant. The car was rigidly attached to the hull by lattice girders, an arrangement first tried on a pressure-airship in 1886 by Wölfert at Tempelhof. No.2's engine, again a 12hp Daimler, was mounted in the car and drove three airscrews through belts, perhaps the weakest feature of the entire design. Two 2m (6ft 6in) diameter airscrews were for propulsion and were mounted as tractors on brackets fixed high on each side of the hull. This was an arrangement first proposed by Gabriel Yon in his airship project of 1864 and was intended to bring the line of thrust as near as possible to the centre of drag. It was also adopted by Zeppelin and Gross in their 'airship-train' project. The third propeller, 2.75m (9ft) in diameter, was mounted as a pusher at the rear of the car and was arranged to swing about a vertical axis under the control of the pilot so that it could be used as a rudder. Originally – as previously advocated by Wölfert – a fourth propeller was to rotate in a horizontal plane below the gondola. This was apparently intended to provide vertical lift but was not fitted for the first flight. The hull had a conical nose and a blunt, slightly convex, stern.

After a test as a tethered balloon, the Schwarz airship No.2 was flown for the first and last time on 3 November, 1897. The

even entirely, financed by their employer Carl Berg (1851–1906), a prominent Westphalian industrialist who played a large part in the early commercial production of aluminium. He supplied all the material required for the airship. (*See* Note 11) Berg's engineers also contributed to the design and manufacture of the longitudinal lattice girders and tubular frames of which the airship was built. The aluminium-sheet covering, which was riveted to the framework, was only a fifth of a millimetre (0.008in) thick. Unfor-

tunately, Schwarz died on 13 January, 1897, but the airship was completed later that year. It had cost 200,000 marks (about £170,000 in present-day values).

At the suggestion of Capt R M W H Bartsch von Sigsfeld (1861–1902), the co-inventor of the Drachen kite-balloon, the inflation problem which had led to the premature destruction of the first Schwarz airship was overcome by adopting exactly the reverse of the procedure used in St Petersburg. On this occasion fitted bags within the hull were

The ZMC-2 Metalclad.

audience at Tempelhof that day did not include Count Zeppelin contrary to some reports. The airship was piloted by Ernst Jaegels, Schwarz's chief engineer. It rose into the air with its engine running but did not give any evidence of being controllable in a brisk 7.5m/s (16.77mph) east-southeast wind. Almost at once trouble arose with the belt drives to the propellers and, after drifting four miles and reaching a height of about 250m (820ft), it landed heavily and was broken up by the wind.

So ends the Schwarz story. But it was not quite the end of the metal-clad airship. In the early 1920s, an American, Ralph H Upson (1888–1968), promoted a design similar in principle to that of Schwarz, having its gas contained directly within its metal envelope. The main differences were that the later ship was made of duralumin, covered with Alclad sheet, and was of better aerodynamic shape. It had innumerable detailed improvements. Upson's design was taken up by a specially formed company, the Airship Development Corporation, which eventually built a single airship (the ZMC-2) to this design for the US Navy. The airship remained in service for 12 years after its first flight on 19 August, 1929, and was rated a complete success. But, as no further examples were ordered, it must have been less satisfactory than equivalent fabric-envelope ships. One other metal-clad airship, the Slate *City of Glendale*, was built, also in the United States, between 1927 and 1931. It was not a success; although flown as a tethered balloon, its steam powerplant was never installed. (*See* Note 12)

The metal-clad airship, with its gas contained directly in its hull, proved to be a dead end, but there is no doubt that the two Schwarz designs were the starting point from which Zeppelin, at the turn of the century, developed the rather different true rigid airship which was to survive for nearly 40 years.

Although Zeppelin's train design was rejected by the aeronautical commission in 1894 and he was unsuccessful in an attempt to join Schwarz when his rival's design was selected for official sponsorship, the commission seems to have been both interested in and impressed by Zeppelin's ideas and made a number of constructive suggestions. These were sent to the Count in a letter from the War Ministry in August 1894 and included the crucial proposals that a single cigar-shaped hull should be adopted and that this should incorporate the principle of the Schwedlar cupola, in place of Zeppelin's earlier discs, between each bay. The Schwedlar cupola (a simple wire-braced polygonal ring which was to act as the main structural member spaced at intervals along the length of the hull and linked by a cage of longitudinals) was the key to the successful and definitive rigid airship design which Zeppelin and Theodor Kober now developed. The key suggestion came from one of the members of the commission, Professor Müller-Breslau. It turned the Zeppelin design of rigid airship hull into one of the classic three-dimensional frame structures of all time. Significantly, this was a field of engineering in which the Germans (Mohr, the two Ritters and Müller-Breslau)

The Slate City of Glendale.

led the world in the second half of the nineteenth century.

While the Schwarz airship was being built in Berlin, Zeppelin and Kober continued their design work in Stuttgart and produced a final layout incorporating these new ideas. It was patented on 28 December, 1897. Earlier in the same month, soon after the destruction of the Schwarz airship, Zeppelin purchased all the Schwarz design rights, patents, etc, from the pioneer's widow. Under the terms of this deal, Zeppelin made an immediate payment of 15,000 marks (£13,000 in present-day values) and agreed to pay a royalty of 10,000 marks (£9,000) on each of the first thirty Zeppelins built. Melanie Schwarz would, therefore, presumably have received a total of some 315,000 marks (£260,000) from the Zeppelin Company over the following seventeen years, had Zeppelin not been released from this commitment when his company went bankrupt in November 1900.

Although he had now arrived at a finalised and potentially practical design, Zeppelin was still a long way from turning this into a workable airship. Indeed, it appears from the fact that he was still taking out airship-train pat-

ents in England in 1898, that his intention may even then have been to use his latest design as prime-mover of a train of airship hulls. Alternatively, he may have been merely trying to mislead the competition. Although the Kaiser had made him a small grant of 6,000 marks (£5,200 in present-day values) early in 1895, in recompense for what he had spent on his project work up to that time, Zeppelin had not yet won any significant support for his ideas. Both Berg, who had financed Schwarz, and the Daimler company, with whose engines Zeppelin had made experiments in airscrew propulsion from 1892, were interested, but neither was prepared to put up the money required which, in 1896, Zeppelin estimated at 300,000 marks (£260,000).

The turning point seems to have been reached in December 1896 when the influential Union of German Engineers came out strongly in favour of Zeppelin's proposals. This did not produce immediate results but, combined with support from an increasing number of important people, it eventually helped Zeppelin to form, in May 1898, a joint stock company 'for the promotion of air navigation with dirigibles'. This company had a capital of 800,000 marks (£700,000) of

which Zeppelin himself subscribed 52$^1/_2$ per cent. Operations started later that year on a site at Manzell on the shore of Lake Constance (Bodensee) not far from Zeppelin's birthplace near the town of Constance which was provided at nominal rent by Zeppelin's friend and Sovereign, King Charles of Württemberg.

Although he apparently did not watch the abortive test of the Schwarz – he is reported to have been in Riga at the time – Zeppelin must have been impressed by accounts of that airship striking the ground heavily at the end of her abortive flight. As a result, he appears to have decided to fly his airship from the surface of Lake Constance. A large hangar on 95 pontoons, designed by a Stuttgart architect, Tafel, was therefore built and moored at Manzell. The hangar was a technical achievement in itself, incorporating workshops, stores, offices, and even sleeping accommodation for night-watchmen. It cost about 200,000 marks (£170,000) and had the great advantage that it could be turned into the prevailing wind when the airship was moved in and out on a separate raft of pontoons. In every other respect, however, it proved unsatisfactory. Experience was to show that the use of floating hangars for the construction of the first five Zeppelins was a mistake and undoubtedly increased the already considerable costs and difficulties.

Schwarz No. 1

Manufacturer: Russian Government

Built at Volkhov near St Petersburg

Number built: one

Chief designers: D Schwarz and Ing Tenzer (at Leidenscheid)

Main structural material: aluminium or Viktoria aluminium alloy

Design began: 23 August, 1892

Construction completed: 27 August, 1894

Powerplant: one 12hp Daimler P1896 two-cylinder inline engine

Gas capacity (100 per cent inflation): 4,545cu m

Overall length: 53.3m

Section: 14m high, 12m wide

Spacing of main frames: 1.5m

Fineness ratio: 3.81–4.44

Number of gas cells: one

Number of main longitudinals: 10

Design empty weight: 4,695kg

Typical design gross lift: 5,270kg (1.16kg/cu m)

Typical disposable load: 575kg

Crew: one

Performance estimates not available

The Schwarz No.1 did not fly and was broken up on 7 February, 1897*

* Dates quoted in data for the breaking up or dismantling of airships are the dates on which work began.

Schwarz No.2

Manufacturer: Prussian Airship Detachment

Built at Tempelhof, Berlin

Number built: one

Chief designers: S Weisspfennig and M von Watzesch-Waldbach

Main structural material: aluminium or Viktoria aluminium alloy

Design began: November 1895

First flight: 3 November, 1897

Powerplant: one 12hp Daimler P1896 two-cylinder inline engine

Gas capacity (100 per cent inflation): 3,700cu m

Overall length: 47.5m

Section: 14m high, 12m wide

Spacing of main frames: 3.5m

Fineness ratio: 3.39–3.96

Number of gas cells: one

Number of main longitudinals: 16

Design empty weight: 3,560kg

Typical design gross lift: 4,300kg (1.16kg/cu m)

Typical disposable load: 740kg

Crew: one

Design maximum speed: 7.5m/s (16.77mph)

Design cruising speed: 6.5m/s (14.5mph)

Cost: DM300,000

Crashed after a few minutes on first flight on 3 November, 1897

Metalclad ZMC-2

Manufacturer: Airship Development Corporation

Built at Grosse Ile, Detroit, Michigan

Number built: one

Chief designer: R H Upson

Main structural material: duralumin and Alclad

Design began: August 1926

First flight: 19 August, 1929

Powerplant: two 220hp Wright J-5

Whirlwind nine-cylinder air-cooled radial engines

Gas capacity (100 per cent inflation): 202,000cu ft (5,720cu m)

Overall length: 149ft 5in (45.54m)

Maximum diameter: 52ft 8in (16m)

Fineness ratio: 2.83

Number of gas cells: one

Number of frames: 15 including five main frames

Number of main longitudinals: 24

Empty weight: 9,116lb (4,135kg)

Typical gross lift: 13,613lb (6,175 kg) (Helium) (1.079kg/cu m)

Typical disposable load: 2,040kg

Maximum fuel: 1,256lb (570kg)

Crew: three

Maximum speed: 61.96 mph (27.7 m/sec)

Maximum range: 683 miles (1,100 km)

Last flight: 19 August, 1939

Hours flown: 2,256hr 30min

The ZMC-2 was broken up on 17 June, 1941

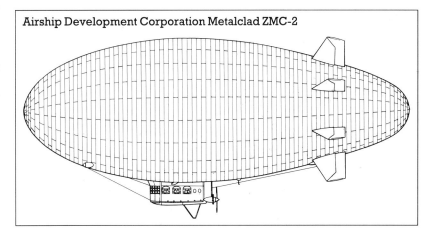

Airship Development Corporation Metalclad ZMC-2

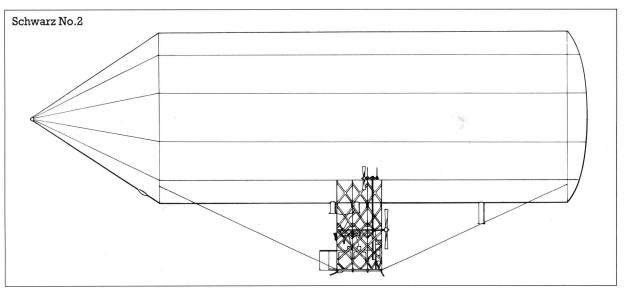

Schwarz No.2

Zeppelins LZ1 and LZ2

The first Zeppelin, LZ1, in original form with suspended weight for pitch control.

Detailed design of the first Zeppelin, LZ1, started in 1898. Kober was soon joined by a young engineer, Ludwig Dürr (1878–1956), whom he originally hired in Stuttgart to undertake the stress calculations for LZ1's structure but who became the key technical figure throughout the entire Zeppelin story. Design of this first airship was largely Kober's work, assisted by Dürr and two others. However, Berg's engineers at the aluminium company, profiting from their previous experience on the Schwarz airship, again helped with both design and manufacture of the structural elements which were shipped by train from the Berg factory at Eveking to Manzell. Berg was able to help Zeppelin in this way only after negotiating with Schwarz's widow for release from an agreement which he had entered into with Schwarz for the exclusive supply of aluminium airship components.

According to contemporary reports, the Schwarz was made of unalloyed aluminium, although an unidentified 'Viktoria' alloy is also mentioned. The LZ1 was constructed of an early aluminium-zinc alloy. This metal, in progressively improved form, was later to be used for all the Zeppelins built up to 1914. Metal salvaged from the Schwarz was said to have been used for the manufacture of the structure of LZ1, so either the Schwarz was made of the same alloy or, more likely, the salvaged aluminium was used to make the alloy for the Zeppelin.

Construction of LZ1 started in April 1899 with a labour force of about 30 men under the direction of Dipl Ing Kübler, who joined the company as works manager. The main structural assembly

LZ1 under construction.

stage was reached early in November and was completed in the spring of the following year. The construction programme was delayed by the floating hangar breaking from its moorings in July 1899 and again in January 1900. On the first occasion it was towed back without serious damage but on the second it was driven ashore and remained stranded until the water level in Lake Constance rose in the spring. As a result, completion of

the airship was delayed more than six months. Repairs to the hangar are said to have cost nearly 100,000 marks (£90,000).

Fitting and installing the 17 gas cells caused much difficulty but even so they were ready for inflation by the middle of June 1900, when the hydrogen arrived in 2,200 steel cylinders from Bitterfeld. Maj Sperling, of the Army balloon establishment at Tempelhof, arrived at the same time in order to supervise the inflation.

As completed, the LZ1 was more than two and a half times as long as the Schwarz, 128m (420ft) compared with 47.5m (155ft 9¹/₂in), although its circular cross-section was rather smaller than the elliptical Schwarz. It had three times the capacity, 11,300cu m (399,056cu ft), and had a 16hp Daimler engine in each of its two cars. There were four propellers arranged on brackets each side of the hull, very like the Schwarz, but the transmission (shafts, universal joints and bevel gears) were a great improvement on the leather belts of the Schwarz. The LZ1 also had control surfaces but these were still far too small to be effective. They consisted of a single rudder each side of the hull fore and aft.

LZ2.

Dr Theodor Kober designed the LZ1.
(Pritchard collection)

Pitch control was by means of a moving weight (300kg or 661lb), a system first proposed for the Pauly and Egg airship of 1816.

Inflation began on 1 July, 1900. It took 12 hours to fill the 17 rubberised-fabric gas cells and the airship was then brought out of her hangar and the engines started. A crew of five, led by Count Zeppelin himself, went on the first flight on 2 July. This lasted about 20 minutes, during which a height of 400m (1,300ft) was reached. Control proved unsatisfactory but a speed of 3.8m/s (8.5mph) was achieved. Lack of control seems to have been due to the inadequate surfaces, to difficulties with the fore and aft weight, to jamming control-runs and to distortion of the main structure. Some bent structural members had to be straightened and strengthened when the ship was safely back in the shed. Two further flights were made about three months later but, although a speed of 7.8m/s (17.5mph) was reached, the overall results were disappointing and the company's

funds had been completely exhausted. There was not enough money left even for another re-fill of gas, which would have cost 8,000–10,000 marks (£7,000–£9,000), a formidable item when account is taken of the fact that osmosis of the hydrogen through the rubberised fabric meant that a filling lasted only three weeks.

The company closed down and went into liquidation in November 1900. Zeppelin acquired all the assets for 124,000 marks (£55,000). He had every reason to feel discouraged, but it was not in the nature of the man to give in. He immediately set to work to win new support. For some time he made little progress: the Union of German Engineers was politely helpful but, like most of the better informed, was not convinced that the trials of LZ1 had proved the feasibility of Zeppelin's concepts, as indeed they had not.

But Zeppelin persisted. He realised that he would have to build a new airship: the weakness of LZ1's structure was probably its most serious deficiency and this could not be overcome by modification. Nevertheless, much had been learnt from building the first airship. Dürr, who had now taken over from Kober, agreed with the Count that a much stronger structure was possible for a similar, or perhaps lower, weight. Two other factors were working in their favour: the petrol engine was rapidly improving, under the impetus of the development of the motor car; and aluminium alloys and hydrogen were getting cheaper as a result of improved and larger-scale production.

At last Zeppelin managed to persuade Berg to provide the structural components for a new airship on credit, and the Daimler company agreed to lend two of its latest engines which developed 80hp each for no more weight than their 16hp predecessors. The War Ministry agreed to provide the hydrogen. Even with this help, Zeppelin estimated that he would still need 400,000 marks (£350,000). Of this sum, 8,000 marks came from a public appeal, 124,000 from profits on a lottery, and 50,000 from the German Chancellor's fund (apparently lottery tickets could not be sold in the State of Prussia and a special grant was made instead). The Count provided the balance of 218,000 marks from his own pocket.

Construction of LZ2 began in April 1905 and was completed in October. It was undertaken in the same floating hangar at Manzell but was under the direction of Dipl Ing Ernst Uhland, who had succeeded Kübler as works manager. It is said that the latter

Dr Ing Ludwig Dürr designed the LZ2 and all subsequent Zeppelins. (Pritchard collection)

parted with the Count because the old man never forgave him not taking part in the flight trials of LZ1. Kübler's excuse for refusing was that he could not afford the associated increased premium on his life insurance.

Kober had also left, and the design work on LZ2 was completed under the direction of young Dürr. He made a fine job of it. Externally, LZ2 was similar to LZ1, having the same length and diameter and the same number of 8m (26ft 3in) bays, although without the closer spacing near the cars and without intermediate frames. The frame bracing was also improved. In most other respects, the layout was similar, with two cars containing the engines and four propellers on brackets each side of the hull. However, LZ2 differed in certain fundamental and vital respects which converted the design from one which was structurally inadequate to one which was to last in progressively improved form for 30 years.

The most important change was in the main structural members. Instead of the flat lattice members of LZ1, with angle-sectioned criss-cross bracing, LZ2 had triangular girders with similar tubular bracing. These were much stronger for their weight, and in fact the complete ship was about one ton lighter. LZ2 had

16, instead of 17, gas cells, reducing the total capacity to 10,400cu m (367,500cu ft). The higher-powered engines drove propellers which were three times the diameter of those on the earlier airship. Research into the best size and type of airscrew continued and resulted in progressive improvements in their design for later Zeppelins. At the same time there were remarkable advances in the successive engines produced first by Daimler and after 1911 by Maybach. The clumsy movable fore-and-aft weight for pitch control was discarded. Instead, box-kite elevator surfaces, no doubt inspired by aeroplane practice, were mounted at the front with triple rudders at the rear. The most important difference was in the keel member. In LZ1 this had been a long, rather flimsy, plate girder, extending the length of the parallel part of the hull but held some distance beneath it by V-bracing. The girder provided a walkway between the two cars. In LZ2, the triangular keel, although still outside and below the hull, was structurally more part of it and the length between the cars was covered in, giving the airship an altogether tidier and more business-like appearance.

There is no doubt that the design of LZ2 was a major *tour de force* by Dürr and firmly established him as the technical mainspring of Zeppelin development, which was to set the pace of rigid airship progress world-wide for the next 35 years. He was to continue to hold this position until the end.

In LZ2, Zeppelin had the makings of a practical airship. Indeed, her sister ship LZ3, which was identical in basic design was sold to the Army in 1909 as ZI. She had been lengthened and had had other detailed improvements incorporated, after her maiden flight on 9 October, 1906. ZI remained in service until as late as 1913.

LZ2 had been ready for her trials in November 1905, and with some reason, Count Zep-

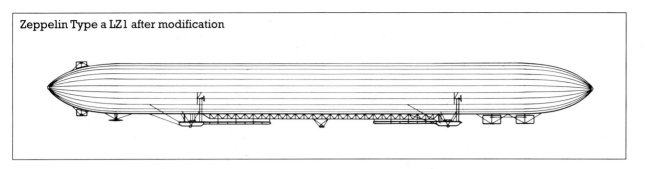

Zeppelin Type a LZ1 after modification

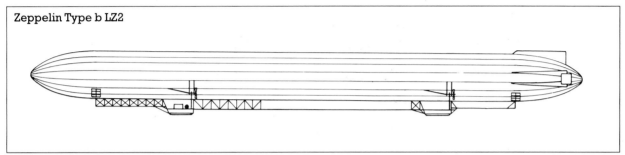

Zeppelin Type b LZ2

pelin had had great hopes of success. However, the trials proved to be a disaster. On the first attempt to bring the airship out of the shed, on 20 November, she was damaged and had to be put back. Protracted repairs delayed the next attempt until 17 January, 1906. On this occasion, with Zeppelin again in command, the airship rose rapidly to about 500m (1,640ft). Stability and control were still unsatisfactory; so much so that when Zeppelin discovered the wind at that height was too strong for the ship to make headway against it, he dared not fly lower, where the wind would have been weaker, because of the lack of control combined, no doubt, with his own limited experience and skill as pilot.

Shortly after this, both engines failed and LZ2 was clearly in trouble. Even so, after drifting with the wind for some distance, a successful 'free balloon' landing was made. It was the first rigid airship to alight successfully on land. By amazing luck, no significant damage was done to the ship. However, she had to be left moored out overnight and the wind got up enough to wreck her completely. The engines and many components were salvaged but LZ2 was a total loss.

Zeppelin LZ1 (Type a)

Manufacturer: Aktiengesellschaft zur Förderung-der Motorluft-schiffahrt (Joint Stock Company for the Promotion of Motor Airship Travel)

Built at Manzell

Number built: one

Chief designer: T Kober; also Tenzer (at Berg's works)

Main structural material: Zn-Al alloy

Design began: May 1898

First flight: 2 July, 1900

Powerplant: two 14hp Daimler N1899 four-cylinder inline engines

Gas capacity (100 per cent inflation): 11,300cu m

Overall length: 128.0m

Maximum diameter: 11.7m

Spacing of main frames: 8.0m

Fineness ratio: 10.21

Number of gas cells: 17

Number of main longitudinals: 24

Empty weight: 10,300kg

Typical gross lift: 13,100kg (1.16 kg/cu m)

Typical disposable load: 2,800kg

Maximum fuel: 100kg

Crew: five

Maximum speed: 7.8m/s (17.39 mph). 7.6m/s (16.99mph) on third flight

Maximum range: 280km at speed of 2.8m/s (6.26mph)

Static ceiling: 650m

Hours flown: 2

Cost: DM200,000

Last flight 21 (possibly 24) October, 1900. Broken up on 30 April, 1901

Zeppelin LZ2 (Type b)

Manufacturer: Aktiengesellschaft zur Förderung-der Motorluft-schiffahrt (Joint Stock Company for the Promotion of Motor Airship Travel)

Built at Manzell

Number built: one

Chief designer: L Dürr

Main structural material: Zn-Al alloy

Design began: April 1905

First flight: 17 January, 1906

Powerplant: two 80hp Daimler H4L four-cylinder inline engines

Gas capacity (100 per cent inflation): 10,400cu m (11,300cu m sometimes quoted)

Overall length: 128.0m

Maximum diameter: 11.7m

Spacing of main frames: 8.0m

Fineness ratio: 10.94

Number of gas cells: 16

Number of main longitudinals: 16

Empty weight: 9,250kg

Typical gross lift: 12,050kg (1.16 kg/cu m)

Typical disposable load: 2,800kg

Maximum fuel: 2,000kg

Crew: seven

Maximum speed: 11.0m/s (24.6 mph)

Maximum range: 1,100km

Static ceiling: 850m

Made two flights, both on 17 January, 1906. Destroyed in storm same day.

Zeppelin over the Alps – LZ3 and LZ4/5

A lesser man would have given up after the loss of LZ2 but the Count was not long dismayed. In a short time he was out arguing and persuading again, now claiming – with some justification – that the last flight had shown that LZ2 was capable of a speed of about 11m/s (25mph) when she had held her own against the wind. Dürr had ideas about curing the instability and lack of control; all they needed was another airship on which to test them.

There was still a little money left and they still had the loaned engines and Berg's credit. Zeppelin found a bit more money of his own and the King of Württemberg agreed to another lottery, the proceeds of which could be spent on the next Zeppelin. They did not wait for this: work began on LZ3 in the floating shed in April 1908 and was completed by October.

LZ3 was basically the same design as LZ2 with the same engines and hull. Some salvaged components of the LZ2 were, in fact, used in the new airship. The only important differences were the addition of quadruplane elevator surfaces forward and aft and of two near-horizontal fins attached to the aft end on each side. These were Dürr's idea, apparently based on wind-tunnel tests on a model, but such surfaces had also been suggested by Charles Renard and Henri Hervé (d.1922) in France in 1903.

With these changes, and slightly up-rated engines which gave 85hp each, LZ3 proved to be a success. Two two-hour flights were made by the Count from Manzell on 9 and 10 October,

LZ3 at the floating shed at Manzell.

1906. These demonstrated complete steadiness and reasonable control which, combined with the Count's increasing experience, enabled the airship to return to its shed on both occasions. A speed of 12.2m/s (27.29mph) was demonstrated.

Both Government and public, who until now had reacted to Zeppelin somewhat sceptically, began to come round to an acceptance of his ideas. The Germans, with their love of the spectacular and particularly, of

LZ4 in original configuration. There was also a bow rudder.

the *kolossal*, responded to the inspiring sight of these great and beautiful ships droning through the sky. These feelings were no doubt linked to the belief, in those nationalistic days before the First World War, that the Zeppelin represented an important potential military advantage to Germany over other nations; particularly, over the traditional enemy, France, a country which had always prided itself on its ascendancy in aeronautics.

Trials of LZ3 had to be suspended after the October flights for lack of funds. The change in the climate of opinion was, at last, to bring official backing. This was something Zeppelin had, until then, largely had to do without ever since he had been turned down in favour of Schwarz by the Helmholtz committee in 1894. Set against the niggardly 6,000 marks awarded to him by the Kaiser for his project work in 1895, Zeppelin had probably spent approximately a million and a half marks (£1.3 million) up to this point. The money had come from various sources, mainly from his own pocket, but there had been no direct financial help from the Imperial Government in Berlin.

Now the position changed. In the autumn of 1906, a Motor Airship Research Committee had been appointed to advise the central Government. This committee paid most attention to the Parseval pressure-airships which were also being developed successfully in Germany at that time, but it did recommend that 500,000 marks (£440,000) should be paid to Zeppelin to enable him to build a replacement for his dilapidated and inadequate floating shed, and to pay for further flight tests with LZ3.

Work appears to have started on the new shed when better weather permitted in the spring of 1907 and was completed in September. LZ3 lay neglected in the old shed until the new one was ready and then flying started again. On 30 September a flight of eight hours was completed during which 350km (217 miles) were covered, nonstop. This flight created a sensation and greatly strengthened Zeppelin's hand in his negotiations with the Government. After this flight, LZ3 made five, shorter trips in just over two weeks during October, before being put away again in the new shed for the winter.

In the latter part of 1907 the Government finally agreed to pay Zeppelin 400,000 marks (£340,000) for the construction and testing of a new airship. Furthermore, it undertook to purchase both LZ3 and the new ship for 2,150,000 marks (£1.84 million), provided the Count first demonstrated a nonstop 24-hour flight during which at least 700km (435 miles) had to be covered. The price agreed for the two ships included compensation of 500,000 marks to Zeppelin for all he had spent on his airship development work over the preceding 15 years.

With prospects of getting his enterprise on to a sounder financial basis, Zeppelin entered into negotiations with Krupps of Essen and with Carl Berg to see if they were prepared to provide more capital and participate in a new Zeppelin company. These negotiations were unsuccessful, however, and Zeppelin remained the sole owner of the enterprise.

LZ3 in her existing form lacked the performance to make the required 24-hour flight, particularly when operating from the 400m (1,300ft) level of Lake Constance. (*See* Note 13) Zeppelin therefore wisely used the excuse of the approaching winter to delay the required demonstration flight, postponing it until the following spring.

The new larger floating shed was damaged in a storm and sank in December 1907. LZ3, housed inside it, was lucky to escape serious damage, but this event put an end to her flying for the time being. When the new shed had been repaired and refloated, LZ3 was moved into the old building so that the assembly of LZ4 could begin in the new, in March 1908. Construction of compo-

LZ4 in original configuration, partly in the Manzell floating shed.

The original tail unit of LZ4.

LZ4 in final configuration.
(Science Museum)

nents for the new ship had started in November and she was completed in June.

The larger shed made possible a larger airship. LZ4 had both a greater diameter, 13m (42ft 73/4in) compared with 11.7m for LZ1–3 and, at 136m (446ft 2in) was longer than her predecessors. Her capacity was 15,000cu m (529,720cu ft) and she was powered by two 105hp four-cylinder J4 Daimlers. A covered-in triangular keel and walkway extended the full length of the ship. Amidships, this gangway expanded into a small passenger cabin at one point.

LZ4 made her first flight on 20 June, 1908. She was an imme-

diate success. The higher-powered engines, combined with larger control and stabilising surfaces, made her steadier and more controllable. When first flown, LZ4 had bow and stern quadruplane elevators, a single rectangular rudder at the stern and one at the bow. This rudder arrangement proved inadequate. The bow rudder was then removed and single port and starboard rudders were added between the horizontal fins. In the final version of the LZ4, the stern rudder was enlarged to an elliptical form, twin port and starboard rudders between the horizontal fins turned as a unit rather than independently, vertical top and bottom fins were added to the stern while the bow elevators were retained.

These progressive changes were an important development exercise aimed at improving control and stability. During her short life of only six weeks, LZ4 made a number of important flights, which identify her as the most notable of the early Zeppelins. At the same time she acted as a test vehicle for improvements in the control arrangements of the Zeppelins.

After a few short local flights, during which a speed of 13.5m/s (30mph) was measured, the Count decided on a longer flight before attempting the 24-hour test required by the Government. Magnificent weather on 1 July encouraged him to make a spectacular 12-hour flight over Switzerland during which he overflew Lucerne and Zürich and made a 380km (236 miles) journey in the Alps.

It is difficult to appreciate today the sensation caused by this flight. For the first time, many thousands of people, in two countries, saw a great airship flying majestically above their heads in the wonderful setting of the lakes and high mountains. The writer himself saw Zeppelins flying in the Swiss mountains many years later. He remembers them as an unforgettable spectacle, even when aircraft had become com-

LZ4's final tail configuration, with dorsal and ventral fins and 26ft high rudder.

monplace. In July 1908, the first public demonstration of controlled heavier-than-air flight by Wilbur Wright at Le Mans was still five weeks in the future. A few, small, pressure-airships had made local flights, principally in France and Germany, but these were as nothing to Zeppelin's great rigid on an extended international cruise over the Alps.

There is no doubt that this flight was a masterstroke of propaganda for the Zeppelins. It was endorsed over the following few days by joy-rides given to the King and Queen of Württemberg and to some of the royal princes.

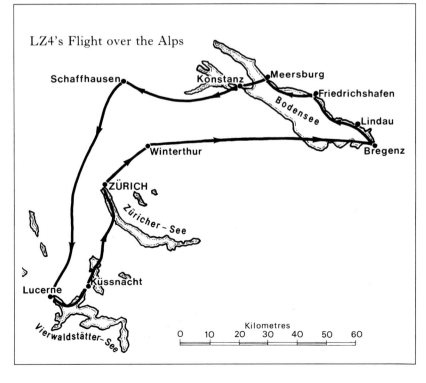

LZ4's Flight over the Alps

LZ4 and the Manzell sheds.

Its impact on the German public was almost certainly the main reason for the extraordinary popular reaction five weeks later when LZ4 was destroyed by fire at Echterdingen near Stuttgart, following the second of two forced landings during an attempt at the 24-hour flight. By great good fortune only two crew members were slightly injured in this incident, the first to a Zeppelin when the hydrogen ignited.

There is no record of the fact, but the Alpine flight was probably suggested by Hugo Eckener (1868–1954), a young journalist who had joined Zeppelin as a part-time public relations adviser in about February 1906. In the future, Eckener was to take up the old Count's mantle after his death and become leader of the Zeppelin enterprise. He had many abilities but, as we shall see, perhaps his greatest was his flair as a publicist. This was to contribute much to the Zeppelin story. Perhaps the first evidence of it was LZ4's memorable flight in the Alps.

Zeppelin LZ3 (Type b)

Manufacturer: Aktiengesellschaft zur Förderung-der Motorluft-schiffahrt (Joint Stock Company for the Promotion of Motor Airship Travel)

Built at Manzell

Number built: one

Chief designer: L Dürr

Main structural material: Zn-Al alloy

Design began: April 1905; converted to LZ3A in October 1908

First flight: 9 October, 1906 (LZ3); 23 October, 1908 (LZ3A)

Powerplant: two 85hp Daimler H4L four-cylinder inline engines (LZ3); two 105hp Daimler J4 four-cylinder inline engines (LZ3A)

Gas capacity (100 per cent inflation): 11,300cu m (LZ3); 12,200cu m (LZ3A)

Overall length: 128.0m (LZ3); 136.0m (LZ3A)

Maximum diameter: 11.7m

Spacing of main frames: 8.0m

Fineness ratio: 10.94 (LZ3); 11.62 (LZ3A)

Number of gas cells: 16 (LZ3); 17 (LZ3A)

Number of main longitudinals: 16

Empty weight: 9,250kg (LZ3); 10,320kg (LZ3A)

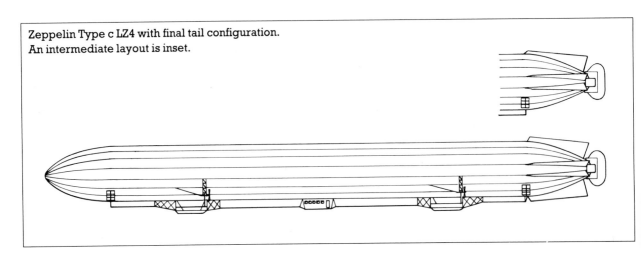

Zeppelin Type c LZ4 with final tail configuration.
An intermediate layout is inset.

Typical gross lift: 13,120kg (LZ3); 14,150kg (LZ3A) (1.16kg/cu m)

Typical disposable load: 3,870kg {LZ3), 3,830kg) (LZ3A)

Maximum fuel: 2,000kg (LZ3)

Crew: seven

Maximum speed: 15.0m/s (33.55 mph) (LZ3A)

Maximum range: 1,100km

Static ceiling: 850m (LZ3); 880m (LZ3A)

Last flight: LZ3 on 12 May, 1908; LZ3A on 7 March, 1913

Hours flown: 20 (LZ3)

Number of flights: 45 (LZ3A)

LZ3A was broken up after March 1913

Zeppelin LZ4 (Type c)

Manufacturer: Aktiengesellschaft zur Förderung-der Motorluft-schiffahrt (Joint Stock Company for the Promotion of Motor Airship Travel)

Built at Manzell

Number built: two (LZ4 and LZ5)

Chief designer: L Dürr

Main structural material: Zn-Al alloy

Design began: November 1907

First flight: 20 June, 1908

Powerplant: two 105hp Daimler J4 four-cylinder inline engines

Gas capacity (100 per cent inflation): 15,000cu m

Overall length: 136.0m

Maximum diameter: 13.0m

Spacing of main frames: 8.0m

Fineness ratio: 10.46

Number of gas cells: 17

Number of main longitudinals: 16

Empty weight: 12,750kg

Typical gross lift: 17,400kg (1.16 kg/cu m)

Typical disposable load: 4,650kg

Maximum fuel: 2,500kg

Crew: 11

Passengers: 14

Maximum speed: 13.5m/s (30.19 mph) (LZ4); 15.5m/s (34.67mph) (LZ5)

Maximum range: 1,450km

LZ4 first flew on 20 June, 1908, and made about eight flights before being destroyed by fire on the ground on 5 August, 1908.

LZ5 first flew on 26 May, 1909, and last flew on 15 April, 1910. It was destroyed in a storm on 25 April, 1910.

Echterdingen – LZ3A and LZ5

The German public's reaction to the destruction by fire of LZ4 on 5 August, 1908, at Echterdingen, marked a turning point in the story of the rigid airship. Public sympathy for the 70-year old Count was such that spontaneous donations came in from all over Germany. These amounted ultimately to a total of at least 6.25 million marks (£5.7 million). This enormous sum converted disaster into triumph and was used to form a trust, the Zeppelin Foundation, of which the Count became chairman. The trust allocated three million marks immediately to establish a new company, Luftschiffbau Zeppelin GmbH, to take over the Zeppelin enterprise. The company was formed on 8 September, 1908. At the same time Alfred Colsman (1873–1966), son-in-law of Carl Berg, was appointed general manager. Previously the works at Manzell had been managed by the Count's nephew.

Following the loss of LZ4, LZ3 was repaired, lengthened by an 8m bay (putting her capacity up to 12,200cu m) and equipped with the more powerful J4 Daimlers of the type used in LZ4. The rebuilt airship (LZ3A) was first flown on 23 October, 1908, and, significantly, was allowed to carry the Crown Prince on a trip to Donaueschingen on 7 November when the Kaiser was paying a visit there. The Kaiser visited Manzell three days later (he had made his first visit on 10 October) and decorated Count Zeppelin with the Order of the Black Eagle. From a boat on Lake Constance he then watched LZ3A make a flight. All this showed that, despite the LZ4 disaster and the previous setbacks, official circles in Germany were being won over to Zeppelin at the same time as popular sentiment swung in his favour.

The German Government were still awaiting completion of the 24-hour flight test and subsequent delivery of its first Zeppelin. With the loss of LZ4, a replacement ship (LZ5) was laid down at Manzell in the autumn of 1908. She was a close replica of LZ4. Indeed, it was reported that she was actually fitted with cars and engines and possibly some other components, salvaged from her sister ship. However, it is believed that the engines were the longer-stroke J4L model which gave 110 hp each. LZ5 was first flown on 25 May, 1909, but, redesignated ZII, she was not delivered to the Army until August.

Meanwhile LZ3A had been taken over by the military and designated ZI (*See* Appendix 6 for explanation of Zeppelin designations). A detachment of 80 men, under the command of Maj Sperling, arrived at Manzell in February 1909, and 9 March the military crew made its first flights with the Count as captain. After he had instructed the Major in the techniques of pilotage, the Count allowed him off in sole charge later the same day. For the first time Zeppelin saw one of his ships in flight from the ground. It is a remarkable fact about this doughty old aristocrat that, in addition to providing the mainspring of the whole development of the rigid airship, he also (starting at the age of 62) acted as captain during all the test flying of his early airships. Up to March 1909 he was, in fact, the only Zeppelin pilot. He then converted Sperling onto ZI. Sperling was from the Army Airship Battalion and had had previous experience on the Gross pressure-airships. Sperling successfully delivered ZI 340km (211 miles) to its base at Metz between 29 June and 3 July.

Before the Army took her away, Zeppelin made a number of further flights on ZI. On 15 March he established a Zeppelin altitude record of 1,720m (5,512ft). On 16 March he made

LZ3A, the modified LZ3, was taken over by the Army as ZI. (Pritchard collection)

the first deliberate alighting on land, probably at the new site on the northern outskirts of Friedrichshafen where his new factory was being constructed. On 19 March he carried 26 people on a cross-country trip of 240km (149 miles) in four hours, which represented an average speed of 16.7m/s (37.35mph). On 1 April he attempted to fly to Munich but was frustrated by strong winds. The ship had to be moored in the open overnight but returned safely to base the fol-

LZ5 on Lake Constance. First flight was on 26 May, 1909.

lowing day. On 5 April he made an attempt on the 24-hour demonstration flight but had to abandon this too, after 11 hours, because of rising wind. The following day he achieved a 13hr 20min flight, much of it in the dark.

Count Zeppelin certainly did his best to show the soldiers what his ship could do. Nevertheless he failed to make the required 24-hour qualifying flight and the Army took over ZI with this requirement still unfulfilled. It remained for Zeppelin to make the demonstration on a later ship.

Once LZ5 had flown on 25 May, either this ship or ZI could be accommodated in the first berth (completed in 1909) of the new, two-berth factory hangar at

Friedrichshafen. No doubt the Army crew practised berthing into this land hangar before they left for Metz at the end of June.

Meanwhile the Count was busy test-flying LZ5, initially from the floating hangar at Manzell where she had been assembled. By 29 May he decided that he was ready to use the new ship for another attempt at the elusive 24-hour flight requirement. Perhaps prompted by Eckener again, he secretly proposed to combine meeting the official test with a flight of 600km (373 miles) to Berlin, a spectacular demonstration of the cross-country capabilities of his airship.

Although Eckener later denied that Zeppelin had planned to fly to Berlin on this occasion, there

seems little doubt that that was indeed his intention. In any case the public and even the Government in Berlin believed this to be the plan and a large crowd, including the Kaiser and other members of the royal family, gathered at Tempelhof to greet him.

LZ5 set off on the great adventure on the evening of Saturday, 29 May. The Count as usual was in command but he was accompanied by a crew of six, including Chief Designer Dürr, whom he was training as a pilot. At first they made good progress but gradually a wind got up and increased in strength. By the time they had covered over 550km (342 miles) it was clear that they would not be able to make it. LZ5's top speed of 15.5m/s (34.67mph) was insufficient for this kind of flight in anything but ideal conditions. On Sunday evening, therefore, they turned back towards Friedrichshafen, having reached Bitterfeld, nearly 160km (100 miles) short of their goal. After flying for 37hr40 min and covering 970km (602 miles) by the route flown, they were running short of fuel. Eventually, towards midday on Monday, they had to make a landing in open country near Göppingen.

The flight was a remarkable effort for a man of nearly 71 as well as for an airship with the limited performance of LZ5. It is hard to realise today the conditions under which the Count and his companions rode in LZ5's open control-car, with a roaring engine just behind them, in continuous and no doubt some of the time bumpy flight, for more than a day and two nights. This was by far the longest flight so far achieved by an airship.

Unfortunately, while refuelling at Göppingen the ship was blown against a pear tree and its nose was seriously damaged. For a while it looked as if this would be another disaster but, by great enterprise, assisted particularly by the presence of Dürr, a rough jury-nose was rigged over the front of the crumpled hull and

LZ5 after the accident at Göppingen. The ship was repaired and went back into service as ZII.

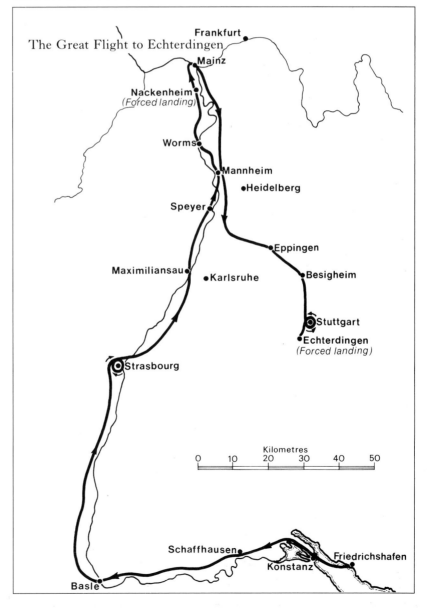

The Great Flight to Echterdingen

LZ6, at its floating shed at Manzell, in its original twin-engined configuration. (Lufthansa)

the ship was then flown 150km (93 miles) back to Friedrichshafen where it was safely hangared two days later.

Turning back from Berlin and the subsequent forced landing resulted in some bad publicity. The Kaiser and the Berlin public were understandably disappointed. This unfavourable effect was offset, to some extent, by the damaged ship's successful return to base after covering about 1,120km (696 miles) by the route taken. Zeppelin promised the Kaiser he would fly one of his ships to Berlin as soon as he could.

LZ5 (now known by its military designation ZII) was repaired and, piloted by the Count, set out for her military base at Cologne on 2 August. When she reached Coblenz, high winds forced the Count to turn back to Frankfurt where he stopped the night. The following day a propeller broke and there was another delay. Finally, on 5 August, after circling Düren the ship reached Cologne, where it was welcomed with great enthusiasm and the Army took over its new acquisition.

Zeppelins for the Army – LZ6 ('ZIII')

Delivery to the Army of ZI in July and of ZII in August 1909 marked a new phase in the history of the Zeppelin. Until then these ships had been purely experimental and we have therefore followed the vicissitudes of their development in some detail. Now they became military weapons, supposedly suitable for daily service with the Army. Soon, for reasons which will shortly be told, the Zeppelin would also become a civil vehicle.

It should be remembered that the rigids of 1909–10, with their top speeds of less than 20m/s (45mph), were not really practical aircraft for anything other than limited local flying over land in good weather. As Eckener himself wrote, the pioneer airship pilots soon discovered that winds of 10m/s (22mph) and more are experienced almost daily at heights of a few hundred metres. A vehicle capable of no more than

about 20m/s is of minimal practical use for getting from place to place in such winds, except when their direction happens to be favourable. Speed over the ground would often be cut to 10m/s or less.

There is continuing confirmation of all this in the modern joy-riding blimps, a few of which are still operating. These aircraft have about the same maximum speed (22m/s; 49mph) as the fastest Zeppelins of 1910–14. They can be used for local flying in a particular area, but even then care must be taken not to get carried downwind of base in conditions of increasing wind. Low speed is also a disadvantage to an airship because it reduces the dynamic effects available to its pilot to compensate for losses or gains in lift. These may be due to temperature changes, consumption of fuel, and rain or snow. Using the extra performance in this way cuts speed but can make an important contribution to efficient operation. Unlike most other rigid airships, however, the Zeppelins were normally flown within five degrees of the horizontal thus minimising dynamic effects on lift.

The year 1909 saw the beginning of a new phase for the Zeppelin enterprise itself. The company now employed about 90 people. Moved from Manzell out of the unsatisfactory lakeside accommodation and the floating sheds, the factory was established in new, specially-built premises on a fine flying ground just north of Friedrichshafen. This site had been purchased for 340,000 marks (£290,000). The new construction hangar, completed by Brückenbauanstalt Flender AG (Flender Bridge Building Company) in September 1909, contained two berths in which two airships could be built simultaneously. It was claimed at this time that Zeppelin would soon have the capacity to build twelve airships a year, although this would clearly have required a considerable increase in the labour force. The new hangar later came to be called the Ring Shed because it was used for the manufacture of the hull frames after it became too small for final assembly of the Zeppelins themselves. However, up to 1915, the next thirty or so Zeppelins were to be assembled in this building.

A new, larger assembly hangar, known as Factory Shed I, was put up alongside it in 1914.

Apart from these much improved facilities at the new Zeppelin works, the design side of the company's activities began to benefit at this time from a wind-tunnel which had been built at Göttingen in the autumn of 1908. Tests were undertaken there on different forms of airship hull, the first aerodynamic experiments at a laboratory which was later to make many major contributions to this field. The research was undertaken at the instigation of Felix Klein, head of the science faculty at the university, and was

LZ6 after fitting of the third engine. LZ6 was later fitted with a cabin and became the second passenger aircraft and the first to make more than one passenger flight.
(Luftschiffbau Zeppelin)

LZ6 in front of the Baden-Oos shed from which Eckener successfully operated it on behalf of DELAG during September 1910. More than 300 passengers were carried on 34 flights in 18 days during that month.
(Lufthansa)

LZ6 flying with three engines. This airship was expected to serve the Army as ZIII but instead was fitted with a cabin and served with DELAG.
(Pritchard collection)

joints and bevel gears, LZ6 went over to a new type of drive using steel belts. This proved to be a mistake; the 'steel band' transmission was not satisfactory and was eventually abandoned in favour of the old system, but not before it had caused a great many problems.

Transmission troubles first appeared on the flight to Berlin. After completing its initial tests LZ6 left Friedrichshafen on 27 August, under the command of Dürr, who was now a fully-qualified pilot and was helping the Count with the flying. He reached Nuremberg (240km, 149 miles) in four hours and then the trouble started. The flight had to be interrupted there while an engine was changed and a propeller, which had come off in flight, replaced. The hazards of such unpremeditated landings were considerable. An airship requires a large handling party on the ground. Without such help, a forced landing in anything but a dead calm involves considerable risks. The flight continued on 28 August but had to stop again, at Bitterfeld, to make adjustments to a transmission which was giving trouble and to pick up the Count so that he could take part in the triumphant arrival in Berlin. They left Bitterfeld on 29 August and, later that day, were tumultuously welcomed at Tegel field, Berlin, by a great crowd headed, by the Kaiser.

LZ6 left Berlin, again under Dürr's command, late that same evening but continued to be plagued by transmission problems on the way home. Near Wittenburg a propeller again flew off, this time piercing the adjoining gas cell, causing it to deflate. The ship had to make a forced landing in open country where repairs were undertaken over the next three days. During this time LZ6

under the direction of the famous Ludwig Prandtl who was a member of the Motorluftschiff-Studien-Gesellschaft, formed in 1906 under the patronage of the Kaiser, to study airship design. MSG concentrated particularly on the development of the Parseval pressure-airships.

The first airship completed at the new works was LZ6, often popularly known as 'ZIII' because Zeppelin had expected to sell her to the Army as its third ship. In the event, the anti-rigid lobby in the Army Airship Battalion (with a vested interest in pressure-airships, which were also being developed rapidly and were achieving some fine performances) prevented further purchase of military Zeppelins at this time. For this reason, LZ6 was mainly used as a development ship by her manufacturers. Later, she became, briefly, the second commercial airship.

To launch LZ6's career Zeppelin decided to use her for the promised flight to Berlin. She flew for the first time on 25 August, 1909, a sister-ship to LZ4 and LZ5, being of the same length, diameter and capacity. Like LZ5, she had two four-cylinder Daimler J4L engines but these had been uprated to give 115hp each. The only important innovation was in the transmission to the bracket-mounted propellers. Instead of the previously-used shafts, universal had a very narrow escape from destruction when a squall passed over the field. Held down by hundreds of soldiers and heavy because of the empty gas cell, she escaped damage. Late on the night of 1 September, Dürr pressed on to Friedrichshafen, getting home safely the following evening, after a flight of 22½ hours.

During September, joy-rides were given both at Friedrichshafen and Frankfurt, where LZ6 was joined by the Army's ZII. Passengers flown from Friedrichshafen included members of the Reichstag and of the Swiss Federal Council. Among the distinguished passengers at Frankfurt was Orville Wright. The demonstrations at Frankfurt were significant because of their effect on the next important development, the formation of DELAG (Deutsche Luftschiffahrts AG), the German Airship Transport Company.

In an unofficial race from Friedrichshafen to Darmstadt on 15 September, the Parseval P.L.3 pressure-airship was claimed to be slightly faster than LZ6.

LZ6 had a rather mixed career after her flight to Berlin in August/September 1909. That flight had shown that a further improvement in performance was essential if airships were to become practical cross-country vehicles. The easiest way to achieve this was to increase total engine power as well as the number of engines and to improve the reliability of the engines themselves. LZ6 was withdrawn from service at the end of September 1909 and a third engine was installed in a new nacell mounted in place of the passenger cabin in the centre of the keel. This engine drove two additional bracket propellers, mounted on the sides of the hull, amidships, through steel-band transmissions. LZ6 was first flown with the third engine on 21 October. The effect on performance was significant: top speed was increased from 13.5m/s (30.19mph) to 15.2m/s (34mph).

The 140hp Maybach A-Z engine which was fitted to LZ6 in a midship position in October 1909.

Karl Maybach whose company was established close to the Zeppelin works at Friedrichshafen. The Maybach engines powered the majority of Zeppelins.
(Pritchard collection)

The new engine was a Maybach A-Z of 140hp, produced by Maybach Motorenbau GmbH which had been formed with Zeppelin's help in November 1908. This company, whose works were later built adjacent to the new Zeppelin factory at Friedrichshafen, was headed by Wilhelm Maybach (1845–1929), partner of Gottlieb Daimler in the development of the motor car. His son, Karl Maybach, provided the technical leadership of the company. It was to specialise in development and manufacture of airship engines and soon took over most of this business from

Daimler, which had previously supplied all Zeppelin's engines.

From this time progress in the development of Maybach engines was to keep pace with that of Zeppelin's airships and was simultaneously to make a vital contribution to that development.

The promise of the trial installation of the third engine in LZ6 suggested that a proper job should be made of the conversion. LZ6's engine in the middle of the keel left no space for passengers and the weight of the third engine and its fuel seriously reduced the useful load.

The answer was to rebuild the ship completely, and on 12 February, 1910, LZ6 was put into the hangar at Friedrichshafen, cut in two and lengthened by the insertion of an extra 8m bay. This bay contained an eighteenth gas cell, in the same way that LZ3 had been enlarged in 1908. This process was to be repeated often with other rigid airships in the future. At the same time, the Maybach engine was moved into the front gondola where it drove a pair of bracket propellers with the original-type transmission, and the two original Daimler engines were put together in the rear gondola, each driving a bracket propeller through a similar transmission. Finally, after it

Zeppelin Type d LZ6

had been decided to let DELAG use LZ6 until the replacement for *Deutschland* was ready, a comfortable cabin for ten to twelve passengers was re-installed in the middle of the keel.

Zeppelin LZ6 (Type d)

Manufacturer: Luftschiffbau Zeppelin GmbH

Built at Friedrichshafen

Number built: one

Chief designer: L Dürr

Main structural material: Zn-Al alloy

Design began: January 1909

First flight: 25 August, 1909

Powerplant: two 115hp Daimler J4L four-cylinder inline engines. In October 1909 fitted with 140hp Maybach A-Z six-cylinder inline as third engine

Gas capacity (100 per cent inflation): 15,000cu m (LZ6)

16,000cu m (LZ6A)

Overall length: 136.0m (LZ6); 144.0m (LZ6A)

Maximum diameter: 13.0m

Spacing of main frames: 8.0m

Fineness ratio: 10.45 (LZ6); 11.08 (LZ6A)

Number of gas cells: 17 (LZ6); 18 (LZ6A)

Number of main longitudinals: 16

Empty weight: 13,550kg (LZ6)

Typical gross lift: 17,400kg (LZ6); 18,600kg (LZ6A) (1.16kg/cu m)

Typical disposable load: 3,850kg (LZ6), 4,370kg (LZ6A)

Crew: seven

Passengers: ten

Maximum speed: 13.5m/s (30.19 mph); 15.2m/s (34mph) (LZ6 with third engine)

Maximum range: 2,000km

LZ6 flew about 59 times up to the end of September 1909 after which it was lengthened as the LZ6A. After conversion it first flew in mid-August 1910 and made 73 flights before being destroyed by fire in its shed at Baden-Oos on 14 September, 1910.

DELAG – LZ7 *Deutschland* and LZ8 Ersatz *Deutschland*

The idea of forming a company to operate civil Zeppelins, at first on pleasure flights and later on regular transport services, had originally been suggested by Zeppelin's general manager, Colsman, in May 1909. There is little doubt that the Count was not keen on the idea in the beginning, and was never entirely reconciled to it. Commercial operations of this type smacked too much of 'going into trade' to appeal to the old aristocrat and soldier. However, he realised that customers and operators must be found for his airships if they were to be developed, as he was convinced they could be, into practical vehicles and important weapons of war. If the armed forces would not purchase them, at that stage of development, he must find other customers.

One scheme was for the use of a Zeppelin in Arctic exploration and a proposal to do this was put to the Kaiser by the distinguished meteorologist, Professor Hergesell on 1 July, 1909. In September a committee, under Hergesell, was formed to promote the idea but after much discussion nothing came of it. Another proposal, put before the town council of Lucerne in Switzerland, was for pleasure flights over the Alps from that town. Although a preliminary contract was signed, the plan did not go ahead. A number

Alfred Colsman, commercial director of Luftschiffbau Zeppelin.

of foreign governments or their agents were interested in doing business with Zeppelin. One of the first seems to have been Gustave A Clement (b.1855) of the famous Clement-Bayard motorcar and airship company who had talks with Zeppelin in Berlin on 7 July, 1909. But although there were discussions with various parties at intervals, right up to 1914, nothing came of them, probably because the German Government would not permit it.

Meanwhile, Colsman resolutely pushed forward his DELAG (Deutsche Luftschiffahrts AG) idea and soon won the support of the local authorities in Frankfurt and in other large towns throughout Germany. Deutsche Luftschiffahrts AG (DELAG) was formed at Frankfurt-am-Main on 16 November, 1909, with a capital of three million marks (£2.5 million). Some of the money was put up by the Hamburg-Amerika shipping line. The original board had 27 directors, most of whom were burgomasters of the cities supporting

DELAG's LZ7 Deutschland *was damaged beyond repair on its first cruise, from Düsseldorf on 28 June, 1910.*
(Luftschiffbau Zeppelin)

LZ7 Deutschland *was one of two Type e Zeppelins.*
(Courtesy Orell Fussli Verlag, Zürich)

the enterprise, which was seen as an important tourist attraction quite apart from its national and local prestige and defence implications. The local authorities which participated also undertook to provide the bases (including sheds) at each participating city from which the airships would operate. Within ten days of its formation, and led by Colsman who was made managing director (he also continued as general manager of the Zeppelin company), DELAG ordered its first airship for delivery the following year. This became LZ7, perhaps rather rashly named *Deutschland*. It was first flown on 19 June, 1910, and was delivered to DELAG at Düsseldorf by the Count three days later. Twenty passengers were carried on this flight at 200 marks a head (£80).

LZ7 was a considerable advance on previous Zeppelins. Diameter was increased to 14m (45ft 10³/₄in) and length to 148m

(485ft 6½in), giving a capacity of 19,300cu m (681,157cu ft). The frames were still spaced 8m apart and the structure was basically unchanged, but a new type of girder was adopted and there was improved longitudinal and frame bracing. Power was provided by three 120hp Daimler J4F engines making LZ7 the first three-engined Zeppelin, following experiments with a third engine in LZ6A, previously described.

At its new base, LZ7 came under the command of Capt Kahlenberg, a Prussian Airship Battalion pilot who had joined DELAG as the company's director of flight operations. Flying started from Düsseldorf because this city was first to have ready its new airship base at Golsheim.

Unfortunately DELAG got off to a disastrous start. Six days after delivery, *Deutschland* set out on its first cruise, carrying 23 journalists in its well-appointed midships passenger cabin in the keel. A trip of about three hours was intended. It became a nightmare journey of nine hours from which those on board were fortunate to escape with their lives. Kahlenberg seems to have been both rash and unlucky. The wind got up and blew him downwind of his base. He was unable to make ground against the wind, even at his top speed of 16.7m/s (37.35mph). Then one of his engines failed and he could not prevent the ship being carried up to 1,100m (3,600ft). After that, heavy from loss of gas and weight of rain, the ship was forced down uncontrollably on to the tops of

The tail configuration of LZ7 shows up well against the shed roof. (Science Museum)

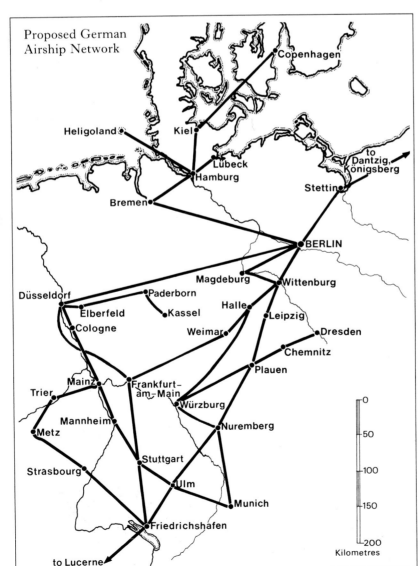

Proposed German Airship Network

DELAG 1912/13 map showing bases, bases under construction, 'routes' and proposed routes.

pine trees near Wallendorf in the Teutoburger Wald. By good fortune there was no fire and the passengers and crew were able to scramble the 30 feet to the ground. The only human injury was a broken leg, but the airship was a total loss and Kahlenberg lost his job.

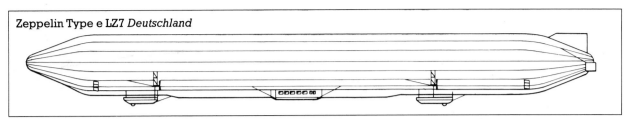

Zeppelin Type e LZ7 *Deutschland*

Zeppelin LZ7 (Type e) *Deutschland*

Manufacturer: Luftschiffbau Zeppelin GmbH

Built at Friedrichshafen

Number built: two

Chief designer: L Dürr

Main structural material: Zn-Al alloy

Design began: September 1909

First flight: 19 June, 1910

Powerplant: three 120hp Daimler J4F four-cylinder inline engines

Gas capacity (100 per cent inflation): 19,300cu m

Overall length: 148.0m

Maximum diameter: 14.0m

Spacing of main frames: 8.0m

Fineness ratio: 10.57

Number of gas cells: 18

LZ7 Deutschland *at Friedrichshafen before its delivery flight to Düsseldorf.*
(Luftschiffbau Zeppelin)

Empty weight: 15,600kg

Typical gross lift: 22,400kg (1.16 kg/cu m)

Typical disposable load: 7,200kg

Crew: eight

Passengers: 20

Maximum speed: 16.7m/s (37.35 mph)

Maximum range: 1,600km

LZ7 flew $20^1/_2$hr before its forced landing and destruction on 28 June, 1910. LZ8 Ersatz *Deutschland*, the second Type e ship, first flew on 30 March, 1911, flew 47hr, made its last flight on 14 May, 1911, and was destroyed leaving its shed at Düsseldorf on 16 May.

LZ8 Ersatz Deutschland.
(Pritchard collection)

HM Airship No.1 *Mayfly*

The British Vickers group was concerned with rigid airships longer than any other manufacturer apart from Luftschiffbau Zeppelin itself. Vickers was involved with airships from 1908. On 21 July of that year Capt R H S Bacon, RN, the Director of Naval Operations at the British Admiralty, submitted proposals to the First Sea Lord (Sir John Fisher) for a rigid airship to be built for the Royal Navy by Vickers, Sons and Maxim Ltd. This recommendation was almost certainly triggered-off by LZ4's great 12-hour flight over the Alps three weeks earlier and by other developments in practical flying which were becoming increasingly evident that memorable summer. Although Wilbur Wright did not make the first public demonstrations of his aeroplane in Europe until the following month, Léon Delagrange (1873–1910) had made flights of about 15 minutes in May and June and Henry Farman (1874–1958) had made one of over 20 minutes on 6 July. It was clear that practical flying machines – whether heavier or lighter-than-air – could not be far away. The greatest

navy in the world could not afford to be left behind in any new technical development which might impinge on the practices of sea warfare.

On 14 August, Vickers was invited to tender for the construction of a rigid airship built on Zeppelin principles. It was to be able to maintain a speed of 40 knots (20.6m/s) for 24 hours, to reach an altitude of 1,500ft (457m), to carry radio and to offer reasonably comfortable crew accommodation. This was, in fact, the same order of performance which was to be achieved by *Schwaben*-type Zeppelins from mid-1911.

Vickers tendered in March and its offer was accepted on 7 May,

HM Airship No.1 Mayfly *at Cavendish Dock, Barrow-in-Furness. The ship is seen in its original form with V keel.*

1909. Meanwhile, Rear Admiral Sir John Jellicoe, who had succeeded Capt Bacon, appointed Capt Murray F Sueter to take charge of the project and of the Admiralty branch specially formed to administer it, although without responsibility for design of the ship itself. Responsibility for the latter was unsatisfactorily shared between the Admiralty

No.1 Mayfly *in original form, showing clearly the tail surfaces. (Pritchard collection)*

Mayfly moored at Barrow-in-Furness.
(Vickers)

and the contractor, the former having prime responsibility for the gas cells, outer cover and control surfaces, while the latter was responsible for the structure. The records are not clear as to who was supposed to be technically in charge at the Admiralty, although the indications are that it was Lieut Neville F Usborne, RN (1883–1916). So far as Vickers was concerned the man in charge was Charles G Robertson, the marine manager at Barrow-in-Furness where the airship was built.

Robertson had had no previous aeronautical experience and the officers at the Admiralty can have known little more of the many problems which had to be overcome if a successful rigid was to be designed, particularly one which was intended to leapfrog more than ten years of intensive development in Germany. The main source of information was, of course, from Germany itself, but this was not easy to obtain. The layout and main structural features could be deduced from external inspection and from photographs of recent Zeppelins, but it was much more difficult to find out anything about the internal details.

The main frames of the new ship were given a spacing which varied between 3.8m and 11.4m (12ft 5$\frac{1}{2}$in and 37ft 4$\frac{3}{4}$in). This compared with the Zeppelin 8m (26ft 3in) bays and there were 17 gas cells, the same number as in LZ4, the latest Zeppelin at that

No.1 Mayfly under construction.
(Pritchard collection)

time. The British designers' most important changes were in the reduced number of longitudinals, 12 instead of the 16 in LZ4, and in the different hull shape. The early Zeppelins were cylindrical with blunt bows and sterns (with a curvature of 1$\frac{1}{2}$ times the diameter). For the British ship a shape worked out by an American, A F Zahm (1862–1954), was chosen. This was still cylindrical but curvature was less blunt at the bow (twice the diameter) and far less at the stern (nine times the diameter), giving a considerably better aerodynamic shape. Another important difference was that the outer cover was made impervious, contrary to Zeppelin practice at the time, which meant that the valves had to be at the top rather than the bottom of each gas cell, where they could vent directly to the exterior. In the early Zeppelins, with valves at the bottom, gas was vented into the ring space and dispersed through the porous outer cover. This seemed to be a potentially dangerous practice, and both Schütte-Lanz and Zeppelin later

went over to impervious outer covers. Gas shafts were then added to carry vented gas to ventilators at the top of the hull.

The tail design of the Vickers ship was an important advance on any previous design. The fixed surfaces were of the simple cruciform layout later adopted by Schütte-Lanz and finally by Zeppelin after 1914. Multiple control surfaces were, however, retained.

The Admiralty requirement for a range of 1,100 miles (1,770km) meant that the Vickers No.1, in characteristic British fashion soon named *Mayfly*, had to be considerably larger than contemporary Zeppelins. Her diameter of 48ft (14.63m) was much greater than LZ4's 13m (42ft 7$\frac{3}{4}$in) and, in fact, larger than any Zeppelin until the L1 of 1912. *Mayfly*'s length of 512ft (156m) was also considerably greater as was her capacity of 663,500cu ft (18,788cu m).

On top of all these bold inno-

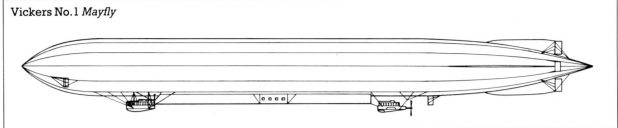

Vickers No.1 *Mayfly*

vations, after much experiment and debate about the material to be used, a decision was taken to go for the new German aluminium alloy, duralumin. The basic sections used to manufacture the structure were supplied from Germany, and as about 75 per cent of these proved to be unusable because of difficulties at the time in rolling the material into the sections required, it is surprising that the British persisted with it. The Germans were to decide against using duralumin in 1910 because of the same problems. The difficulties of working duralumin were not overcome until 1914, when Zeppelin finally went over to the new material.

Use of duralumin which was not properly worked and the difficulty of obtaining information about the design of the Zeppelin girders and structural framework were most likely at the root of the failure of the British ship. As first completed and brought out of her

Mayfly *was wrecked on being brought out of the shed on 24 September, 1911, after modifications including removal of parts of the V keel.*
(Pritchard collection)

shed on 22 May, 1911, she was so heavy that there was no disposable load. In this condition, in winds of up to 45mph, she remained moored out for three days to a 38ft (11.58m) mast in Cavendish Dock at Barrow-in-Furness, where she had been erected. She was then put back into the shed and extensively modified to reduce weight. Among changes made was removal of parts of the external triangular-section keel and this probably seriously weakened the structure. Whatever the reasons, the hull collapsed as the ship was being brought out of the shed for a second time on 24 September, and that was the end of the project.

Because it initially drew its inspiration directly from the Zeppelins, *Mayfly* was built to operate from water and was also constructed in a shed on water. The only real justification for copying this Zeppelin practice (which Zeppelin was, in fact, on the point of abandoning) was that it enabled the shed to be turned into wind whenever the ship was being taken in or out. The British apparently failed to appreciate the importance of this point and the Vickers shed was built rigidly on to the side of Cavendish Dock, a

fact which may have contributed to the final disaster.

The story of the *Mayfly* epitomises the entire story of rigid airship development outside Germany. Directly inspired by progress in Germany, it was an attempt to capitalise on that progress by imitation and by improvement where this seemed feasible. *Mayfly* incorporated a number of original ideas, some of which the Germans were later to adopt themselves, but it suffered sadly from the lack of structural knowledge which the Germans had accumulated and had applied to their Zeppelins. This lack was particularly critical in relation to the design of the built-up girders and of the hull framework.

For over 20 years the British, the French and the Americans sought to obtain from Germany this, and other, information about the design of rigid airships. Their failure to do so adequately, or to develop an equivalent capability of their own, meant that they were never able to produce airships as good as contemporary Zeppelins. It also meant that up to 1918 there was continuous espionage activity in attempts to learn the latest Zeppelin secrets, as well as major efforts to get all

possible information from such Zeppelins as fell into Allied hands. After the Armistice, the Allies did everything they could to acquire German rigid airship technology. They were not entirely successful in this, judging by the structural failures and other deficiencies of postwar, non-German rigids, including even the last two American ships designed by an ex-Zeppelin team which had emigrated to the United States.

HM Airship No.1, *Mayfly*

Manufacturer: Vickers, Sons & Maxim Ltd (initially), Vickers Ltd (from April 1911)

Built at Cavendish Dock, Barrow-in-Furness

Number built: one

Chief designer: C G Robertson

Main structural material: duralumin

Design began: February 1909

Design completed: 24 September, 1911

Powerplant: two 160hp Wolseley eight-cylinder vee engines

Gas capacity (100 per cent inflation): 663,500cu ft (18,788cu m)

Overall length: 512ft (156m)

Maximum diameter: 48ft (14.63m)

Spacing of main frames: 12ft $5^1/_2$in–37ft $4^3/_4$in (3.8m–11.4m)

Fineness ratio: 10.7

Number of gas cells: 17

Number of main longitudinals: 12

Number of transverse rings: 40

Empty weight: 43,872lb (19,900 kg)

Typical gross lift: 45,195lb (20,500 kg) (1.09kg/cu m)

Typical disposable load: 600kg

Maximum fuel: 3,086lb (1,400kg)

Crew: 22

Maximum speed: 42.05mph (18.8 m/s) (estimated)

Maximum range: 1,087 miles (1,750 km) at speed of 18.8m/s (estimated)

Static ceiling: 1,475ft (450m)

Cost: £41,000

Mayfly was brought out of her shed for the first time on 22 May, 1911, but was not flown. After modification, she was destroyed on being brought out of the shed on 24 September, 1911.

French Rigid – Zodiac Spiess

Not surprisingly, perhaps, the second non-German rigid airship was French. As events turned out, it proved to be the only French rigid airship built. Designed by Joseph Spiess, it was built by the long-established firm of balloon manufacturers, Maurice Mallet, which had been reorganised as the Société Zodiac in 1908 and which later became well known as a manufacturer of pressure-airships.

Following the disaster to the Lebaudy pressure-airship *République* on 25 September, 1908, Joseph Spiess offered to develop a small rigid airship at his own expense and to present it to the French Army as a replacement. The Spiess was built as Zodiac's Type No.13 (later No.13A) and was first announced as being under development in April 1909. In September, a model was shown at the Paris Salon. Spiess claimed that his ideas for rigids pre-dated those of Zeppelin, the basis of his claim being a patent (No.100695), taken out in Paris on 27 February, 1873. He also took out a German patent (No.98580) in 1895. However, the device described in both these patents was a monstrosity which bore no relationship to the later 1909 design. It is evident that the latter was as much a copy of Zeppelin as was the Vickers No.1.

Although a variety of figures

The Zodiac Type 13 Spiess as originally built with only the forward engine.
(Pritchard collection)

were quoted, it appears that the Spiess was originally projected with a diameter of 12m (39ft $4^1/_3$in), a length of 88m (288ft $8^1/_2$in) and a capacity of only 7,000 or 8,000cu m (247,200–282,500cu ft). The structure was clearly modelled on Zeppelin with the same frame spacing of 8m (26ft 3in) but it was built of wood held together by aluminium ferrules. The use of wood was proposed by Schütte in Germany at about the same time but the first Schütte airship had an entirely original structure. Only later did the wooden German ships adopt Zeppelin-type structures.

As originally envisaged, the Spiess was considerably smaller than any other rigid airship. It appears that Spiess soon realised that he would have to make his ship larger if it were to have any chance of success. By 1910, projected capacity had risen to 10,000cu m (352,147cu ft) and, at some stage, the frame spacing seems to have been increased to 9m (29ft 6in) and the diameter to 13.5m (44ft $3^1/_2$in). It is probable that the design was then known as Type No.13.

Early in 1911, a sufficiently large construction shed was completed by the French Government at Saint-Cyr, on the outskirts of Paris. It was 160m (525ft) long, 25m (82ft) wide and 24m (78ft $8^3/_4$in) high. Assembly of the airship itself probably still known as the Type 13, started in April. The framework was just

The Type 13 Spiess after modification to Type 13A with increased gas capacity and two engines. (Pritchard collection)

about complete by the end of the year but it now seems to have been lengthened to 113m (370ft 8³/₄in) to give a capacity of 12,800cu m (452,000cu ft). The ship was reported to be finished in May 1912 but, after unsatisfactory trials with two 120hp Panhard-Levasseur engines, a decision was taken to fit more powerful Chenu engines. These were delivered in August, and later the first flight was promised for November. However, trouble with the gas cells prevented this and the airship did not fly until April 1913 (13, 17 and 30 April have all been quoted) with the Comte de la Vaulx in charge. It is believed that at this stage only a single 210hp Chenu engine was fitted because of a lack of useful lift. The single engine was mounted in the forward car and drove two 4.5m (14ft 9in) bracket propellers on each side of the hull, on the Zeppelin pattern.

The Spiess flew again on 2 May but was already completely outclassed by Zeppelin development. This fact was dramatically brought home to the French by an event of considerable import-ance in the history of rigid airships. On 3 April, 1913 – some weeks before the Spiess's first flight – the military Zeppelin ZIV made a forced landing at Lunéville in France. The crew of ZIV had lost its way and, probably trapped by a strong east wind, found that they could not get back to Germany. This was just the sort of opportunity for which the French had been waiting and they seized it to copy and photograph every possible detail of the ship before returning it to the Germans.

The result of this unexpected windfall meant that the French had all the latest data on the ZIV, an L1 Class ship which had flown for the first time only the previous month. No doubt this contributed to the Spiess being grounded in May after only a few flights. By November, under the designation No.13A, she had been enlarged by no less than three 9m (29ft 6in) bays, thus increasing her length to 140m (459ft 3¹/₂in) and her capacity to 16,400cu m (579,156cu ft). With the greater disposable lift which resulted, the second engine could be installed and the ship was eventually flown, in her definitive form, on 9 or 11 December, 1913. After testing, which demonstrated a maximum speed of 70km/h (43.5mph), she was delivered to the French military authorities on 1 February, 1914, and was reported to have continued in service until about the outbreak of war in August. Earlier, on 16 January, 1914, the Spiess made a three- to four-hour flight over Paris and caused considerable patriotic enthusiasm. The pilot was André Schelcher with a crew of six. But the Spiess was the only rigid airship to be built in France. Two German-built Zeppelins went to the French after the First World War, as reparations, but they did not survive long as we shall see in later chapters.

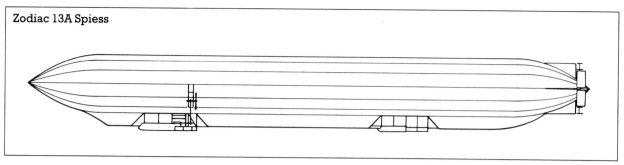

Zodiac 13A Spiess

Zodiac Type 13 and 13A Spiess

Manufacturer: Société Zodiac

Built at Saint-Cyr, Paris

Number built: one

Chief designers: J Spiess and M Mallet

Main structural material: wood with aluminium ferrules

Design began: 25 September, 1909

First flight: 13, 17 or 30 April 1913 (No.13)

Powerplant: two 120hp Panhard-Levasseur replaced by two 210hp Chenu AE.6 six-cylinder inline engines. Originally tested with front engine only

Gas capacity (100 per cent inflation): 12,800cu m (No.13); 16,400cu m (No.13A)

Overall length: 113.0m (No.13); 140.0m (No.13A)

Maximum diameter: 13.5m

Spacing of main frames: 9.0m

Fineness ratio: 10.4

Number of gas cells: 17 (No.13A)

Number of main longitudinals: 14

Empty weight: 16.070kg (No.13A)

Typical gross lift: 19,000kg (No.13A) (1.6kg/cu m)

Typical disposable load: 2,930kg

Maximum fuel: 1,090kg

Crew: seven

Maximum speed: 18.0m/s (40.26 mph)

Maximum range: 1,560km at speed of 13.9m/s (31.09mph)

No.13 made a few flights up to 2 May, 1913, after which it was lengthened as No.13A. As No.13A it first flew on 9 or 11 December, 1913. It made a few flights until about August 1914 and was broken up at the end of the year.

Britain Tries Again – Vickers No.9

Meanwhile there had been another change of policy in Britain. Following the *Mayfly* fiasco, the Admiralty had decided not to pursue its requirement for airships. This attitude did not last long. After much argument and discussion, both in the Committee of Imperial Defence and in the Service departments, it was decided, in September 1912, that a new rigid airship should be ordered. The Admiralty issued a new invitation to tender to Vickers, after attempting, without success, to buy a Zeppelin.

This decision was, of course, primarily due to German progress with Zeppelins. In November 1911, Sir John Jellicoe, accompanied by the British Naval Attaché in Berlin, Capt Sir Hugh D Watson RN, had flown in *Schwaben* and had reported favourably to the Admiralty. Eight months later, in June 1912, Capt Murray Sueter and Lieut-Col Mervyn O'Gorman (superintendent of the Royal Aircraft Factory) flew in *Viktoria Luise* and reported favourably to the Committee of Imperial Defence. It was clear that Britain could not afford to ignore the German airship developments. Ironically, Colsman used the British interest in Zeppelins in his efforts to persuade the German naval authorities to acquire Zeppelins.

The Vickers airship department, which had been closed down after the *Mayfly* episode, was re-constituted early in 1913. In April, a small design office was set up in Victoria Street, London, under Hartley B Pratt, a young engineer who had been working for Vickers at Barrow on its lightweight marine diesel engines for submarines and who had taken part, for a time, in the design of *Mayfly*. With Pratt were two other young men, B N (later Sir Barnes) Wallis (1887–1980) and J E Temple. They had not got very far with their new design when drawings, made from photographs, of all parts of ZIV's structure and other details of that airship began to reach them from France. The new ship, called No.9 (being the ninth British naval airship, including pressure-ships, officially numbered since No.1), was therefore broadly based on the Zeppelin L1 class of 1912. Like two of the lengthened ships in that class, No.9 had 17 gas cells and 17 main longitudinals plus the usual prominent external V-section keel, standard on Zeppelins at that time. However, her diameter was considerably greater 53ft (16.15m), as against 14.9m (48ft 10$\frac{1}{2}$in) and her frame spacing 30ft (9.14m) was intermediate between the 8m (26ft 3in) of the early Zeppelins (including ZIV) and the 10m (32ft 9$\frac{1}{2}$in) adopted by the Germans from 1914.

As finally completed in 1916, No.9 – like the wooden Shütte-Lanz S.L.II – had two light, intermediate frames dividing the bays between each two main frames. This was a feature of much later Zeppelins with 15m (49ft 2$\frac{1}{2}$in) bays (L53 class and

Vickers No.9, built at Walney Island, Barrow-in-Furness.
(Vickers via Pritchard collection)

later) but no Zeppelin with a 10m frame-spacing had more than a single full intermediate frame in each bay. The first Zeppelin to have the single intermediate frame had been ZXII of 1914. The Allies had become aware of the fact that Zeppelins had intermediate frames from the wreckage of various L10 class, and later ships, which came into their hands in the early years of the war.

The shape of No.9's hull was also a compromise between the Zahm profile of No.1 and the blunt-ended cylindrical hull of the L1 class Zeppelin. Curvature at the bow was $1^3/4$ times the diameter and the tapering stern had a radius of 5.8 times the diameter. Capacity of the hull was 889,300cu ft (25,181cu m), again considerably larger than L1 class which had ranged from 19,500 to 22,470cu m.

Power was provided by four 150hp Maybach C-X engines, purchased from Germany. The two engines, in both gondolas, were geared to swivelling propellers which could be used to develop vertical thrust when required. For a long time it was incorrectly rumoured that the Zeppelins were fitted with such propellers, but Nos.1 and 9 were actually the first rigids to have them. They were fitted because of their use in the British Army's pressure-airships. One pair of swivelling propellers on No.9 was, however, removed to save weight, soon after flight trials began.

The frames and longitudinals were built of triangular girders, following Zeppelin practice, and the design of these girders and of the hull framework, was directly based on the L1 class design information obtained from ZIV.

When the design was nearly completed in 1914, Hartley Pratt decided that it would be a good idea if they could check the information from ZIV against latest Zeppelin practice. Accordingly, he made a private trip to Friedrichshafen. While snooping around the Zeppelin works, he managed to make pencil rubbings of the cross sections of the various standard Zeppelin girders which he found on railway wagons in a siding in Friedrichshafen station. These rubbings provided valuable confirmation of the correctness of the earlier data.

L1 class ships were, in fact, built of zinc-aluminium alloy (*See* Note 14), as were all Zeppelins made at Friedrichshafen until March 1915. The Vickers designers decided, on the other hand, to continue to use duralumin which, by 1914, could at last be rolled satisfactorily into the required sections. Duralumin is considerably stronger than the zinc-aluminium alloy, so that the Vickers girders, based on the earlier Zeppelin design in the lower strength material, were probably unnecessarily heavy when made of duralumin. This may have been one of the reasons why No.9 and the ships derived from her were all heavy.

No.9 was ordered by the Admiralty on 19 June, 1913. The Vickers design was submitted for Admiralty approval in December 1913 and the contract was finally signed in March 1914. The re-

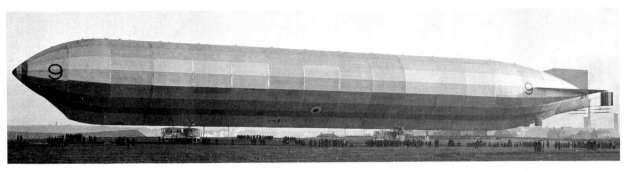

The Vickers No.9 owed much to Zeppelin design practices.
(Vickers via Pritchard collection)

Impressive view of No.9, showing keel section, control car, forward propellers and red, white and blue bow masking.
(Vickers via Pritchard collection)

quirements to which the ship was designed made her about a third larger than *Mayfly* and included:

1. A speed of at least 40 knots (20.6m/s) at full power.
2. A minimum disposable lift of 5 tons (5,080kg) for movable weights.
3. Capability to attain a height of at least 2,000ft (610m).

Work began soon afterwards on a new hangar on Walney Island near Barrow (*See* Note 18), and construction of the ship started in August 1914 after the

This view shows the complex tail structure of Vickers No.9.
(Vickers via Pritchard collection)

start of the war. The failure of the Germans to make any visibly effective use of their airships in the early months of the war undoubtedly affected thinking in Britain. Winston Churchill, then First Lord of the Admiralty, ac-

cordingly stopped the airship programme in March 1915. Work on No.9 was restarted by A J Balfour, who succeeded Churchill in June of the same year, and manufacture began that autumn. No.9 was finally completed in

Vickers No.9

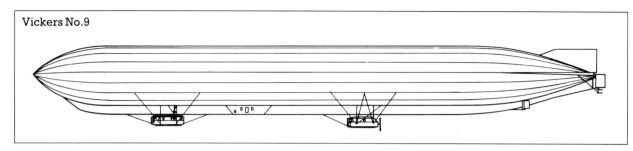

November 1916, important changes having been made at the request of Constructor-Cdr C I R Campbell, of the Air Department at the Admiralty, as late as March of that year. At some stage, one – and possibly two – further ships of the same design (to be designated Nos.14 and possibly 15) are reported to have been mooted for construction by Armstrong Whitworth, but they were never ordered.

No.9 was first flown by Wing Capt E A D Masterman on 27 November, 1916. She was so heavy that the Navy refused to accept her and Vickers had to make extensive modifications to reduce weight. These included simplification of the control surfaces, and substitution, for the original rear twin-engined gondola, of an engine-car containing a single 250hp Maybach H-S-Lu. The latter had been recovered from the wreckage of L33 when she was forced down at Little Wigborough, Essex, on 24 September, 1916, and burned by her crew. The ship was accepted on 12 December, subject to the incorporation of further modifications. She was finally delivered on 4 April, 1917. By then, of course, she was hopelessly old-fashioned, but she flew a couple of hundred hours, mainly on training flights, before being damaged in a ground-handling accident on 28 June, 1918, and, subsequently, broken up.

Vickers No.9

Manufacturer: Vickers Ltd
Built at Walney Island, Barrow-in-Furness
Number built: one
Chief designer: H B Pratt
Main structural material: duralumin
Design began: April 1913

First flight: 27 November, 1916
Powerplant: four 150hp Wolseley-Maybach C-X six-cylinder inline engines; two later replaced by one 250hp Maybach H-S-Lu of the same layout
Gas capacity (100 per cent inflation): 889,300cu ft (25,181cu m)
Overall length: 530ft (161.54m)
Maximum diameter: 53ft (16.15m)
Spacing of main frames: 30ft (9.14m)
Fineness ratio: 9.89
Number of gas cells: 17
Number of main longitudinals: 17
Number of main transverse frames: 18
Empty weight: 59,745lb (27,100 kg)
Typical gross lift: 60,560lb (27,470 kg) (1.09kg/cu m)
Typical disposable load: 370kg
Crew: 14
Maximum speed: 45mph (20.1 m/s)
Maximum range: 1,615 miles (2,600 km)

No.9 flew 198hr 16 min. It made its last flight on 28 June, 1918, and was broken up that same month

The Schwaben class – LZ9, 10 and 12

After the loss of *Deutschland*, it was obvious that it would take time to build a new ship for DELAG. Meanwhile, all operations would have to be suspended. In the face of this dilemma it was decided that LZ6 should be taken over as an interim solution until the new ship could be delivered.

Since the Berlin flight in August/September 1909, LZ6 had been used for a number of demonstration flights and for development of her controls. In

This view of Schwaben *at Potsdam shows to advantage the tail configuration.*
(Lufthansa)

LZ10 Schwaben *at Friedrichs-hafen was the first of three Type f Zeppelins.*
(Luftschiffbau Zeppelin)

September 1909, LZ6 was withdrawn from service and, as described in Chapter X, used for a trial installation of a three-engine layout. This involved putting the third engine in the passenger compartment in the middle of the keel. The experiment was sufficiently successful to justify adoption of a more elaborate engine arrangement and the lengthening of LZ6's hull by the addition of an 8m bay containing an additional gas bag. Thereafter the ship was re-designated LZ6A. To meet DELAG's requirements a cabin for ten to twelve passengers was restored to the keel.

In this greatly improved form, LZ6A was ferried on 21 August to the new DELAG hangar at Baden-Oos where she restarted the commercial flights. The problem of replacing the unlucky Kahlenberg was solved by appointing Hugo Eckener (1868–

1954) as the new director of flight operations. Ever since he began working for Zeppelin as public relations adviser in 1906, Eckener had become increasingly involved in the destiny of the airship. By the time of the loss of *Deutschland*, he felt himself to be one of those chiefly responsible for persuading the local authorities of cities all over Germany into supporting DELAG. He had, for

Schwaben *with mooring lines trailing.*

example, prepared and publicised the economic forecasts of airship operating costs on which the case for the formation of DELAG had been based. When it was suggested he should become an airship pilot, he began taking instruction from Count Zeppelin. Later, when he was asked to ac-

Schwaben *leaving the shed at Baden-Oos.*
(Luftschiffbau Zeppelin)

cept the DELAG job, he considered himself morally obliged to do so. Thus it was Eckener who ferried LZ6A to Baden in August 1910 and, in this way, started the most distinguished flying career of any airship pilot.

He began cautiously. This, together with the fact that the site of Oos near Baden-Baden, where he was based, was particularly favourable to airship operations, helped him learn quickly the many difficult tricks of his new trade. Passenger flights were made almost daily; sometimes more frequently. After a total of thirty-four flights in a little over three weeks, fate intervened. On a flight to Heilbronn, on 14 September, an engine failed and the ship had to return to base. She was safely hangared but an accidental petrol fire was started by someone working on the failed engine. Within seconds the hydrogen was alight and the ship and hangar were gutted. Once again, by amazing good fortune, there was no loss of life.

LZ6A, and possibly the *Deutschland*, had been insured with Lloyds of London. Perhaps

Schwaben *over Johannisthal aerodrome, Berlin.*

Schwaben *at Friedrichshafen.*
(Lufthansa)

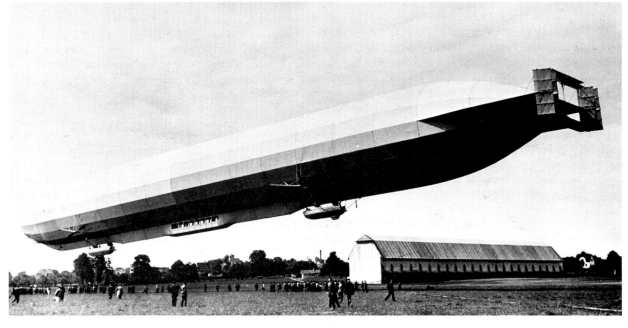

Schwaben's *control car*.
(Lufthansa)

the cover was for ground risks only, in which case DELAG was paid for the loss of LZ6A but not for the LZ7. In any case, the insurance money was used for the replacement ship, LZ8, Ersatz *Deutschland*, ordered immediately after Kahlenberg's accident. Very similar to LZ7, she was first flown on 20 March, 1911, and delivered by the Count to Düsseldorf on 11 April after visits to the new sheds at Stuttgart, Baden-Baden and Frankfurt.

Eckener had no responsibility for the loss of LZ6A and again took charge of flying. Unfortunately, the Düsseldorf shed was far less satisfactory than that at Baden. Eckener continued to be cautious but nearly came to grief within three days, when the ship was caught by the wind and damaged while being brought out of the shed. A month later, on 16 May, after twenty-four successful passenger flights, his luck ran out. Passengers were waiting to fly and so an attempt was made to bring the ship out of the shed in a cross-wind. Despite a ground handling party of 250–300 men, she was blown against a windbreak and was so badly damaged that she had to be written off. Only a few structural components were salvaged for use in later Zeppelins.

This appeared to be the end of the road for DELAG, if not for the Zeppelin company itself. The first DELAG ship had survived one week in service; the second, three weeks; and the third, five. It would be hard to imagine a more disastrous record. The only saving grace was that nobody had been killed. For some time, the DELAG board wavered before making up its mind. Then, by an unrecorded majority it decided to have one more try; a fourth airship was ordered for delivery later in the year.

This decision was remarkable evidence of faith in the Count and his ideas when one considers that DELAG was mostly com-

posed of local bureaucrats, representing such diverse interests. Of all the crucial stages in the Zeppelin's story, this was surely the most important. The DELAG board's apparently unreasonable faith was justified, in the event. The next commercial airship, LZ10, *Schwaben*, was flown for the first time on 26 June, 1911. Following the *Deutschland's*, the name *Schwaben* had a special meaning for the Swabians of Württemberg, the southern German state which often resented Prussian overlordship from Berlin and regarded Zeppelin as a symbol of its local identity.

Schwaben survived for a year and two days before she was burnt on the ground at Düsseldorf after racing a squall back to

This historic photograph shows Count Zeppelin on the left and Dr Hugo Eckener on the right. Taken in the summer of 1911 it was the occasion on which Eckener flew Schwaben *to take his examination for qualification as an airship pilot.* (Friedrich Moch collection)

base and unloading her passengers just in time. Again, no lives were lost although Dürr and several others on board were injured. (Dürr appears to have stopped flying as pilot after this accident, even though he was not in command at the time; the ship's captain had been Dipl Ing W E Dörr.)

The primary cause of *Schwaben's* destruction was never clearly established. Some reports

Zeppelin Type f LZ10 *Schwaben*

A royal group aboard Schwaben. *Left to right: Prince Frederik Karl, Prince Frederick Sigismund, Prince Joachim, Prince Eitel Frederik, Prince von Hohenzollern, Prince Oscar, Prince and Princess August Wilhelm, Prince George of Greece, Herr von Bretenbach (Minister of Railways) and Zeppelin director Alfred Colsman.*

ZIII (LZ12), third of the Type f Schwaben *class.*
(Pritchard collection)

said that she started to break up in the violent wind before she caught fire. The official conclusion, however, was that ignition was due to a spark caused by 'frictional electricity', set up by the flapping and chafing of the rubberised cotton fabric of which the gas cells were made. As a result, the Luftschiffbau Zeppelin went over to goldbeaters' skin for the gas cells of their future airships. This material had, in fact, already been tried by Zeppelin but had not been adopted because of its high cost, its tend-

ency to absorb moisture and thus increase in weight, and its vulnerability to damp and tearing. The first cells of this material used by Zeppelin are said to have been supplied by the British balloon manufacturers, C G Spenser and Sons Ltd, as early as 1902. One cell of ZII in 1909 had been, experimentally, of goldbeaters' skin. (*See* Note 4)

At first, gas cells were made of seven layers of goldbeaters' skin. Later, 'skinned fabric' cells were adopted and became standard practice until synthetic materials

began to be adopted in the 1930s. The skinned fabric cells had one or more (commonly three) layers of goldbeaters' skin stuck with rubber solution to the inside of cotton fabric. The first Zeppelin with skinned fabric cells was LZ24 (L3), which made her maiden flight in May 1914.

Although *Schwaben* was ultimately lost in an accident, her year of successful operations provided the evidence that was so badly needed to prove rigid airships could be flown regularly under suitable conditions: at this stage, it is true, only locally from sheltered inland sites or on rather slow cross-country journeys in favourable weather

Schwaben proved to be the classic design of early rigid airship. She represented the optimum combination of various features which had been evolved in previous ships. Basically her hull was the same as those of the *Deutschlands*' except that she was shorter by an 8m bay and thus had seventeen instead of eighteen gas cells, giving a capacity of 17,800cu m (628,600cu ft). Her reduced length of 140m (459ft 3$\frac{1}{2}$in), combined with her improved control surfaces, made her handier in the air and easier to manage on the ground. Perhaps most important of all, she was the first ship with three of the more reliable and powerful Maybach engines. Her top speed of 19.5m/s (43.62mph) was the best yet, and brought her almost into the category of a fully practical airship for local flying.

Apart from the characteristics of *Schwaben* herself there were four factors which contributed to her success. These were the exceptionally fine, almost windless summer of 1911; the favourable situation and siting of the hangar at Baden-Oos from which she operated much of the time; the rapidly increasing skill of Hugo Eckener, who soon began to show an instinctive skill as airship pilot; and the adoption of docking rails and trolleys to restrain the ship while leaving and entering the shed.

The passenger accommodation in the early DELAG airships consisted of a 'coach' near the ship's centre of gravity created by enlarging to about 2m width a section of the external keel. About 25 lightweight seats were arranged in a longitudinal row each side of a centre aisle. Large windows in the sides of the cabin provided a magnificent view of the ground passing slowly close beneath. The passengers were sufficiently distant from the engine cars to have a pleasantly quiet ride. Accommodation included two lavatories – very necessary on the long slow journeys – and a rudimentary galley.

As became standard practice in DELAG, *Schwaben* was laid up for about four months during the winter. She resumed flying at the end of March 1912 and continued her successful career until the accident in June. During her one year of operating life, *Schwaben* made 234 passenger flights during which she carried nearly 2,000 revenue passengers in 480 hours of flying. She was notable, also, as the first aircraft to carry a steward, Heinrich Kubis, who served refreshments and meals in flight. Kubis continued as a steward in Zeppelins until 1939.

Zeppelin LZ10 (Type f) *Schwaben*

Manufacturer: Luftschiffbau Zeppelin GmbH

Built at Friedrichshafen

Number built: three

Chief designer: L Dürr

Main structural material: Zn-Al alloy

Design began: January 1911

First flight of type: 26 June, 1911

Powerplant: three 145hp Maybach A-Z six-cylinder inline engines

Gas capacity (100 per cent inflation): 17,800cu m

Overall length: 140.0m

Viktoria Luise *at Friedrichshafen.* (Pritchard collection)

Maximum diameter: 14.0m

Spacing of main frames: 8.0m

Fineness ratio: 10.0

Number of gas cells: 17

Number of main longitudinals: 17

Empty weight: 13,600kg

Typical gross lift: 20,650kg (1.16kg/cu m)

Typical disposable load: 7,050kg

Maximum fuel: 1,400kg

Crew: eight

Passengers: 20

Maximum speed: 21.0m/s (46.97 mph)

Maximum range: 1,450km at speed of 19.5m/s (43.62mph)

Static ceiling: 2,450m

Cost: DM650,000

LZ10 *Schwaben* flew 480hr and was destroyed by fire on the ground at Düsseldorf on 28 June, 1912.

The other Type f *Schwaben* class ships were LZ9 Ersatz ZII and LZ12, the Army's ZIII. LZ9, with 16,550cu m gas capacity, first flew on 2 October, 1911. Her last flight was on 21 October before being converted to LZ9A with 17,800cu m capacity. In enlarged form the first flight was on 23 November, 1911, the last flight on 1 August, 1914, after which she was dismantled at Gotha. LZ12, with 17,800cu m capacity, first flew on 25 April, 1912, last flew on 10 July, 1914, and was dismantled at Metz in August 1914.

Civil Zeppelin Operations – LZ11 *Viktoria Luise* and LZ13 *Hansa*

The evidence of practicality provided by *Schwaben* was decisive. DELAG was encouraged to order further airships. The first, LZ11, named *Viktoria Luise*, first flew on 14 February, 1912, and was in service before *Schwaben* was lost. On 30 July, a month after the *Schwaben* accident, a sister-ship to the *Viktoria Luise*, the LZ13 (*Hansa*), first flew and entered service on 3 August. Both *Viktoria Luise* and *Hansa* were similar to the two *Deutschlands*, having basically the same structure. However, their gas cells were reduced in capacity to 18,700cu m (660,380cu ft), their bows were more rounded and their sterns more pointed. Their control surface configurations also differed. *Viktoria Luise* had three Maybach

LZ11 Viktoria Luise *was the first of two Type g ships operated by DELAG.*
(Luftschiffbau Zeppelin)

engines like *Schwaben* but these were of improved B-Y type, developing 150hp, later up-rated to 170hp.

Hansa reverted to 120hp J4F Daimlers, although perhaps up-rated to 160hp. She is believed to have been re-engined later with Maybachs, like her sister-ship. Finally, DELAG ordered one more ship in the latter part of 1912. This was to be of the 'improved *Schwaben*' type which became the L1 class, the first of which was the first Zeppelin supplied to the German Navy.

These ships were of a larger, 14.9m (48ft 10½in) diameter and had 16, 17 and 18 eight-metre bays. LZ15 had 16 bays, which gave her a capacity of 19,500cu m (688,637cu ft) She was, however, diverted to the Army (as Ersatz ZI) while still under construction, in December 1912, and was replaced for DELAG by LZ17, named *Sachsen* (*Saxony*). With the same number of gas cells as LZ15, *Sachsen* was of similar capacity but had a hull two metres shorter. She flew for the first time on 3 May, 1913, and entered service in June.

These last three DELAG ships all remained in service until

the war. They were then taken over by the armed forces and used for training, a function they had performed most of the time they were in commercial service. It was standard practice, before the war, for DELAG to have naval or military officers and men on board on most commercial flights. These men were under instruction from the regular DELAG crews, many of whom were, in any case, reservists. By the time they were finally retired in late 1915–16 these three ships had each flown between 1,000 and 1,500 hours, probably more than any rigid until the *Los Angeles* and *Graf Zeppelin* of the later 1920s.

Although the prewar DELAG operations never became regular scheduled services as had originally been hoped (the performance of the ships was inadequate for this), they were the first properly organised commercial air transport operations. Most of DELAG's flying consisted of short, local joy-rides, of an average duration of about two hours. Interspersed with these local flights were some longer trips, when airships were deployed from one base to another.

During the period of its operations, from 22 June, 1910, to 31 July, 1914, DELAG carried 33,722 passengers and crew including about 10,000 revenue passengers, an average of about

6.5 revenue passengers per flight. A total of 3,139 hours was flown in 1,588 flights with 172,535km (107,205 miles) travelled, without injury to a passenger.

Although Eckener had forecast that the operation could be profitable, it lost money heavily so far as the passenger operations were concerned. From such figures as are available, the high fares charged – they worked out at about 100 marks or £84 in today's values per hour flown – generated an average revenue which covered rather less than half of the operating costs. This meant a probable loss, over the four-year period, of about 2,240,000 marks (£1,900,000). This was a better revenue/expenditure ratio than that achieved by aeroplanes before the early 1930s. The comparison is not strictly fair because the airships did not contribute to the cost of their bases, nor did they attract all the costs associated with scheduled services over a route network. The operation was viable because the German armed forces presumably subsidised DELAG for crew-training. (*See* Appendices 2 and 3)

Schwaben's successful flying season in 1911 not only led to the subsequent years of successful DELAG operations but also encouraged the Army, reluctant since the delivery of ZII in August 1909, to purchase more rigid airships.

LZ13 Hansa, *second Type g, on the lake at Potsdam.*
(Popperfoto)

ZII herself had been lost in an accident on Army service on 26 April, 1910. After taking part in manoeuvres, in which the *Gross I* and *Parseval II* Army pressure-airships also participated, she was forced down by a rising wind on her way back from Hamburg to Cologne. After being held, precariously moored, in the open, overnight, she broke away in a strong wind, the following morning, and was destroyed at Weilburg near Limburg. A replacement was finally ordered in February 1911. LZ9, Ersatz ZII, was similar to *Schwaben*. Although bearing an earlier works

(*Above*) Hansa, *a view showing well the forward propellers and passenger cabin.*
(Science Museum)

(*Below*) Hansa *after being transferred from DELAG to the VII Army Corps for crew training.*
(Pritchard collection)

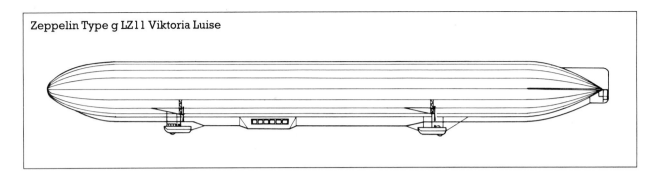

Zeppelin Type g LZ11 Viktoria Luise

number, *Ersatz ZII* made her first flight after *Schwaben*'s, on 2 October, 1911. As completed, she was one 8m bay shorter than her sister-ship but was extended to the same length before being delivered to the Army on 23 November.

Zeppelin LZ11 (Type g)
Viktoria Luise

Manufacturer: Luftschiffbau Zeppelin GmbH

Built at Freidrichshafen

Number built: two

Chief designer: L Drr

Main structural material: Zn-Al alloy

Design began: probably mid-1911

First flight of type: 14 February, 1912

Powerplant: three 150hp Maybach B-Y six-cylinder inline engines (later 170hp)

Gas capacity (100 per cent inflation): 18.700cu m

Overall length: 148.0m

Maximum diameter: 14.0m

Spacing of main frames: 8.0m

Fineness ratio: 10.57

Number of gas cells: 18

Number of main longitudinals: 18

Empty weight: 15,150kg

Typical gross lift: 21,700kg (1.16kg/cu m)

Typical disposable load: 6,550kg

Crew: eight

Passengers: 25

Maximum speed: 21.0m/s (46.97 mph) (22.7m/s (50.77mph) sometimes quoted)

Maximum range: 1,100km

LZ11 *Viktoria Luise* last flew on 12 October, 1915, had flown 1,550hr and was destroyed coming out of its shed at Liegnitz on 18 October.

LZ13 *Hansa* first flew on 30 July, 1912, and last flew on 5 August, 1916, completing 1,227hr. It was then dismantled.

Hansa, in passenger configuration, with the entrance to the Potsdam airship station (Potsdamer Luftschiffhafen).
(Courtesy Philip Jarrett)

Das Zeppelin-Luftschiff „Hansa" über dem Potsdamer Luftschiffhafen.

Military and Naval Zeppelins

Schwaben's success did more than put new life into Zeppelin's civil operations. It finally convinced the armed forces that they should buy more Zeppelins. The Minister of War, General von Moltke, called for the ordering of nine more ships and even the Navy began to change its attitude.

The first new Army ship was ZIII (LZ12), another *Schwaben*-type vessel, ordered in March 1912, flown on 25 April and finally delivered on 23 July. The Navy had rightly claimed, up to now, that the Zeppelins were too slow to be used over the sea. As we have seen, they barely had sufficient speed to be practical vehicles over land; the wind is always stronger at sea and so more speed was clearly essential. Even the *Schwaben*-type, which was significantly faster than its predecessors, was not fast enough.

Ever since a naval officer, Fregattenkapitn Robert Mischke, had had a flight in LZ3 on 30 September, 1907, the Navy had been pressing Zeppelin to produce larger and faster ships for its use. The Zeppelin designers had been cautious in their response. They felt, with some justification, that higher-powered engines were required and that bigger airships could be safely developed only in a series of progressive steps. When the first naval Zeppelin was at last ordered in April 1912, the designers had gone some way

LZ9 was a Type f Zeppelin which went to the Army as Ersatz ZII.
(Pritchard collection)

towards meeting the Navy's requirements. Orders for a further four ships were mooted, delivery to be spread over the following three years.

L1 (LZ14), the first naval airship, was of a new larger diameter, 14.9m (48ft 10^1/$_2$in), and her capacity of 22,470cu m (793,518cu ft) made her bigger than any previous airship. She had a hull length of 156.0m (492ft 1^1/$_2$in) but, like LZ15 and LZ16, a longer fin gave an overall length of 158.0m (518ft 4^1/$_3$in). L1's structure consisted of one 16.0m (52ft 6in) bay at the stern, sixteen 8.0m (26ft 3in) bays and a 12.0m (39ft 4^1/$_2$in) bay in the bow. The last three ships in the class introduced a structural innovation: they had single intermediate semi-frames, linking the six lowest longitudinals. These semi-frames were inserted between the main frames to strengthen the structure.

With three 165hp Maybach engines of the new B-Y type, first fitted in *Viktoria Luise*, L1 had a top speed of 21.2m/s (47.42mph). She flew, for the first time, on 7 October, 1912. Following an impressive 30-hour proving flight under the command of Count Zeppelin (13/14 October), which covered 1,600km (1,000 miles), L1 went into service with the Navy. She gave a good account of herself, mainly in the training role but was lost at sea near Heligoland on 9 September, 1913, with most of her crew and the head of the Naval Airship Division. In that period of nearly a year, L1 showed clearly that her speed, although higher than any previous airship, was still inadequate for naval use. As a result, the Zeppelin company agreed, in January 1913, to build a larger, higher-powered ship to naval designs, and no more L1 class ships were ordered.

L1 might be called the first production-type Zeppelin. Five other ships of the same class were

built during 1913. Four of them, Ersatz ZI, ZIV, Desatz ZI and ZV, were for the Army, and one, *Sachsen*, for DELAG. ZV and *Sachsen* were later lengthened by one 8m bay containing an additional gas cell, and one other ship, ZVI, was built from the

Ersatz ZII at Friedrichshafen.
(Pritchard collection)

L1 (LZ14) was the first Type h Zeppelin. It flew on 7 October, 1912.
(Pritchard collection)

Count Zeppelin and Korvetten-kapitän Peter Strasser in L1 (LZ14).

then combined to carry her uncontrollably into the sea. The same sort of accident was to be repeated again and again through the story of the rigid airship. In some cases, structural failure, usually resulting from rapid ascent or turbulence, occurred before the airships involved hit the surface. On the evidence of 40 years and nearly 80,000 hours of rigid airship flying, the strong up- and down-draughts commonly associated with cold fronts and thunderstorms represented a quite insurmountable hazard to large airships and were probably responsible for the loss of most rigids destroyed in flying accidents. Of the twenty rigids destroyed in fatal flying accidents (other than those lost by enemy action), it appears that well over half were lost from this cause or from associated phenomena such as lightning strikes or static discharge. (*See* Appendix 3)

Properly trained rigid airship captains of sufficient experience (perhaps only the select band of Zeppelin commanders of the 1920s and 1930s really come into this category) did their best to avoid such weather and usually managed to do so on the routes they operated. However, even they ran grave risks of getting

start to this lengthened standard. Finally, two more Army ships, ZVII and ZVIII (LZ22–23), were built early in 1914. They were still broadly of the same type but were lengthened, having two additional 8m (26ft 3in) bays, each containing another gas cell. The single intermediate semi-frames, introduced on the later L1 class ships, were extended to link the eight lowest longitudinals. The external keel on these two ships blended more smoothly into the bow of the hull, improving appearance and reducing drag. These ships each had three 180hp Maybach C-X engines.

The loss of L1 was not directly attributable to any deficiency in performance, marginal as this still was for extended patrols over the sea. The accident was similar to Kahlenberg's crash in *Deutschland* more than three years earlier. Caught in a squall, L1 was lifted far above her pressure height. The resulting loss of gas and a subsequent down-draught

ZIV (LZ16), the third Type h ship.

ZIV (LZ16) after its forced landing at Lunéville in France on 3 April, 1913. French authorities closely examined the ship and made drawings available to Britain and the USA.

caught out by inadequate fore-casting of stormy conditions. It was not realised at that time that in many parts of the world wide-spread thunderstorm activity is prevalent at certain times of the year. Even in less affected areas, such activity can occur frequently in a bad year. Modern aero-planes, even with the aid of radar and vastly improved forecasting techniques, still get involved in dangerous conditions from time to time – this, despite the fact that their high performance helps them overfly or circumvent the worst of the weather. Occasions when the consequences are seri-ous are fortunately rare because aeroplanes are incomparably less vulnerable than any airship.

Two views of DELAG's LZ17 Sachsen, *a Type h ship.* (Science Museum and courtesy Peter Bowers)

The also ill-fated second naval Zeppelin, L2 (LZ18), was built at Friedrichshafen in one of the berths of the Ring Shed. The size limitations of this building and of the operating sheds available had an important and, as it tran-spired, disastrous effect on her design. Until now, the prominent external V-section keel had been a feature of all Zeppelins. The first Schtte-Lanz rigid, discussed later, which had a wooden struc-ture, completely unlike that of the Zeppelins, did not have an external keel when it appeared in 1911. This may well have in-fluenced Felix Pietzker, the naval designer of L2, into inverting the keel member in his design and enclosing it within the hull. At the same time, the two power-gondolas, each containing two of the new type 180hp Maybach C-X engines, were brought up much closer to the hull than ever before. There was a third, separ-ate control-gondola near the bow. The effect of these changes made it possible to increase the ship's diameter to 16.6m (54ft 5^1/$_2$in) and its capacity to 27,000cu m (953,500cu ft) within the same overall dimensions as the earlier, smaller ships. Significantly, the length of 158m (518ft 4^1/$_3$in) just fitted inside the existing sheds.

As it turned out, L2's top speed of 21m/s (46.97mph) was slightly less than L1's, and it was

certainly still inadequate for naval use. On the other hand, the new C-X engines, which had been first fitted for tests in L1 earlier in the year, held promise of de-velopment to higher powers and this would have given a useful in-crease in speed in due course.

But this was not to be. After flying for the first time on 6 Sep-tember, 1913, L2 made eighteen test flights and was moved to Johannisthal, the early Berlin aerodrome. On her tenth flight, on 17 October, with a mainly naval crew of twenty-eight on board, she caught fire in flight shortly after leaving the ground. She was completely destroyed along with her entire crew and her designer, Pietzker.

The accident was attributed to some of the new features of L2's design. The subsequent inquiry concluded that hydrogen, over-flowing into the internal keel, was ignited by the engines which were so much nearer the hull than previously. The accident

might have been avoided if Pietz-ker had adopted another feature which Schtte-Lanz introduced on S.L.II in 1914, namely gas ex-haust shafts between the valves at the bottom of the gas cells and ventilators on the top of the hull. These were incorporated in later Zeppelins, together with an im-permeable outer cover. However, the first ship with these innova-tions, LZ78 (L34), did not fly until 22 September, 1916.

The L2 disaster, coming so soon after the L1's, and like that accident, involving heavy loss of life, was a severe blow to the whole airship cause. These were the first accidents to Zeppelins which resulted in fatalities, and they seem to have had a signifi-cant effect on Count Zeppelin who, in spite of his age – he was now 75 – had, until this time, continued to play the leading role in his organisation. Although he did not retire immediately, he handed over the executive direc-tion of the company to Colsman

Zeppelins Go to War – Types h, i, k, l and m

in the latter part of 1913. He still did much of the test flying, at least until early 1914, and he seems to have gone on with some flying after that. He remained chairman of the company and of the Zeppelin Foundation but, increasingly, he withdrew from the day-to-day activities at Friedrichshafen. After the war started in August 1914, he devoted a large part of his time to political and policy matters. He was disappointed at Germany's failure to make early effective use of its airships for strategic bombing; by the time operations of this type were built up on any scale, it was too late. The development of higher-performance aeroplanes and of new types of incendiary ammunition had rendered the airship too vulnerable.

Count Zeppelin appears to have realised this sooner than most. Although in February 1915 he made the sweeping claim that the Zeppelin airship's development 'will govern the future of war', he had already started manufacturing aeroplanes in the previous year. By early 1917 he was saying that 'airships are an antiquated weapon. The aeroplane will control the air'. He particularly advocated large aero-

L2 (LZ18) was a Type i Zeppelin designed for the German Navy,

planes. Even before the war, he had realised the significance of the Russian Igor Sikorski's (later Sikorsky) first large, multi-engined aeroplane, the *Bolshoi Baltiski* of 1913, and had taken steps to encourage similar developments in Germany. Mainly as a result of his initiative, Germany led in the development of large aeroplanes throughout the First World War and also pioneered the all-metal monoplane which later led to the evolution of the very large, modern, long-range aeroplane. The Count died of pneumonia on 8 March, 1917. The great jet airliners of today are an ironic, but not unfitting, memorial to a remarkable man.

When the war began in August 1914, the German Army had seven rigid airships in service, the Zeppelins ZIV, ZV, ZVI, ZVII, ZVIII and ZIX, plus the wooden Schtte-Lanz S.L.II. The Navy had only one rigid, the Zeppelin L3. Two of the civil DELAG ships, *Hansa* and *Sachsen*, went to the Army and the third, *Viktoria Luise*, went to the Navy. On the face of it, therefore, the Army had a formidable fleet of rigids, while the Navy was lamentably weak in the new weapon.

The Allies over-rated the capabilities of the German rigid airships and were afraid they would be used right away for bombing attacks on their towns and cities. They did not realise that the German High Command had different ideas. It is true that there was a school of thought in the German Navy, led by Peter Strasser, the leader of the Naval Airship Division, which advocated the use of rigid airships for strategic bombing attacks, but it did not have the support of the High Command which was, in any case, prevented from adopting such a policy by orders from the Kaiser. These banned any bombing attacks on non-military targets. Strasser also had ambitious ideas for the use of his airships in support of the Navy at sea, but with only one operational airship, he lacked the means to put them into effect. Once again, the Allies greatly over-estimated the Germans' preparedness at this time.

Incredibly enough at the beginning of the war, the German High Command believed that the main role of rigid airships should be in support of the Army at the front. It thought they could be

ZV (LZ20), the last Type h ship, over Johannisthal aerodrome, Berlin.

ZVI (LZ21), Type k, at Brunswick.
(Popperfoto)

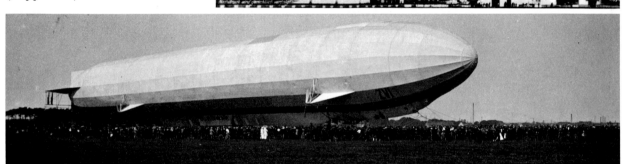

used for close-support bombing. As events swiftly proved, this concept was utterly wrong. As a result of it, four Army rigids were lost in the first month of the war. They were shot down by fire from the ground while trying to bomb the enemy near the front: three in the west and one over Poland in the east.

After such a disastrous beginning, the High Command had second thoughts and the rigids were stopped from flying low over battle areas. However, the idea that airships could be used for tactical purposes in support of the armies died hard, and both rigid and pressure-airships continued to be used for this purpose, although mainly at night, for several years. The German Army seems to have decided that it had no further use for rigids after LZ77 was shot down by anti-aircraft fire on 21 February, 1916,

at Révigny. It closed down its airship operations on 1 August, 1917.

Partly because of this preoccupation with tactical applications, and partly because of the Kaiser's reluctance to allow cities to be bombed, the Germans made the serious mistake of not using their airships for strategic bombing on any scale until May 1915. In the first months of the war the Allies had no effective defence against

airship attack, particularly at night. Even by May 1915, their defences were still pathetically weak. The Germans not only started late but they also took a long time to develop and exploit appropriate techniques and weapons for such attacks. By the time these began to have some chance of being effective, Allied defences had been greatly improved. Thereafter, despite remarkable technical improvements

L3 (LZ24), first of the Type m L3 class.
(Pritchard collection)

ZVII (LZ22), Type l, at Fried-richshafen in early 1914.

This view of L3 (LZ24) shows well the outrigged propellers.

ZIX (LZ25), second of the Type m L3 class. It first flew at the end of July 1914.

than five similar ships, thus giving the Navy, for the first time, a strong airship force which became more potent than the Army's.

L3 was basically a further development of the L1 class with a diameter of 14.9m (48ft 10½in). Like L1, the L3 class ships were all of 22,470cu m (793,518cu ft) capacity with 18 gas cells and were 158m (518ft 4⅓in) long. The frames had an 8m (26ft 3in) spacing. There were intermediate semi-frames linking the eight lowest of the longitudinals, as on ZVII and ZVIII. L3 and the rest of the m and m2 type airships had a 10m (32ft 9½in) bay amidships with a full intermediate ring in place of one of the 8m bays with the intermediate semi-frame. Top speed was 22.4m/s (50mph). The engines were the up-rated 180hp version of the Maybach C-X which had become available from early 1914. These Zeppelins were the first with sufficient speed to have a genuine cross-country flying capability. The performance was still marginal for maritime use but they were employed for reconnaissance over the North Sea and for a few of the early tentative attacks on targets such as Paris and England's east coast during the first part of 1915. A typical offensive load for the L3 class was five 50kg (110lb) high explosive bombs and twenty 3kg (6.5lb) incendiary bombs.

Despite their inadequacies, these ships were built in quantity at the start of the war because they were the best that could be quickly produced in numbers. During the latter half of 1914 and the beginning of 1915, they were being built in the Ring Shed at Friedrichshafen at a rate of one every five or six weeks. (Luft-

in airships, the Allies managed to keep ahead so that the airship campaign had been completely defeated before the end of the war.

Strategic attacks, when they were at last launched on a significant scale, were mainly made by the German naval airships, although the Army also participated. Before strategic bombing started, there was much political haggling between the two Services over which was to be responsible for this type of warfare. The heavy losses suffered by the Army's fleet of rigids, at the beginning of the war, were partly made good by the end of 1914 by the addition of three new Zeppelins. Two were of the powerful new L3 class which had been authorised in June 1913, ordered in October and developed for the Navy as a result of experience with L1 and L2. L3 herself, the first of the class, was the only naval Zeppelin at the outbreak of war (she had first flown on 11 May, 1914) but she was joined, before the end of 1914, by no less

schiffbau Zeppelin now employed nearly 1,000 people.) Six ships of this class were delivered to the Army, three of them being among the first Zeppelins manufactured away from Friedrichshafen, at Potsdam-Wildpark, near Berlin, where a second production source was established in late 1914 in a former operating shed.

The fourth L3 class Army ship, LZ34, instead of being called ZXIII when she was commissioned, continued, for superstitious reasons, to be known by her works number. This new practice, once adopted, was adhered to for Army Zeppelins thereafter. In mid-1915, for reasons of security, the ship with the LZ44 works number was renumbered LZ74 in the Army, and all later Army Zeppelins continued to be given a number which was their works number plus 30, a cause of much confusion to historians but also, as was no doubt intended, to the Allied intelligence services. (*See* Appendix 6).

Although L3 herself (designated Type m) had the older type of tail unit with multiple control surfaces, the second ship (ZIX)

This view of ZIX shows the much improved tail surfaces compared with all previous Zeppelins including sistership L3. ZIX was designated Type m2.
(Pritchard collection)

and the remainder of the class had much simplified cruciform tail units, similar to those already fitted by Schtte-Lanz to its rigids. They were identified as Type m2. This much better looking type of tail was standardised on Zeppelins from then. The aerodynamically cleaner tail unit raised the top speed of later L3 class ships to about 23.4m/s (52.34mph). The improved streamlining of the tail, and other refinements such as better fairing of the keel into the nose of the hull and a more tapered line to the stern, resulted from the application of steadily increasing research in aerodynamics and structures within the Zeppelin organisation and at Göttingen and elsewhere. The influence of the Navy's technical people was also significant from 1913 when they had been involved in the design of L2.

Zeppelin LZ14 (Type h), L1

Manufacturer: Luftschiffbau Zeppelin GmbH
Built at Friedrichshafen
Number built: six
Chief designer: L Drr
Main structural material: Zn-Al alloy
Design began: April 1912
First flight of type: 7 October, 1912
Powerplant: three 180hp Maybach B-Y six-cylinder inline engines
Gas capacity (100 per cent inflation): 22,740cu m (LZ14); 19,500cu m (LZ15, 16, 17, 19, 20)
Overall length: 158m (LZ14); 142m (LZ15 and 16); 140m (LZ17, 19, 20)
Maximum diameter: 14.9m
Spacing of main frames: 8.0m
Fineness ratio: 10.6 (LZ14)
Number of gas cells: 18 (LZ14); 16 (LZ15, 16, 17, 19, 20)
Number of main longitudinals: 17
Empty weight: 17,900kg (LZ14)
Typical gross lift: 26,100kg (LZ14); 22,700kg (LZ16) (1.16kg/cu m)
Typical disposable load: 8,200kg (LZ14), 4,800kg (LZ16)
Crew: 20

Zeppelin Type h LZ14

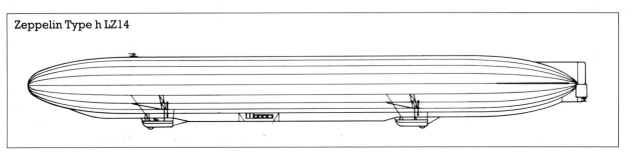

Zeppelin Type i LZ18

Maximum speed: 21.2m/s (47.42 mph)

Maximum range: 2,300km

LZ14	L1	First flight 7.10.1912, last flight 9.9.1913, 68 flights, destroyed in storm 9.9.15
LZ15	Ersatz ZI	First flight 16.1.1913, last flight 19.3.1913, 33 flights, destroyed in storm 19.3.1913
LZ16	ZIV	First flight 14.3.1913, last flight 20.10.1916, 419 flights, broken up late 1916
LZ17	*Sachsen*	First flight 3.5.1913, last flight 6.5.1914, 980hr, converted to LZ17A with 20,870cu m gas capacity
LZ17A	*Sachsen*	First flight 1.8.1914, last flight 5.11.1916, broken up late 1916
LZ19	Desatz ZI	First flight 6.6.1913, last flight 13.6.1914, destroyed in storm 13.6.1914
LZ20	ZV	First flight 8.7.1913, last flight 12.1913, converted 12.1913 to LZ20A with 20,870cu m gas capacity, last flight 27 or 28.8.1914. Shot down by anti-aircraft fire

Zeppelin LZ18 (Type i), L2

Manufacturer: Luftschiffbau Zeppelin GmbH

Built in Friedrichshafen

Number built: one

Chief designers: L Drr and F Pietzker

Main structural material: Zn-Al alloy

Assembly began: June 1913

First flight: 9 September, 1913

Powerplant: four 180hp Maybach C-X six-cylinder inline engines

Gas capacity (100 per cent inflation): 27,000cu m

Overall length: 158.0m

Maximum diameter: 16.6m

Spacing of main frames: 8.0m

Fineness ratio: 9.52

Number of gas cells: 18

Empty weight: 20,250kg

Typical gross lift: 31,350kg (1.16 kg/cu m)

Typical disposable load: 11,100kg

Crew: 23

Maximum speed: 21.0m/s (46.9 mph)

Maximum range: 2,100km

LZ18 was flown for ten hours but burned in flight on 17 October, 1913

Zeppelin LZ21 (Type k), ZVI

Manufacturer: Luftschiffbau Zeppelin GmbH

Built at Friedrichshafen

Number built: one

Chief designer: L Drr

Main structural material: Zn-Al alloy

Assembly began: July 1913

First flight: 10 November, 1913

Powerplant: three 180hp Maybach C-X six-cylinder inline engines

Gas capacity (100 per cent inflation): 20,870cu m

Overall length: 148.0m

Maximum diameter: 14.9m

Spacing of main frames: 8.0m

Fineness ratio: 9.93

Number of gas cells: 17

Empty weight: 15,450kg

Typical gross lift: 24,250kg (1.16kg/cu m)

Typical disposable load: 9,800kg

Crew: 18

Maximum speed: 20.5m/s (45.85 mph)

Maximum range: 1,900km

LZ21 made its last flight on 6 August, 1914, when it was shot down by anti-aircraft fire

Zeppelin LZ22 (Type l), ZVII

Manufacturer: Luftschiffbau Zeppelin GmbH

Built at Friedrichshafen

Number built: two

Chief designer: L Drr

Main structural material: Zn-Al alloy

Assembly began September 1913

First flight of type: 8 January, 1914

Powerplant: three 180hp Maybach C-X six-cylinder inline engines

Gas capacity (100 per cent inflation): 22,140cu m

Overall length: 156.0m

Maximum diameter: 14.9m

Spacing of main frames: 8.0m

Fineness ratio: 10.47

Number of gas cells: 18

Empty weight: 16,850kg

Typical gross lift: 25,700kg (1.16kg/cu m)

Typical disposable load: 8,850kg

Crew: 18

Maximum speed: 20.0m/s (44.73 mph)

Maximum range: 1,900km

LZ22 ZVII was shot down by anti-aircraft fire on 23 August, 1914.

LZ23 ZVIII first flew on 21 February, 1914, and was also shot down by anti-aircraft fire on 23 August, 1914

Zeppelin LZ24 (Type m and m2), L3 class

Manufacturer: Luftschiffbau Zeppelin GmbH

All built in the double shed at Friedrichshafen except LZ30, LZ34 and LZ37 built at Potsdam

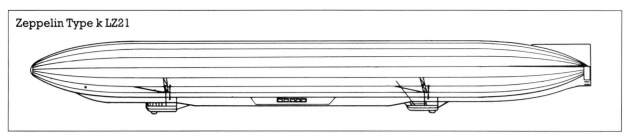

Zeppelin Type k LZ21

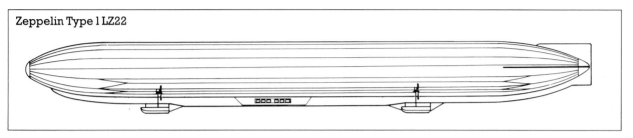

Zeppelin Type l LZ22

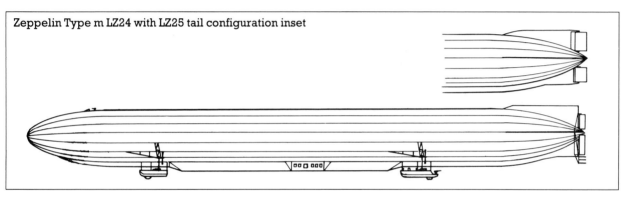

Zeppelin Type m LZ24 with LZ25 tail configuration inset

Number built: 12
Chief designer: L Drr
Main structural material: Zn-Al alloy
Design began: October 1913
First flight of type: 11 May, 1914
Powerplant: three 180hp Maybach C-X six-cylinder inline engines
Gas capacity (100 per cent inflation): 22,470cu m
Overall length: 158.0m
Maximum diameter: 14.9m
Spacing of main frames: 8.0m
Fineness ratio: 10.61
Number of gas cells: 18
Number of main longitudinals: 17
Empty weight: 16,900kg
Typical gross lift: 26,100kg (1.16kg/cu m)
Typical disposable load: 9,200kg
Maximum fuel: 4,000kg
Crew: 16
Maximum speed: 23.4m/s (52.34 mph)
Maximum range: 2,200km at speed of 22.4m/s (50mph)
Static ceiling: 2,800m
Cost: DM850,000

Production

C/n		First flight	Last flight	Flights	Disposal
LZ24	L3	11.5.14	17.2.15	141	Wrecked. Forced landing on Fan [Is, Denmark]
LZ25	ZIX	29.7.14	7/8.10.14		Bombed in shed at Dsseldorf 7/8.10.14
LZ27	L4	28.8.14	17.2.15	48	Forced landing in Denmark 17.2.15
LZ28	L5	22.9.14	6.8.15	92	Forced down by anti-aircraft fire in Russia 6.8.15
LZ29	ZX	13.10.14	21.3.15		Forced down by anti aircraft fire at St Quentin 21.3.15
LZ30	ZXI	11.11.14	20.5.15		Burned on ground after blowing away at Posen 20.5.15
LZ31	L6	3.11.14	16.9.19	419	Burned in shed at Hamburg 16.9.16
LZ32	L7	20.11.14	4.5.16	164	Shot down by British cruisers off Horns Reef 4.5.16
LZ33	L8	17.12.14	5.3.15	21	Shot down in Belgium by anti-aircraft fire 5.3.15
LZ34	LZ34	6.1.15	21.5.15		Forced down by anti-aircraft fire 21.5.15 in E Prussia
LZ35	LZ35	11.1.15	13.4.15		Forced down in Belgium by anti-aircraft fire 13.4.15
LZ37	LZ37	28.2.15	7.6.15		Shot down by British aircraft over Ghent 7.6.15

Zeppelin Types n and o

One of Count Zeppelin's great qualities was his ability to pick good men and, having picked them, he was able to hold their loyalty. In the technical field during the period 1910–14, the Zeppelin organisation was joined by a number of extremely able engineers, several of whom later became well-known in their own right. They included Claude Dornier, Paul Jaray, Karl Arnstein and Adolf Rohrbach.

The results of the increased technical effort going into basic research and into the design and development of new Zeppelins began to show more clearly with the appearance of the next new design. This was LZ26 (ZXII), the third new Zeppelin to join the Army before the end of 1914.

There had been reports as early as 1910 that future Zeppelins would be made of a new ma-terial to replace the zinc-aluminium alloy used until then. In that year, LZ7 *Deutschland*, the first of the ships built for DELAG introduced a new type of girder in the old material. (*See* Note 14) Even while LZ7 was under construction, incorporating the new girder, there was talk of her being the last ship to be built in zinc-aluminium alloy. But the new girder in the old material continued to be used on all Zeppelins down to, and including, the L3 class which remained in production until early 1915.

ZXII (LZ26), the only Type n Zeppelin.
(Popperfoto)

The first British rigid, the un-successful Vickers No.1 *Mayfly* which was directly inspired by the Zeppelin, was under construction during the period May 1909 to May 1911. The structure of this ship was of duralumin, a new, stronger, age-hardened aluminium alloy (containing small quantities of copper, manganese

The sub-cloud car of ZXII invented by Oblt Ernst Lehmann.

L9 (LZ36), one of two Type o ships, was one of the first to have 10m bays.

Ernst A Lehmann the wartime Zeppelin commander continued with Zeppelin operations after the war, became a director of Deutsche Zeppelin-Reederei, and was fatally injured in the Hindenburg disaster at Lakehurst in 1937.

and silicon) which had been discovered by the German, Alfred Wilm, in the autumn of 1909. The patent rights for the alloy were held by Düren Metallwerke AG of Düren, which put the metal on the market in 1910. The Zeppelin engineers were apparently dissatisfied at this time with the methods then available for rolling the new material into sheets and strips.

By 1914 these difficulties had been largely overcome and Luftschiffbau Zeppelin introduced a new duralumin girder for ZXII. The basic sections were similar to the earlier type but the built-up girder was larger in cross-section. Apart from the new girders, ZXII also introduced several other important innovations. First of all, the diameter, 16m (52ft 6in), was greater than on previous Zeppelins. Second, the main-frame spacing was increased to 10m (32ft 10^1/$_2$in) and a full intermediate frame was introduced dividing the bay between the main frames. Thirdly, the continuous external V keel was inverted and built into the inside of the hull. This had been tried in the ill-fated L2. Now, however, a partial, four-sided external keel-like structure, which would have contained the passenger cabin if ZXII had become a civil ship as originally intended, was added outside the hull, but extended over only the middle part of its length. ZXII also had the simple cruciform tail unit fitted to most of the L3 class. Finally,

while the two engines in the rear gondola drove bracket propellers, the single engine in the front gondola drove its pusher propeller direct for the first time in a Zeppelin, an arrangement which had been used previously on Schütte-Lanz airships. The gondolas were enclosed. They had been intended to be open, originally, as in previous civil ships.

ZXII was 161.2m (528ft 10^1/$_3$in) long and had a capacity of 25,000cu m (882,870cu ft) in 15 larger gas cells. Three 180hp Maybach C-X engines gave a top speed of 22.5m/s (50.33mph). Because the Zeppelin works at Friedrichshafen and the new works at Potsdam were fully taken up with production of the L3 class, ZXII was assembled in the large operating shed at Frankfurt, the only Zeppelin to be built there. ZXII flew, for the first time, on 14 December, 1914. She had originally been ordered by DELAG but was now delivered straight to the Army, with which she gave good service on both the eastern and western fronts and bombed Paris on 17 March, 1916. During part of her career she was commanded by Ernst A Lehmann (1886–1937) who was to become famous as a postwar Zeppelin commander.

Lehmann first tried out the sub-cloud car on ZXII. This was a small, streamlined gondola, designed to carry an observer. It could be lowered a considerable distance below the airship on a cable. The ship could then fly in,

or above, the clouds with only the small, practically invisible sub-cloud car hanging into the clear air below. The observer could then direct the ship over a target by telephone. This device was used for the first time to bomb Calais on 17 March, 1916.

Towards the end of her career, ZXII seems to have been used for test purposes. An experimental biplane glider-bomb was launched from her on 27 April, 1917. ZXII was to have made her last flight on 8 August that year, but she survived the war and was ultimately broken up by order of the Allies.

ZXII represented the biggest single technical advance since the start of rigid airship development. She combined most of the results of all that had been learnt in Zeppelin development up to the war. In spite of this, only two other ships basically similar to ZXII were built: L9 for the Navy and LZ39 for the Army. They were assembled at Friedrichshafen and were completed in

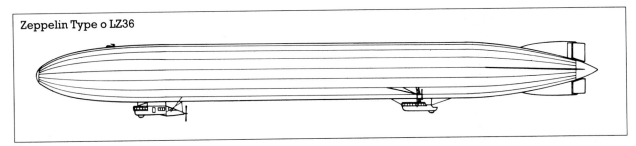

Zeppelin Type n LZ26

Zeppelin Type o LZ36

March–April 1915. Because these ships were intended for military purposes from the beginning, ZXII's external, keel-like structure for the passenger cabin was deleted. L9 was thus the first Zeppelin without any visible keel since L2. Its removal gave a useful reduction in drag so that, with three 180hp Maybach C-X engines, these ships had a top speed of 23.6m/s (52.79mph).

Within a few weeks of entering service on 17 May, 1915, LZ39 had a narrow escape over Ostend when she was attacked by Cdr A W Bigsworth of the RNAS in an Avro 504. Bigsworth got above the airship and dropped four 9kg (20lb) bombs which hit and damaged the hull but failed to ignite the gas. The airship escaped to make a heavy landing. Three weeks later Flight Sub-Lieut R Warneford made a similar attack on the L3 class LZ37 in the same area and sent her down in flames. He was awarded the Victoria Cross.

To take full advantage of the new technology incorporated in ZXII, a new, larger and higher-powered airship was required; this was something which the Navy had, in any case, been demanding for a long time. In August 1914, the Navy took steps to get what it was sure would be its first practical naval airship. While this was being developed, it would have to put up with the interim L3 class which would,

meanwhile, continue in production at the highest rate possible. The new naval airship requirement led to the development of two new types of rigid airship, both in the million cubic feet class, the wooden Schütte-Lanz S.L.3 class and the Zeppelin L10 class. In August, examples of both were ordered by the Navy which also agreed to pay for the larger construction hangars both manufacturers would require in order to be able to build them.

Zeppelin LZ26 (Type n) ZXII

Manufacturer: Luftschiffbau Zeppelin GmbH

Built at Frankfurt-am-Main

Number built: one

Chief designer: L Dürr

Main structural material: duralumin

Design began: August 1914

First flight: 14 December, 1914

Powerplant: three 180hp Maybach C-X six-cylinder inline engines

Gas capacity (100 per cent inflation): 25,000cu m

Overall length: 161.2m

Maximum diameter: 16.0m

Spacing of main frames: 10.0m

Fineness ratio: 10.1

Number of gas cells: 15

Empty weight: 16,800kg

Typical gross lift: 29,000kg (1.16kg/cu m)

Typical disposable load: 12,200kg

Crew: 18

Maximum speed: 22.5m/s (50.33 mph)

Maximum range: 3,300km

After more than 127 flights, LZ26 made its last flight on 8 August, 1917, and was broken up on 11 July, 1919, at Jüterbog

Zeppelin LZ36 (Type o) L9

Manufacturer: Luftschiffbau Zeppelin GmbH

Built at Friedrichshafen

Number built: two

Chief designer: L Dürr

Main structural material: duralumin

Assembly began: December 1914

First flight of type: 8 March, 1915

Powerplant: three 180hp Maybach C-X six-cylinder inline engines

Gas capacity (100 per cent inflation): 24,900cu m

Overall length: 161.4m

Maximum diameter: 16.0m

Spacing of main frames: 10.0m

Fineness ratio: 10.09

Number of gas cells: 15

Empty weight: 17,800kg

Typical gross lift: 28,900kg (1.16kg/cu m)

Typical disposable load: 11,100kg

Crew: 16

Maximum speed: 23.6m/s (52.79 mph)

Maximum range: 3,300km

LZ36 made its 148th and last flight on 16.9.16 and was accidentally burned in its shed at Hamburg that day.

LZ39 first flew on 24.4.15 and was forced down by anti-aircraft fire at Kovno, Russia, on 16.12.15

Wooden Rigids – Schütte-Lanz S.L.1–20

The Schütte-Lanz company had been started in Mannheim as early as 1909 to manufacture rigid airships out of wood. The moving spirit was Johann Schütte (1873–1940), a professor of shipbuilding at the Danzig Technical High School. He obtained the support of Karl Lanz and probably of other Mannheim industrialists. Schütte's first airship differed in most respects from Zeppelin practice although general principles and basic configuration clearly derived from it. The streamlined shape was modelled on the Parseval pressure-airships.

The S.L.1 was started in September 1909 with the encourage-

The first Schütte-Lanz airship, S.L.1. It first flew in October 1911 and, unlike Zeppelins, had a wooden structure.
(Popperfoto)

The S.L.1. The 'geodetic' structure is just visible through the outer covering.

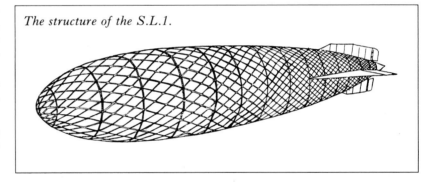

The structure of the S.L.1.

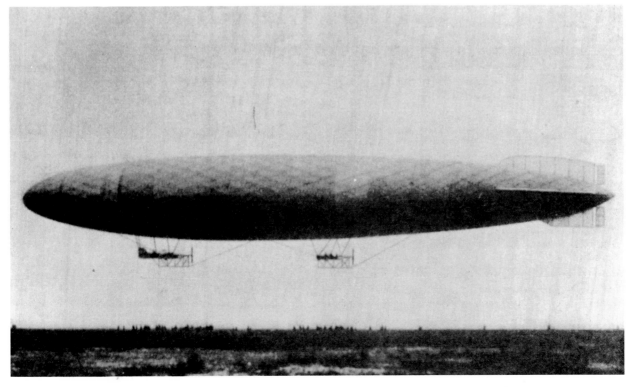

The Schütte-Lanz S.L.1 under construction. The crossed spiral wooden girder construction was unique to this ship.

ment of the Army, which was keen to see the appearance of a competitor to Zeppelin. As originally designed in the winter of 1908, and as first built, S.L.1 had elevator surfaces, each side of the hull both fore and aft, together with fixed fins at the tail, all similar to Zeppelin practice at that time. In other respects, notably the streamline shape in place of Zeppelin's blunt-ended cylinders, S.L.1 represented an important advance. The two large 270hp Daimler J8L eight-cylinder engines were installed in two cars and drove pusher propellers direct, a much tidier arrangement than Zeppelin's bracket propellers. The ship was very large for its time, having a capacity of 20,500cu m (723,950cu ft), but she had only seven gas cells.

The most unusual feature of S.L.1 was the structure which was designed by Schütte and Carl Huber (d.1911), a civil engineer. This was built up of crossed spirals of wooden girders, forming a wire-braced cage of the required

S.L.1 before fitting of lower fin and rudder.

Professor Johann Schütte.
(Deutsches Museum)

*S.L.2, the Schütte-Lanz Type 'b',
was the first successful four-engined
rigid airship. It became the Army's
S.L.II.*

*S.L.II flying the German Ensign
from its stern.*

shape. It was similar to the geo-detic design in metal, developed twenty years later by B N Wallis, and used in a number of Vickers aeroplanes, including the Wellington bomber of the Second World War. (*See* Note 15) A similar form of construction was also used for a small British rigid, the MacMechan/Marshall Fox airship, partly built, but not completed, in 1915. S.L.1 had an

S.L.4, the second Type 'c' S.L.3 class.

S.L.3 Type 'c' S.L.3 class.

Schütte-Lanz Type 'e' S.L.8 class with lengthened tail cone and gunner's position.

S.L.16 ('e'9) of the S.L.8 class.

S.L.15 (S.L.XV) of the S.L.8 class.

internal passageway along the bottom of the hull but this was structurally less important than Zeppelin's external V keel. The wood used for the structure was variously reported as Russian white fir, American pine, ash, poplar and laminated aspen wood.

S.L.1 flew for the first time on 17 October, 1911, and, following various vicissitudes, including an accident on an early test flight in which she dived into the ground, was modified several times. S.L.1 was finally wrecked on 17 July, 1913, when forced down while returning to Berlin after a trip to Königsberg. As with the early Zeppelins, trouble was experienced initially with instability and lack of control. This was put right by the adoption of a simple cruciform tail unit, the first of a type which was later to be adopted for all rigid airships.

The spiral form of construction also proved unsatisfactory and the glued joints gave trouble because Scotch glue, which is affected by damp, seems to have been used. As a result, when construction of S.L.2 started in February 1913, she had a new form of structure, basically similar to that of the Zeppelins with radially-braced frames and longitudinals, but made of wooden trellis girders with aluminium fittings. The number of gas cells (fifteen) was similar to that in the Zeppelins. Schütte-Lanz may

have switched to casein cement (*Kaltleim*) for this airship; they certainly did so for all their later airships. This new glue had been invented in Switzerland and was patented in 1892. It was adopted in Germany at about this time as the standard aircraft glue because of its resistance to damp, and it continued to be used for aircraft until the discovery of ureaformaldehyde resin glues in Britain, in the 1930s.

S.L.2 was the first successful four-engined rigid airship. She had 180hp (later 210hp) Maybach C-X engines, mounted in four separate cars, two of which were in 'wing' positions away from the centreline, a practice which was to be generally adopted in later airships. S.L.2, like her predecessor, was of good streamlined shape and had a capacity of 25,000cu m (882,870cu ft), which made her second in size when she first flew on 28 February, 1914, only to the unsuccessful L2. Her structure, despite being basically

of Zeppelin type, but in wood, also introduced an arrangement whereby there were three 12m (39ft 4¹/₃in) bays and other frames, spaced at 8 and 5m (26ft 3in and 16ft 4³/₄in) intervals. The 12m bays were each divided by two light intermediate frames.

S.L.2, purchased by the Army in May 1914 (and thereafter designated S.L.II) operated with some distinction on both eastern and western fronts after the war began. In April 1915, she was withdrawn from service and enlarged to a capacity of 27,000cu m (953,500cu ft), her length being increased from 144m (472ft 5in) to 156m (511ft 9¹/₂in). She returned to service in August and was subsequently used intensively on operations, including a bombing attack on eastern England on 7–8 September, 1915. She was destroyed in a storm on 10 January, 1916.

Schütte-Lanz proposed a 31,500cu m (1,112,407cu ft) design based on S.L.II, to the Navy

S.L.9, second of the Type 'e' S.L.8 class.

S.L.22, third, and last, of the Type 'f' S.L.20 class.

in October 1913, but this was not ordered, partly – it was alleged – because Schütte was not liked by Admiral von Tirpitz. However, this submission led to the order from the Navy in August 1914 for S.L.3 to be delivered by the end of the year.

S.L.3 was also four-engined (Maybach C-X) and of 32,410cu m (1,144,549cu ft) capacity. She was like S.L.II with her stream-lined hull but she had seventeen, instead of S.L.II's original fifteen gas cells. She was 153.1m (502ft 3^1/$_2$in) long with a maximum diameter of 19.75m (64ft 9^1/$_2$in). Her speed was 23.5m/s (52.56mph).

There were delays while the Navy enlarged in metal the Schütte-Lanz wooden shed at Mannheim-Rheinau. But once

this work had been completed, S.L.3 was rapidly assembled and flew, for the first time, on 4 February, 1915. She was handed over to the Navy soon afterwards, being at that time the largest air-ship in the world and thus two months ahead of the competitive first 'million cubic feet' Zeppelin. Two other S.L.3 class ships were ordered by the Navy and de-livered later in 1915 but the wooden Schütte-Lanz were never popular with Peter Strasser, head of the Naval Airship Division, who was convinced that the wooden girders were inherently weak and suffered from faulty workmanship. The third ship, S.L.5, was diverted to the Army where it became S.L.V. S.L.3 and S.L.4 had an appalling suc-

cession of girder failures, collapse of fins and rudders and separ-ation of ring joints. All three ships were lost in bad weather in the Baltic theatre over s seven-month period.

Two further Schütte-Lanz ships appeared in 1915, the Navy's S.L.6 and the Army's S.L.VII. These were simple 'stretches' of the S.L.3 class, having one extra 9m (29ft 6in) bay which gave them a capacity of 35,130cu m (1,267,600cu ft).

The S.L.8 class, the first of which flew on 30 March, 1916, was a further development of the same design. The first two ships of this class, which were de-livered to the Navy, have been reported – probably incorrectly – to have been of the same capacity as S.L.6/VII. It is more likely that these two ships were of the same design as the remaining eight ships in the class, two of which went to the Navy. These had a 12m (39ft 4^1/$_3$in) bay, added at their greatest diameter, and thus achieved an increase in maximum diameter as well as being longer. The capacity was increased to 38,780cu m

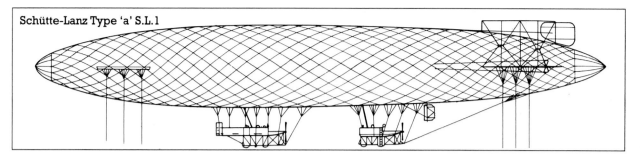

Schütte-Lanz Type 'a' S.L.1

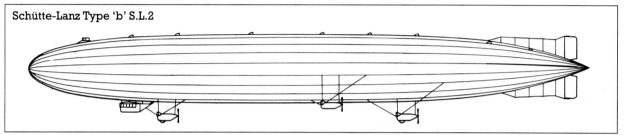

Schütte-Lanz Type 'b' S.L.2

(1,369,504cu ft). Some of these ships did a great deal of flying but they never converted the Navy into exhibiting any real enthusiasm for wooden rigids. An Army ship of this class, S.L.XI, suffered a terrible fate when she became the first rigid to be shot down in flames near London on 3 September, 1916, the first victim of the recently invented Pomeroy incendiary ammunition. (*See Note 16*). Capt Leefe Robinson, who made the successful attack, was awarded the VC.

The first airship of Schütte-Lanz's last class, the S.L.20s (Type 'f'), made its maiden flight at Rheinau in September 1917. Delivered to the Navy, she was one of the five airships destroyed in the disastrous explosion at the Ahlhorn base in January 1918. Two other ships in this class were built: S.L.XXI for the Army and S.L.22 for the Navy. Although both were flown, neither took part in operations. They were the first airships to have rectangular wooden girders instead of the triangular type used in S.L.20 and previous ships.

Schütte-Lanz may have originally intended to adopt a tubular duralumin structure for the S.L.20 class but, in the event, the first metal Schütte-Lanz airship (S.L.24) was not completed by the end of the war and was never flown.

Schütte-Lanz S.L.1 (Type 'a')

Manufacturer: Luftschiffbau Schütte-Lanz GmbH
Built at Rheinau near Mannheim
Number built: one
Chief designers: J Schütte and C Huber
Main structural material: wood
Design began: September 1908
First flight: 17 October, 1911
Powerplant: two 240hp Daimler J8L eight-cylinder inline engines
Gas capacity (100 per cent inflation): 20,500cu m
Overall length: 131.0m
Maximum diameter: 18.4m
Spacing of main frames: 12.0m
Fineness ratio: 7.1
Number of gas cells: seven
Number of longitudinals: 48
Empty weight: 19,300kg
Typical gross lift: 23,800kg (1.16kg/cu m)
Typical disposable load: 4,500kg
Maximum fuel: 1,100kg
Crew: 12
Maximum speed: 19.7m/s (44.06 mph)
Maximum range: 1.060km at speed of 14.7m/s (32.88mph)
Static ceiling: 1,700m
Cost: DM500,000

S.L.1 was wrecked on 17 July, 1913, after 53 flights

Schütte-Lanz S.L.2 (Type 'b') S.L.II

Manufacturer: Luftschiffbau Schütte-Lanz GmbH
Built at Rheinau near Mannheim

Number built: one
Chief designer: J Schütte
Main structural material: wood
Design began: February 1913
First flight: 28 February, 1914
Powerplant: four 180hp Maybach C-X six-cylinder inline engines (later 210hp)
Gas capacity (100 per cent inflation): 25,000cu m; 27,500cu m (lengthened)
Overall length: 144.0m; 156m (lengthened)
Maximum diameter: 18.2m
Spacing of main frames: 12.0m
Fineness ratio: 7.92
Number of gas cells: 15
Number of main longitudinals: 20
Empty weight: 21,000kg
Typical gross lift: 29,000kg (1.16kg/cu m). 31,800kg (lengthened)
Typical disposable load: 8,000kg, 10,800kg (lengthened)
Maximum fuel: 4,000kg
Crew: 19
Maximum speed: 24.5m/s (54.8 mph)
Maximum range: 2,100km at speed of 24.5m/s (54.8mph)
Static ceiling: 2,000m
Cost: DM1,000,000

S.L.2 (S.L.II) made its last flight in April 1915 before being lengthened by 12m (39ft 4^1/3in) and capacity increased by 2,000cu m (70,629cu ft). In lengthened form, still with the same designation, S.L.2 flew in August 1915 and made six war flights before being wrecked in a storm at Luckenwalde on 10.1.1916

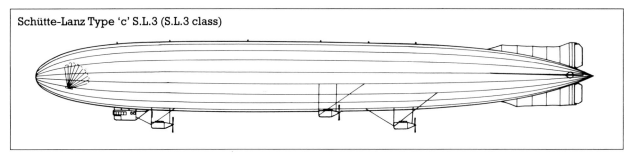

Schütte-Lanz Type 'c' S.L.3 (S.L.3 class)

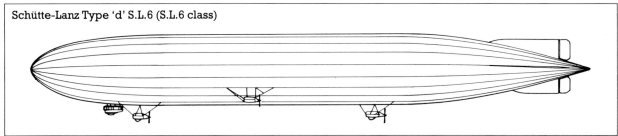

Schütte-Lanz Type 'd' S.L.6 (S.L.6 class)

Schütte-Lanz (S.L.3 (Type 'c') (S.L.3 class)

Manufacturer: Luftschiffbau Schütte-Lanz GmbH

First of type built at Rheinau near Mannheim, S.L.4 built at Sandhofen near Mannheim and S.L.5 at Darmstadt

Number built: three
Chief designer: J Schütte
Main structural material: wood
Design began: August 1914
First flight of type: 4 February, 1915
Powerplant: four 210hp Maybach C-X six-cylinder inline engines
Gas capacity (100 per cent inflation): 32,410cu m
Overall length: 153.1m (156m sometimes quoted)
Maximum diameter: 19.75m
Spacing of main frames: 9.0m
Fineness ratio: 7.77
Number of gas cells: 17
Empty weight: 24,400kg
Typical gross lift: 37,600kg (1.16 kg/cu m)
Typical disposable load: 13,200kg
Crew: 19
Maximum speed: 23.5m/s (52.56 mph)
Maximum range: 2,500km

Schütte-Lanz S.L.6 (Type 'd') (S.L.6 class)

Manufacturer: Luftschiffbau Schütte-Lanz GmbH

First of type built at Mockau near Leipzig, S.L.7 built at Rheinau near Mannheim

Number built: two

Production (S.L.3 class)

C/n		First flight	Last flight	Flights	Disposal
S.L.3	S.L.3	4.2.15	1.5.16	71	Wrecked in Baltic 1.5.16
S.L.4	S.L.4	25.4.15	15.12.15	32	Wrecked in shed at Seddin by storm 5.12.15
S.L.5	S.L.V	21.5.15	5.7.16		Destroyed in storm at Giessen 5.7.16

Chief designer: J Schütte
Main structural material: wood
Design began: about January 1915
First flight of type: 19 September, 1915
Powerplant: four 210hp Maybach C-X six-cylinder inline engines
Gas capacity (100 per cent inflation): 35,130cu m
Overall length: 162.1m
Maximum diameter: 19.7m
Spacing of main frames: 9.0m
Fineness ratio: 8.23
Number of gas cells: 18
Empty weight: 24,900kg
Typical gross lift: 40,700kg (1.16kg/cu m)
Typical disposable load: 15,800kg
Crew: 16
Maximum speed: 25.8m/s (57.71 mph)

S.L.6 (Navy S.L.6) made seven flights with the Navy. Exploded after leaving shed at Seddin 18.11.15.

S.L.7 (Army S.L.VII) first flew on 3.9.15, last flew on 6.3.17 and was then broken up at Jüterbog

Schütte-Lanz S.L.8 (Type 'e') (S.L.8 class)

Manufacturer: Luftschiffbau Schütte-Lanz GmbH

First of type built at Mockau near Leipzig, others at Rheinau and Zeesen

Number built: 10 or 12
Chief designer: J Schütte
Main structural material: wood
Design began: March 1915
First flight of type: 30 March, 1916
Powerplant: four 240hp Maybach H-S-Lu six-cylinder inline engines
Gas capacity (100 per cent inflation): 38,780cu m (S.L.10–19); 35,130 cu m sometimes quoted for S.L.8/9)
Overall length: 174.0m
Maximum diameter: 20.1m
Spacing of main frames: 9.0m
Fineness ratio: 8.66
Number of gas cells: 18 (S.L.8/9); 19 (S.L.10–19)
Empty weight: 22,000kg
Typical gross lift: 40,750kg (S.L.8/9); 45,000kg (S.L.10–19). (1.16kg/cu m)
Typical disposable load: 18,750kg (S.L. 8/9); 23,000kg (S.L.10–19)
Crew: 16
Maximum speed: 26.9m/s (60.17 mph)

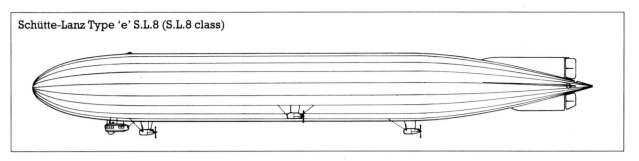

Schütte-Lanz Type 'e' S.L.8 (S.L.8 class)

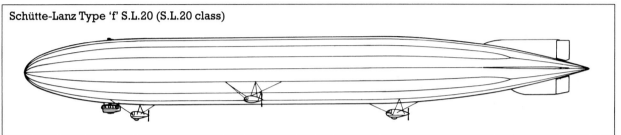

Schütte-Lanz Type 'f' S.L.20 (S.L.20 class)

Schütte-Lanz S.L.20 (Type 'f') (S.L.20 class)

Manufacturer: Luftschiffbau Schütte-Lanz GmbH

First and last of type built at Rheinau near Mannheim. S.L.21 built at Zeesen

Number built: three

Chief designer: J Schütte

Main structural material: wood

Design began: July 1915

First flight of type: 10 September, 1917

Powerplant: five 240hp Maybach H-S-Lu six-cylinder inline engines

Gas capacity (100 per cent inflation): 56,000cu m

Overall length: 198.3m

Maximum diameter: 22.96m

Spacing of main frames: 10.0m

Fineness ratio: 8.66

Number of gas cells: 19

Number of main longitudinals: 17

Empty weight: 27.100kg

Typical gross lift: 65,000kg (1.16kg/cu m)

Typical disposable load: 37,900kg

Crew: 16

Maximum speed: 28.5m/s (65.4 mph)

Static ceiling: 5,000m

Production (S.L.8 class)

C/n		First flight	Last flight	Flights	Disposal
S.L.8	S.L.8	30.3.16	20.11.17	90	Broken up at Seddin
S.L.9	S.L.9	24.5.16	30.3.17	48	Burned in flight (lightning)
S.L.10	S.L.X	17.5.16	28.7.16		Lost in Black Sea
S.L.11	S.L.XI	2.8.16	3.9.16		Shot down near London by RFC
SL.12	S.L.12	9.11.16	28.12.16	9 with Navy	Forced landing at Ahlhorn
S.L.13	S.L.XIII	19.10.16	8.2.17		Burned in shed at Leipzig
S.L.14	S.L.14	23.8.16	11.5.17	20	Forced landing at base and broken up
S.L.15	S.L.XV	9.11.16	25.4.17		Broken up 8.17
S.L.16	'e'9	18.1.17	7.4.17		Broken up 8.17
S.L.17	'e'10	22.3.17	25.4.17		Broken up 8.17
S.L.18	'e'11		8.2.17		Completion unconfirmed
S.L.19	'e'12				Completion unconfirmed

Production (S.L.20 class)

C/n		First flight	Last flight	Flights	Disposal
S.L.20	S.L.20	10.9.17	5.1.18	15	Destroyed in Ahlhorn explosion
S.L.21	S.L.XXI or 'f'2	26.11.17	February 1918	Trials only	Broken up 2.18
S.L.22	S.L.22	5.6.18	June 1920	Trials only	Broken up 6.20

LZ38, Type p, first of the L10 class.
(Pritchard collection)

L10 (LZ40), the second L10 class ship.

L11 (LZ41) of the L10 class with L8 dimly seen in the background.

Million Cubic Feet Zeppelins – L10 and L20 classes

The first million cubic feet Zeppelin was an Army ship, LZ38, which first flew on 3 April, 1915, but the majority of the L10 class were supplied to the Navy. The first had been promised by January 1915, but delivery of ships in this class was much behind programme. A total of sixteen were built in the new Friedrichshafen Factory Shed I (constructed by the Navy for the purpose), and in the operating hangars at Potsdam, near Berlin, and at Löwenthal, near Friedrichshafen – these last two hangars having been turned over to manufacture in order to accelerate production. In addition, six other L10 class ships were built at Löwenthal and Potsdam but were converted almost at once, by lengthening by one 10m and one 5m bay, to L20 class standard. The L20 class, of which twelve further ships were built, was simply a 'stretched' L10 class, with

The wreckage of LZ85 (c/n LZ55) after being shot down by anti-aircraft fire near Salonika in May 1916.

L13 (LZ45).

The Army's LZ90 (c/n LZ60) emerging from its shed.

L20 (LZ59), first of the Type q L20 class, after being wrecked on the Norwegian coast in May 1916. (Pritchard collection)

improved 240hp Maybach H-S-Lu engines. At the peak, L10 and L20 class ships were being produced at the rate of more than one a month from each of the production lines at Friedrichshafen, Löwenthal and Potsdam. This was a considerable industrial achievement.

The L10 class was the first Zeppelin to break away from the blunt-ended cylindrical configuration which had been retained since the earliest designs. Advancing aerodynamic knowledge had established, soon after research into optimum hull shapes had begun at Göttingen in 1908, that fatter, streamlined shapes were superior to long, thin cylinders, because of the importance of skin friction. This knowledge seems to have influenced Schütte-Lanz from the beginning. It now began to be taken into account by the Zeppelin designers also. Some compromise with a purely cylindrical shape was, however, retained to ease production problems.

The original L10 class had a gas capacity of 31,900cu m (1,126,533cu ft) and the 10m main frame spacing and other structural features of ZXII, although apparently the keel was of less structural importance. The hull had a larger diameter, 18.7m (61ft 4½in). These ships had sixteen gas cells and were 163.5m (536ft 4¾in) long. The first nine ships had four 210hp Maybach C-X engines which gave a top speed of 25.0m/s (55.92mph). Later ships had the 240hp H-S-Lu motor which first became available in August 1915. One engine was in the front gondola and drove a pusher propeller direct. The other three were in the rear gondola; one drove a pusher propeller direct and the other two drove bracket propellers on each side of the hull. The H-S-Lu engines gave a great deal of trouble at first, and in March 1916, five of the class had to be withdrawn from service with the Navy for engine modifications. The problems were eventually solved and the new engines gave good service. They increased the speed of L10 class to 26.7m/s (59.72mph) which gave a reasonable cross-country performance.

From an operational point of view, the L10 and L20 classes were probably the most important rigid airships of the war. They were very handy ships with a just-adequate speed for long-

Three great Zeppelin personalities – Dr Hugo Eckener, Count Ferdinand von Zeppelin and Korvettenkapitän Peter Strasser.

A contemporary painting of L19 (LZ54), an L10 class ship, with a boarding party launched to examine the papers of a Scandinavian ship.
(Popperfoto)

distance sorties. Their smaller size, compared with the larger ships which came later, was always remembered as a good point, easing the handling on the ground that was always the biggest problem with any airship.

Although their military loads, range, speed and climb were inferior to later ships, they were able to undertake more in the military sense than their successors because they were operating in a less hostile environment. That is

to say, the Allied defences were less developed, both relatively and in absolute terms.

This point is brought out if the numbers of bombing raids against the United Kingdom by each class of airship are compared:

Class of Airship	Percentage of total raids
S.L. types	2 per cent
L3	3 per cent
L10	40 ⎫ 59 per
L20	19 ⎭ cent
L30 Super-Zeppelin	19 ⎫
L48 Height-climber	3 ⎬ 28 per cent
L53 Height-climber	6 ⎭
L70	2 per cent
Various LZ prototypes	6 per cent

Furthermore, because of the steadily increasing effectiveness of the defence against airships, more than half of all airship attacks made on Britain, and these mainly the more effective ones, occurred in 1916 when the L10 and the L20 class ships undertook about 80 per cent of the successful sorties.

L10 and L20 class ships achieved a great deal. The Army's LZ38 was the first air-

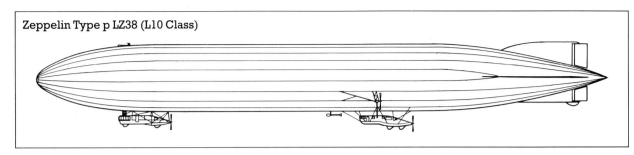

Zeppelin Type p LZ38 (L10 Class)

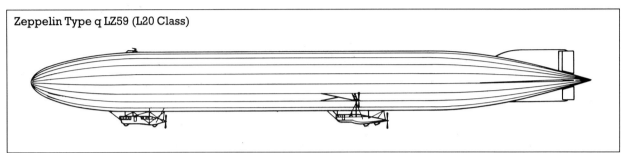

Zeppelin Type q LZ59 (L20 Class)

ship to bomb London. Five L10 class and four L20 class ships took part in the Battle of Jutland, although ineffectively. L14 was probably the most successful military airship ever built. (Apart from being one of the airships at Jutland, she made no less than twenty-four attacks on Britain and, after starting her career in August 1915, survived the war, having made 526 flights.) In the technical field, these ships exploited advances in the use of radio and navigational aids. Radio had been installed in Zeppelins since the earliest tests with LZ6 in September 1909, but it had been greatly developed since then and had become an essential contributor to the Zeppelin's effectiveness for patrol work over the sea as well as providing communications and navigational aid during long-range bombing attacks. Direction-finding radio was used from early in the war on L3 class ships and a radio compass was fitted to some L10 class ships.

Zeppelin LZ38 (Type p) L10 class

Manufacturer: Luftschiffbau Zeppelin GmbH

First of type and seven others built at Friedrichshafen. Seven built at Löwenthal and seven at Potsdam

Number built: 22

Chief designer: L Dürr

Main structural material: duralumin

Design began: August 1914

First flight of type: 3 April, 1915

Powerplant: four 210hp Maybach C-X six-cylinder inline engines

Gas capacity (100 per cent inflation): 31,900cu m

Overall length: 163.5m

Maximum diameter: 18.7m

Spacing of main frames: 10.0m

Fineness ratio: 8.68

Number of gas cells: 15

Number of main longitudinals: 19

Empty weight: 20,800kg

Typical gross lift: 37,000kg (1.16kg/cu m)

Typical disposable load: 16,200kg

Maximum fuel: 4,800kg

Crew: 18

Maximum speed: 26.7m/s (59.72 mph) after re-engining

Maximum range: 4,300km at speed of 25.0m/s (55.92mph)

Static ceiling: 2,800m

Price: DM1,360,000

Zeppelin LZ59 (Type q) L20 class

Manufacturer: Luftschiffbau Zeppelin GmbH

First of type and LZ65 built at Friedrichshafen. Four built at Löwenthal and six at Potsdam

Number built: 12

Chief designer: L Dürr

Main structural material: duralumin

Design began: October 1915

First flight of type: 21 December, 1915

Powerplant: four 240hp Maybach H-S-Lu six-cylinder inline engines

Gas capacity (100 per cent inflation): 35,800cu m

Overall length: 178.5m

Maximum diameter: 18.7m

Spacing of main frames: 10.0m

Fineness ratio: 9.55

Number of gas cells: 18

Empty weight: 23,650kg

Typical gross lift: 41,550kg (1.16kg/cu m)

Typical disposable load: 17,900 kg

Crew: 16

Maximum speed: 26.5m/s (59.27 mph)

Maximum range: 4,300km

Production (L10 class)

C/n		First flight	Last flight	Flights	Disposal
LZ38	LZ38	3.4.15	7.6.15		Bombed in shed at Evère 7.6.15
LZ40	L10	13.5.15	3.9.15	28	Burned in flight
LZ41	L11	7.6.15	25.4.17	394	Broken up
LZ42	LZ72	15.6.15	16.2.17		Broken up
LZ43	L12	21.6.15	10.8.15	14	Burned at Ostend after AA damage over England
LZ44	LZ74	8.7.15	8.10.15	2 bombing raids	Hit mountain 8.10.15
LZ45	L13	23.7.15	30.4.17	159	Broken up
LZ46	L14	9.8.15	23.6.19	526	Broken up, 23.6.19
LZ47	LZ77	24.8.15	21.2.16		Shot down by AA, 21.2.16
LZ48	L15	9.9.15	1.4.16	36	Shot down by aircraft
LZ49	LZ79	2.8.15	30.1.16		Shot down by aircraft
LZ50	L16	23.9.15	19.10.17	235	Destroyed landing
LZ51	LZ81	7.10.15			Converted to LZ51A
LZ51A	LZ81	3.3.16	27.9.16		Shot down by AA fire
LZ52	L18	3.11.15	17.11.15	4	Burned in shed
LZ53	L17	20.10.15	28.12.16	73	Burned in shed
LZ54	L19	27.11.15	2.2.16	14	Shot down by AA fire
LZ55	LZ85	12.9.15	5.5.16		Shot down by AA fire
LZ56	LZ86	10.10.15			Converted to LZ56A
LZ56A	LZ86	21.1.16	4.9.16		Wrecked on landing
LZ57	LZ87	6.12.15			Converted to LZ57A
LZ57A	LZ87	1.5.16	28.7.17		Broken up
LZ58	LZ88	14.11.15		61	Converted to LZ58A
LZ58A	LZ88	3.2.16	15.9.17		Broken up
LZ60	LZ90	1.1.16			Converted to LZ60A
LZ60A	LZ90	29.4.16	7.11.16		Destroyed in storm
LZ63	LZ93	23.2.16			Converted to LZ63A
LZ63A	LZ93	18.4.16	July 1917		Broken up

Converted ships with A-suffix c/ns had 35,800cu m capacity. LZ44 and LZ45 had 31,600cu m capacity. All other ships in the L10 class were of 31,900cu m capacity.

Production (L20 class)

C/n		First flight	Last flight	Flights	Disposal
LZ59	L20	21.12.15	3.5.16	15	Wrecked in Norway
LZ61	L21	10.1.16	28.11.16	70	Wrecked off Yarmouth by AA fire
LZ64	L22	2.3.16	14.5.17	81	Shot down by British aircraft off Terschelling
LZ65	LZ95	31.1.16	22.2.16		Forced down by AA fire near Namur
LZ66	L23	8.4.16	21.8.17	101	Shot down by RFC
LZ67	LZ97	4.4.16	5.7.17		Broken up
LZ68	LZ98	28.4.16	Summer 1917	50	Broken up, 5.8.19
LZ69	L24	20.5.16	28.12.16	45	Burned entering shed at Tondern 28.12.16
LZ71	LZ101	29.6.16	Autumn 1917		Broken up, 20.9.19
LZ73	LZ103	8.8.16	Summer 1917		Broken up, 12.8.19 at Königsberg by Allies
LZ77	LZ107	16.10.16	Summer 1917		Broken up, 6.8.19 at Darmstadt by Allies
LZ81	LZ111	20.12.16	Summer 1917		Broken up, 10.8.19 at Dresden by Allies

Super-Zeppelins – L30 class

The operational success of the L10 and L20 classes encouraged the development of the next Zeppelin in the series, the famous L30 class which was known to the Allies as the Super-Zeppelin. If L10 and L20 were operationally the most successful, L30 was historically the most important rigid to be produced in the whole forty years of the rigid airship's history. Technically, it was outstandingly successful, not only in itself but also as the basis of all other types of Zeppelin produced during the war. Furthermore, rigid airships built in both the United Kingdom and the United States, were direct copies of either L30 or its derivatives.

Design started in April 1915 to meet a Navy request to the two rigid airship manufacturers for the largest airship which could be accommodated in existing sheds. A formal requirement was issued in April and a contract signed in July. Assembly of the prototype began in Factory Shed I at Friedrichshafen in February 1916 and she was flown, for the first time, on 28 May.

L30 was the first six-engined, two million cubic feet airship. Although remaining completely independent, Zeppelin and Schütte-Lanz were induced to pool their experience, exchange patents and compare results of their research in about May 1915. L30 thus incorporated all that had been learned in Germany about rigid airship design up to that time, and she also benefitted from the extensive research and development in related fields which had intensified since the start of the war. To begin with, the shape of the hull represented a careful compromise between the ideal streamlined shapes which had been favoured by Schütte-

L31 (LZ72) second of the Type r L30 class Super-Zeppelins.

L30 (LZ62), the prototype Type r which first flew at the end of May 1916.

Lanz and some of the pressure-airship designers, and the need to use as many standard frames as possible to ease production problems. The structure of the hull represented a significant step forward from the ZXII type which had been used in the L10–L20 class. Not only was an entirely new form of girder adopted, of much larger cross-sectional dimensions and built up from new basic sections, but the structure itself was radically new, with a marked reduction in the number of main longitudinals (nineteen in L10 now reduced to only thirteen). Twelve lighter intermedi-

ate longitudinals between the main members gave the outside cover a better profile. The diameter was increased to 23.9m (78ft 5in) but the main-frame spacing was kept to 10m with single intermediate frames. The main-frames themselves were strengthened by king-posted trussing. The only major innovation was the addition of a wire along the axis of the airship. This passed through the gas cells and anchored the radial wiring in the plane of each main-frame.

The L30 had six 240hp Maybach H-S-Lu engines, four arranged as in the L10 class ships

and two more in wing cars (a Schütte-Lanz innovation). Although the L30 prototype (LZ62) was slightly smaller, production ships had nineteen gas cells of a total capacity of 55,200cu m (1,949,373cu ft). The fifth L30 class ship (L34), introduced an impermeable outer cover and gas shafts, features deriving directly from Schütte-Lanz experience.

L30 caused something of a sensation when she first appeared. She was the first airship to exceed 100km/h, with a speed of 28.7m/s (64.19mph). With her ceiling of 3,900m (12,795ft) and a permitted maximum rate of climb of 10m/s (1,968ft/min), she was reckoned to be fully capable of dealing with the ever stronger defences of the Allies. Her military load could include up to sixty assorted bombs to a total weight of nearly 5,000kg (11,000lb). Peter Strasser, who had done much to encourage

Ludwig Dürr and his engineers to develop the new ship, was confident that he had a potent new weapon in his hands. The need was for production in order to put a useful number into service with the Naval Airship Division as soon as possible.

Count Zeppelin travelled in L30 when she was delivered from Friedrichshafen to her operational base at Nordholz on 30 May, 1916. He died nine months later. By then, fourteen of the new ships had been completed, at Friedrichshafen, Löwenthal or at a new works in Berlin-Staaken. A second, new, construction hangar, Factory Shed II, had been completed and was in use at Friedrichshafen. A total of seventeen L30 class ships were eventually completed, all but two going straight to the Navy, and even those two being transferred to the Navy when the Army airship service closed down later that year. The peak rate on any one production line was an airship every two months.

L35 (LZ80) first flew in October 1916 and survived the war.

L50 (LZ89), in night camouflage, was lost in the Mediterranean.

The German Army's LZ120 (c/n LZ90) went to Italy in 1920 as Ausonia.

This view of L40 (LZ88) shows the gun position atop the forward hull.

L33 (LZ76) was forced down at Little Wigborough, Essex, on 24 September, 1916, and burned by her crew. Future British rigid airships were based on the L33 which was carefully studied.

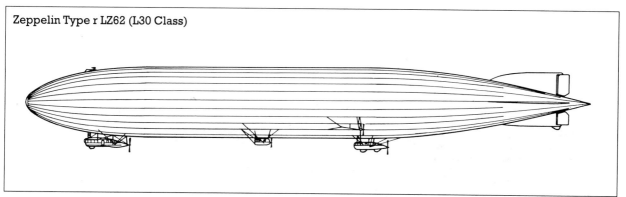

Zeppelin Type r LZ62 (L30 Class)

Zeppelin LZ62 (Type r) L30 Super-Zeppelin

Manufacturer: Luftschiffbau Zeppelin GmbH

First of type built at Friedrichshafen

Number built: 17

Chief designer: L Dürr

Main structural material: duralumin

Design began: April 1915

First flight of type: 28 May, 1916

Powerplant: six 240hp Maybach H-S-Lu six-cylinder inline engines

Gas capacity (100 per cent inflation): 55,200cu m; 55,000cu m (LZ62)

Overall length: 198.0m

Maximum diameter: 23.9m

Spacing of main frames: 10.0m

Fineness ratio: 8.24

Number of gas cells: 19

Number of main longitudinals: 13

Number of intermediate longitudinals: 12

Empty weight: 31,400kg

Typical gross lift: 63,800kg (1.16kg/cu m)

Typical disposable load: 32,400kg

Maximum fuel: 6,250kg

Crew: 17

Maximum speed: 28.7m/s (64.19 mph)

Maximum range: 7,400km at speed of 22.4m/s (50.1mph)

Static ceiling: 3,900m

Price: DM2,800,000

Production

C/n		First flight	Last flight	Flights	Disposal
LZ62	L30	28.5.16	16.7.20	115	Broken up 1920
LZ72	L31	12.7.16	2.10.16	19	Shot down at Potters Bar by RFC
LZ74	L32	4.8.16	24.9.16	13	Shot down near Billericay by RFC
LZ75	L37	9.11.16	August 1920	45	To Japan as components
LZ76	L33	30.8.16	24.9.16	10	Forced down at Little Wigborough by RFC
LZ78	L34	22.9.16	28.11.16	11	Shot down off West Hartlepool by RFC
LZ79	L41	15.1.17	23.6.19	54	Wrecked by airship crew. Components to Japan 11.7.19
LZ80	L35	12.10.16	September 1918	98	Broken up 23.6.19
LZ82	L36	1.1.16	7.2.17	20	Lost in forced landing
LZ83	LZ113	22.2.17	8.10.20		Surrendered in France. Broken up
LZ84	L38	22.11.16	29.12.16	10	Wrecked in forced landing in Russia
LZ85	L45	2.4.17	20.10.17	27	Forced landing in France
LZ86	L39	11.12.16	17.3.17	24	Shot down in France by AA
LZ87	L47	11.5.17	5.1.16	44	Burned in shed at Ahlhorn
LZ88	L40	3.1.17	17.6.17	30	Wrecked in forced landing
LZ89	L50	9.6.17	20.10.17	19	Lost in Mediterranean
LZ90	LZ120	31.1.17	25.12.20	28+	To Italy, 25.12.20 as *Ausonia*. Dismantled June 1921

Height-climbers – L48 and L53 classes and the Afrika-Zeppelins

Long before the last L30 was delivered, in June 1917, it was clear that, good as she was, the L30 was no match for the Allied defences. The writing was on the wall so far as the future of the airship, as a bomber, was concerned. Four L30 class ships had been shot down over England, three of them in flames, in a little over two months during the latter part of 1916. A fifth suffered the same fate over France in March 1917. These losses were additional to those of earlier ships that were still operating. The big enemy was the aeroplane which was responsible for most of the losses.

The only answer to this was height. Hence the intensive effort in the first half of 1917 to produce Zeppelins with greatly increased operating ceilings. Strasser's indomitable will gave this effort impetus; his refusal to admit that his beloved Zeppelins were being defeated was absolute.

He realised that the only way to produce a more effective Zeppelin bomber quickly was to develop improved versions of the L30 class and it was in its capacity for such improvement that this classic design showed itself remarkable. At a meeting between representatives of the Navy and the manufacturers, on 17 January, 1917, it was agreed that a programme to develop new versions of the L30 class, which came to be known as Height-climbers, should be immediately pursued.

Four prototype airships, L42, 43, 44 and 46, were flown between February and April 1917

L43 (LZ92), first flown in March 1917, was the second of the Type s Height-climbers.
(Pritchard collection)

to explore possibilities. All four had one fewer gas cell than the L30 class but, in spite of this, slightly increased total capacities of 55,500cu m (1,959,967cu ft), for the first two, and 55,800cu m (1,970,561cu ft) for the others. They were all fitted with five, instead of six, H-S-Lu engines, the engine driving the pusher propeller direct in the rear gondola being omitted from L42 and L43, and an entirely new two-engined

L44 (LZ93) was the Type t Height-climber prototype.
(Pritchard collection)

L48 (LZ95), first production Type u L48 class Height-climber. (Pritchard collection)

rear gondola substituted in L44 and L46. In these last two, the two engines were geared to one pusher propeller, and bracket propellers were not used. The ships were modified to different successive standards as various expedients and improvements were tested. The same applied to the production Height-climbers and also to a lesser extent to the L30 class itself. The L48 and L53 class production Height-climbers were initially built – and many were subsequently modified – to a variety of standards during their careers. All Height-climbers, however, were painted matt black on their lower surfaces to reduce their visibility in the rays of searchlights.

L53 (LZ100) first of the Type v L53 class – the second Height-climber class.

L53 leaving its shed.

L63 (LZ110) and L42 (LZ91) wrecked by their crews at Nordholz in 1919 were respectively Type v and Type s Height-climbers – L42 being the first prototype.

L57 (LZ102) Type w was the first Afrika-Zeppelin.
(Pritchard collection)

Eventually, two classes of Height-climbers were produced in numbers: five of the L48 class (the first of which flew on 22 May 1917) and ten of the L53 class (first flight 8 August, 1917). Like all the others, the L48 class differed from the basic L30 mainly in changes to save weight. As in the prototypes, capacity was slightly increased to 55,800cu m (1,970,561cu ft) by omitting a frame at the bow and combining two of the gas cells. One engine was removed and the two engines left in the rear gondola were now geared to a single pusher propeller. The bracket propellers were not fitted. Smaller, streamlined engine wing-cars and a smaller, lighter control-car saved more weight. The various changes saved more than 5,000kg (11,000lb), compared with the original L30. This increased the

ceiling to 5,500m (18,000ft). In spite of the fewer engines, speed increased slightly to 29.9m/s (66.88mph) and to 31.8m/s (71.13mph) for the last two ships in the class which were fitted with the new 245hp Maybach Mb IVa 'altitude motors'. These were high-compression engines gated below 1,800m (5,900ft).

The second class of Height-climber, the L53s, went a lot further in the search for height. To begin with, their structures were radically altered. Instead of the basic 10m main frame spacing with single intermediate frames which had been used for all Zeppelins since ZXII, nine 15m (49ft 2½in) bays were substituted with two intermediate frames per bay. Five 10m bays were included at the ends of the ship. Although the new hull was somewhat shorter than that of L30, the altered

structure accommodated fourteen larger gas cells in place of the L30's nineteen. The cells themselves were of lighter material: silk, with only two layers of goldbeaters' skin. By these means, capacity was increased to 56,000cu m (1,977,620cu ft) and further weight was saved. All but the first three of the L53 class had the new Maybach 'altitude motors' and the first and third were re-engined. With these, the speed (31.8m/s; 71.13mph), was the same as the last two L48 class ships which had similar engines. The L53 class achieved a ceiling of 6,500m (21,325ft), a remarkable technical achievement, resulting from many – mostly small – improvements to the basic L30 design. L65, last of the L53 class, introduced a notable innovation which was to become standardised on later Zeppelins. This

L59 (LZ104) was the Afrika-Zeppelin which made the outstanding flight from Bulgaria to the Sudan and back in November 1917.
(Pritchard collection)

was the so-called 'streamlined' fins. The tail surfaces which, up to now, had been extensively braced externally, became semi-cantilever structures (with only three bracing wires) about 1.8m (5ft 10³/₄in) thick at the root.

Although the Height-climber Zeppelins' greater operating height carried them above the ceiling of the obsolete aeroplanes used by the Allies up till then for air defence, it was still insufficient against the latest fighters which were soon deployed against them. The rigid airship's fate was sealed, as a strategic bomber, just as it already was for tactical attack, although Peter Strasser would still not acknowledge the fact.

For its other role of sea patrol, the L30 class Zeppelin and its developments and successors were barely more suitable than the earlier, smaller Zeppelins, despite their most desirable higher speeds. This was because their larger size made them more difficult to handle on the ground and, in particular, to move in and out of their sheds. In addition, to

save weight for altitude performance, the Height-climbers were structurally weak and sacrificed much equipment, armament and crew comfort.

The adverse effect of increased size, and therefore of greater difficulty in leaving and entering sheds, on the utility of the airship for reconnaissance, is borne out by the percentage of days on which German naval airships were unable to undertake patrol flights over the North Sea during the war years:

1914   23.6 per cent
1915   34.0 per cent
1916   24.3 per cent
1917   26.3 per cent
1918   17.5 per cent

Thus, except for the fact that the 1916 percentage is depressed by the emphasis on raiding during that year, there is a clear trend after truly usable airships were introduced in 1915, towards reduced utility as the composition of the airship fleet changed from the 32–36,000cu m L10–20 class to the 55–56,000cu m L30 and Height-climber classes. The fact is that these low rates of utility meant that, contrary to widespread belief, the rigid airship was of strictly limited value for sea patrol work. Where there was enemy air opposition, it was rapidly becoming as ineffective in this role as it was as a bomber.

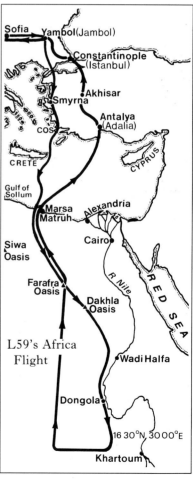

L59's Africa Flight

Between the wars Allied naval authorities were also misled by inadequate reports of Zeppelin involvement in the battles of Heligoland Bight (1914), Dogger Bank (1916) and Jutland (1916). Unfortunately, these facts were

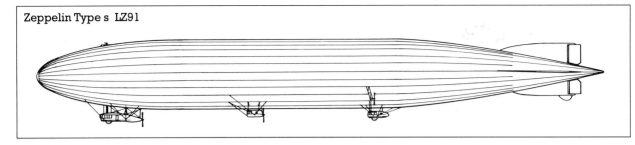

Zeppelin Type s LZ91

Production

C/n		First flight	Last flight	Flights	Disposal
LZ91	L42	22.2.17	23.6.19	65	Wrecked by airship crews at Nordholz 23.6.19
LZ92	L43	6.3.17	14.6.17	14	Shot down by anti-aircraft fire and RFC

not fully driven home before the end of the war. Had they been, a great deal of money and effort might have been saved, and loss of life avoided, during the following twenty years.

Ships of the L30 class and its derivatives were used for a number of purposes, in addition to sea patrol and bombing. L35 replaced L25, an L20 class ship (LZ88), transferred from the Army, as the experimental airship used for various trials. She was employed, among other duties, for development flying of the 'altitude motors' and to make tests (on 27 January, 1918) of the carriage and launching, in flight, of an Albatross D III fighter. (*See* Note 17) Another experiment was the launching of a glider-bomb.

One Height-climber class ship, L61, was handed over to Italy as a war reparation, on 30 August, 1920. She was then named *Italia*. She did not do much flying and was broken up at Ciampino in January 1921.

Special derivatives of the L53 class were L57 and L59, the 'Afrika-Zeppelins'. With two more 15m bays added, these ships had the tremendous length of 226.5m (743ft 1¼in) and a capacity of no less than 68,500cu m (2,419,057cu ft), making them easily the largest airships in the world at that time. Propelled by five H-S-Lu motors, they were reckoned to have a speed of 28.6m/s (63.97mph) and a range of 16,000km (9,942 miles) in still air.

Range was the main objective. A repatriated German prisoner of war, a Doctor Zupitza, had suggested that badly needed supplies, arms and ammunition should be flown by Zeppelin to General von Lettow-Vorbeck,

commander of the beleaguered German forces in East Africa. On 30 October, 1917, after some delay, the Kaiser gave his approval for the flight to be attempted. By then, tests had been made with a specially modified Zeppelin. L57 was converted during assembly as an L53 class ship in Factory Shed II at Friedrichshafen, and was first flown on 9 September, 1917. However, she was accidentally destroyed by fire a couple of weeks later while being put into her shed. The size of these ships made them particularly difficult to handle and this was aggravated by the fact that they were under-powered. Nevertheless, a replacement was chosen: L59 being built at Staaken.

L59 was first flown on 19 October and was ferried to Yambol* in Bulgaria, the southernmost base of the Central Powers, on 3 November, 1917. Loaded with 13,870kg (30,578lb) of special supplies and under the command of Ludwig Bockholt, she left Yambol on 21 November after two previous unsuccessful attempts. Shortly after her departure, information from East Africa indicated to the German Government that it was. now too late for the Zeppelin to hope to be able to find Lettow-Vorbeck, who had moved with his small force into Mozambique.

Attempts were made to recall L59 by radio but these failed until she had covered 3,200km

(1,988 miles) and had reached a position some 200km (124 miles) west of Khartoum†. She then returned safely to Yambol, completing a flight of 95 hours during which 6,700km (4,163 miles) were covered. (It is interesting that her position near Khartoum was established by radio bearings from three stations in Asia Minor) L59 was then modified and used as a bomber in the Mediterranean theatre. She burned, in flight, on 7 April, 1918, while flying over the Gulf of Otranto.

* Yambol has normally been reported as Jambol or Jamboli, but the reason for this appears to have been the German use of J instead of Y.

† Reported as 16.30N 30.00E

Zeppelin LZ91 (Type s) L42 Height-climber Prototype

Manufacturer: Luftschiffbau Zeppelin GmbH

Both built at Friedrichshafen

Number built: two

Chief designer: L Dürr

Main structural material: duralumin

Design began: 17 January, 1917

First flight of type: 22 February, 1917

Powerplant: five 240hp Maybach H-S-Lu six-cylinder inline engines

Gas capacity (100 per cent inflation): 55,500cu m

Overall length: 196.5m

Maximum diameter: 23.9m

Spacing of main frames: 10.0m

Fineness ratio: 8.22

Number of gas cells: 18

Zeppelin Type t LZ93

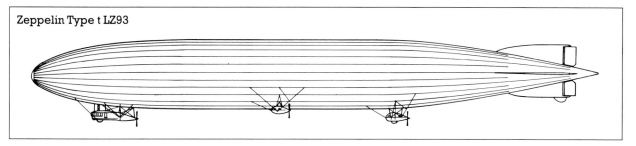

Zeppelin Type u LZ95

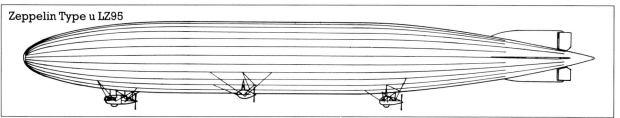

Empty weight: 28,100kg

Typical gross lift: 64,500kg (1.16kg/cu m)

Typical disposable load: 36,400 kg

Crew: 23

Maximum speed: 27.7m/s (61.96 mph) (28.7m/s/64.19mph sometimes quoted)

Maximum range: 10,400km

Static ceiling: 5,000m

LZ91 (L42) made 65 flights and was wrecked by airship crews at Nordholz 23.6.19. LZ92 (L43) first flew 6.3.17 and was shot down by AA and RFC 14.6.17 after 14 flights

Zeppelin LZ93 (Type t) L44 Height-climber Prototype

Manufacturer: Luftschiffbau Zeppelin GmbH

LZ93 built at Löwenthal, LZ94 built at Friedrichshafen

Number of type built: two

Chief designer: L Dürr

Main structural material; duralumin

Design began: 17 January, 1917

First flight of type: 1 April, 1917

Powerplant: five 240hp Maybach H-S-Lu six-cylinder inline engines

Gas capacity (100 per cent inflation): 55,800cu m

Overall length: 196.5m

Maximum diameter: 23.9m

Spacing of main frames: 10.0m

Fineness ratio: 8.22

Number of gas cells: 18

Empty weight: 26,900kg

Typical gross lift: 64,750kg (1.16kg/cu m)

Typical disposable load: 37,850kg

Crew: 23

Maximum speed: 28.9m/s (64.64 mph)

Maximum range: 11,500km

Static ceiling: 5,200m

LZ93 (L44) made 25 flights and was shot down by anti-aircraft fire at St Clement on 20.10.17.

LZ94 (L46) first flew on 24.4.17, made 36 flights and was destroyed in an explosion in her Ahlhorn shed on 5.1.18

Zeppelin LZ95 (Type u) L48 First Height-climber class

Manufacturer: Luftschiffbau Zeppelin GmbH

First and third of type built at Friedrichshafen, LZ96 built at Löwenthal and last two at Staaken

Number of type built: five

Chief designer: L Dürr

Main structural material: duralumin

Design began: January 1917

First flight of type: 22 May, 1917

Powerplant: five 240hp Maybach H-S-Lu six-cylinder inline engines. LZ98 and LZ99 re-engined with 245hp Maybach Mb IVas March–May 1918

Gas capacity (100 per cent inflation): 55,800cu m

Overall length: 196.5m

Maximum diameter: 23.9m

Spacing of main frames: 10.0m

Fineness ratio: 8.22

Number of gas cells: 18

Empty weight: 25,750kg

Typical gross lift: 64,750kg (1.16kg/cu m)

Typical disposable load: 39,000kg

Crew: 19

Maximum speed: 29.9m/s (66.88 mph); 31.8m/s (71.13mph) LZ98 and LZ99 after being re-engined

Static ceiling: 5,500m

Zeppelin LZ100 (Type v) L53 Second Height-climber class

Manufacturer: Luftschiffbau Zeppelin GmbH

First of type and three others built at Friedrichshafen. Three built at Löwenthal and three at Staaken

Number of type built: ten

Chief designer: L Dürr

Main structural material: duralumin

Design began: January 1917

First flight of type: 8 August, 1917

Powerplant: five 240hp Maybach H-S-Lu six-cylinder inline engines (LZ100–103). The others had 245hp Maybach Mb IVas and LZ100 and LZ103 were re-engined April–July 1918

Gas capacity (100 per cent inflation): 56,000cu m

Production (L48 class)

C/n		First flight	Last flight	Flights	Disposal
LZ95	L48	22.5.17	17.6.17		Shot down by RFC
LZ96	L49	13.6.17	20.10.17	15	Forced down by AA fire
LZ97	L51	6.7.17	5.1.18	21	Burned in shed, Ahlhorn
LZ98	L52	4.7.17	23.6.19	40+	Broken up by airship's crew at Wittmund 23.6.19
LZ99	L54	13.8.17	19.7.18	43+	Bombed at Tondern by RAF

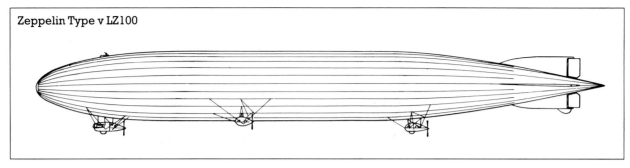

Zeppelin Type v LZ100

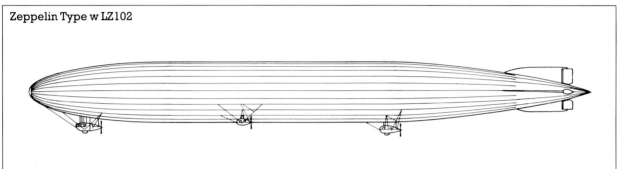

Zeppelin Type w LZ102

Overall length: 196.5m
Maximum diameter: 23.9m
Spacing of main frames: 15.0m
Fineness ratio: 8.22
Number of gas cells: 14
Empty weight: 25,000kg
Typical gross lift: 65,000kg
(1.16kg/cu m)

Typical disposable load: 40,000kg
Crew: 19
Maximum speed: 29.9m/s (66.88 mph) increasing to 31.8m/s (71.13 mph) for LZ110 and LZ111
Maximum range: 13,500km
Static ceiling: 6,500m

Production (L53 class)

C/n		First flight	Last flight	Flights	Disposal
LZ100	L53	8.8.17	11.8.18	53?	Shot down off Terschelling by RAF
LZ101	L55	1.9.17	20.10.17	6+	Forced landing and dismantled
LZ103	L56	24.9.17	23.6.19	35+	Broken up by airship crews at Wittmund 23.6.19
LZ105	L58	29.10.17	5.1.18	10+	Burned in shed at Ahlhorn
LZ106	L61	12.12.17	28.8.20	32	To Italy 30.8.20 as *Italia*, broken up at Ciampino January 1921
LZ107	L62	19.1.18	10.5.18	19	Lost in explosion off Heligoland
LZ108	L60	18.12.17	19.7.18	17+	Bombed in shed at Tondern by RAF 19.7.18
LZ109	L64	11.3.18	21.7.20	26?	Surrendered to United Kingdom 21.7.20; broken up, 21.6.21
LZ110	L63	4.3.18	23.6.19	37?	Broken up by airship crews at Nordholz 23.6.19
LZ111	L65	17.4.18	9.11.18	28	Broken up

Production (Afrika-Zeppelins)

C/n		First flight	Last flight	Flights	Disposal
LZ102	L57	9.9.17	7.10.17	4	Burned on ground at Jüterbog 8.10.17
LZ104	L59	19.10.17	7.4.18	23	Burned over Gulf of Otranto

Zeppelin LZ102 (Type w) L57 Afrika-Zeppelin

Manufacturer: Luftschiffbau Zeppelin GmbH

First of type built at Friedrichshafen. LZ104 built at Staaken

Number built: two

Chief designer: L Dürr

Main structural material: duralumin

Design began: August 1917

First flight of type: 29 September, 1917

Powerplant: five 240hp Maybach H-S-Lu six-cylinder inline engines

Gas capacity (100 per cent inflation): 68,500cu m

Overall length: 226.5m

Maximum diameter: 23.9m

Spacing of main frames: 15.0m

Fineness ratio: 9.52

Number of gas cells: 16

Number of main longitudinals: 13

Number of intermediate longitudinals: 12

Empty weight: 27,400kg

Typical gross lift: 79,500kg (1.16kg/cu m)

Typical disposable load: 52,100kg

Maximum fuel: 21,700kg

Crew: 22

Maximum speed: 28.6m/s (63.97 mph)

Maximum range: 16,000km at speed of 22.4m/s (50.1mph)

Static ceiling: 6,600m

Price: DM3,264,000

Last Military Zeppelins – L70 class

Before recording the final wartime developments of the Zeppelin, the history of the last Schütte-Lanz rigid airships must be told. Schütte-Lanz, like Zeppelin, responded to the Navy's request in March 1915 for a two million cubic feet airship. A contract for the first ship, S.L.20, was signed in July.

S.L.20 had five Maybach H-S-Lu engines (although six were originally intended) and a capacity of 56,000cu m (1,977,620cu ft). She did not, however, fly until 10 September, 1917, fifteen months later than Zeppelin flew L30. Thus, while Schütte-Lanz had been quicker than Zeppelin in developing the first million cubic feet ship, they were hopelessly beaten in the later competition. The triangular wooden girders used in previous ships gave trouble in this size of vessel. As a result, a change to rectangular girders was made for the other

two ships in the Class: S.L.XXI for the Army and S.L.22 for the Navy, neither of which was delivered. The latter first flew on 5 June, 1918, the last Schütte-Lanz airship to fly. Apparently, however, S.L.22 was not the last Schütte-Lanz airship to be built.

During 1918, Schütte-Lanz was at last persuaded that wood was inferior to duralumin as a structural material. It therefore designed a new type of structure, the main elements of which were built of duralumin tubes. The

L70 (LZ112), first of the Type x L70 class.

first design in the new material seems to have been S.L.23, which was not built. However, S.L.24, a stretched version with a capacity of 77,970cu m (2,753,348cu ft) was under construction in 1918. She would have been 25 per cent

L71 (LZ113A) arriving at Pulham in July 1920.
(Pritchard collection)

One of the engine cars of L70. The engine is a Maybach Mb IVa.

larger than the largest Zeppelin completed during the war.

The last Zeppelins of the war were the L70 class which were really production versions of the two 'Afrika-Zeppelins' (*See* page 100) and were therefore the ultimate German development of the famous L30, as modified in the L53 class. The first two L70s (flown on 1 July and 29 July, 1918) were originally designed and built with one 15m bay less than the 'Afrika-Zeppelins', giving them a capacity of 62,200cu m (2,196,574cu ft), but they had no less than seven 245hp Maybach Mb IVa 'altitude motors', giving a speed of 36.4m/s (81.42mph). After L70 was lost, the second ship, L71, was lengthened by an extra bay and the third ship was completed with the additional bay incorporated so that they then both had essentially the same hulls as L57 and L59. With seven engines, the ships had clearly been over-engined causing vibration and flexural troubles in the hull. Fatigue of the structure was feared. The deficiencies were partly overcome by removing one engine and by

Korvettenkapitän Peter Strasser, commander of the German Naval Airship Division. Strasser was killed when the L70 was shot down off the English coast by Maj Egbert Cadbury and Capt Robert Leckie in a D.H.4 operating from Yarmouth.

the introduction of 'stirrup wires' which, through sleeves in the gas cells, braced the top of each main frame to the mid-point of the internal keel between each frame. Even in this form, a good deal of flexibility in the hull was still apparent in flight in turbulent air, as the British and French noticed when they each took delivery of one of these ships as reparations after the war. The front engine on L71 had reversing gear so that reverse thrust was available for manoeuvring.

The British, wisely, did not fly L71 but the French made a number of flights over the Mediterranean and North Africa with L72, which they renamed *Dixmude*. On 21 December, 1923, she apparently suffered structural failure and fell, burning, into the Mediterranean off Sciacca in Sicily, with the loss of her entire crew of fifty. This was perhaps not surprising, these ships having been deliberately lightened and, therefore, weakened to the limit in the search for ultimate performance. They may have been just strong enough for a short, operational life in wartime, flown mainly at high altitudes; they were certainly too weak, as civil ships, in the denser air at low levels, particularly in turbulent air over North African deserts. Lost with *Dixmude* was her commanding officer, Lieutenant de Vaisseau Jean J A J du Plessis de Grenédan (1892–1923), France's greatest protagonist of the rigid airship.

L70 herself, tragically but fittingly, provided the funeral pyre of the German naval airship service and of their exceptional and gallant leader, Peter Strasser. Nobody had done more than he to try to make the rigid airship into an effective weapon of war. Determined to the last that his airships would win their battle, even though the war itself was all but lost, he led his airships once more against Britain. He was shot down in L70 on 5 August, 1918, by a D.H.4 of the RAF, and fell into the North Sea off Norfolk.

L72 (LZ114) went to France as Dixmude.
(Pritchard collection)

Production (L70 class)

C/n		First flight	Last flight	Flights	Disposal
LZ112	L70	1.7.18	5.8.18	7?	Shot down by RAF
LZ113	L71	29.7.18	3.10.18	7 or 8	Converted to LZ113A
LZ113A	L71	28.10.18	1.7.20	2	Flew to Pulham July 1920, then broken up 1923
LZ114	L72	9.7.20	21.12.23	10	To France as *Dixmude* 9.10.20; burned in flight 21.12.23

Zeppelin LZ112 (Type x) L70 (L70 class)

Manufacturer: Luftschiffbau Zeppelin GmbH

First two built at Friedrichshafen, LZ114 built at Löwenthal

Number of type built: three

Chief designer: L Dürr

Main structural material: duralumin

Design began: April 1918

First flight of type: 1 July, 1918

Zeppelin Type x LZ112

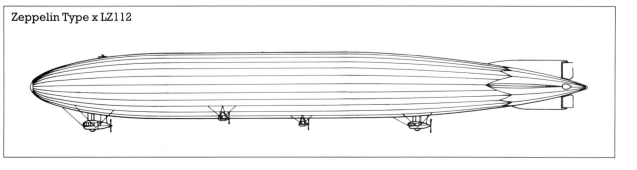

Lieut de Vaisseau Jean du Plessis de Grenedan was commander of the Dixmude, *formerly L72 (LZ114). He was killed when the* Dixmude *burned in flight on 21 December, 1923.*
(Pritchard collection)

Powerplant: seven (later six) 245hp Maybach Mb IVa six-cylinder inline engines

Gas capacity (100 per cent inflation): 62,200cu m (62,600cu m sometimes quoted); 68,500cu m (LZ113A and LZ114)

Overall length: 211.1m (LZ112/113); 226.5m (LZ113A/114)

Maximum diameter: 23.9m

Spacing of main frames: 15.0m

Fineness ratio: 8.83

Number of gas cells: 15 (LZ112 and LZ113); 16 (LZ113A and LZ114)

Number of main longitudinals: 13

Number of intermediate longitudinals: 12

Empty weight: 24,700kg

Typical gross lift: 72,200kg (LZ112 and LZ113); 79,460kg (LZ113A and LZ114) (1.16kg/cu m)

Typical disposable load: 47,500kg (LZ112 and LZ113); 54,760kg (LZ113A and LZ114)

Maximum fuel: 12,000kg

Crew: 30

Maximum speed: 36.4m/s (81.42 mph)

Maximum range: 12,000km at speed of 30.5m/s (68.22mph)

Static ceiling: 6,200m

British Rigids During and After the War – 23, 23X and 31 classes

The experience gained by Vickers in the development of No.9 made this firm the obvious choice as main contractor for the next type of British rigid. When, in June 1915, interest in rigid airships again revived at the Admiralty, it was proposed that four additional ships should be ordered. On 28 August Vickers was asked to undertake the design of a development of No.9 to be known as the 23 class. The first ship, No.23, was to be built by Vickers in its existing Walney shed (*See* Note 18) and this, therefore, dictated the maximum dimensions of the airship. One of the other three ships (R26) was also to be built by Vickers (there was room for two ships, side by side, in the Walney shed) and the other two, Nos.24 and 25, were to be built by Beardmore in a new shed at Inchinnan, on the Clyde, and by Armstrong Whitworth in a new shed at Barlow, near Selby in Yorkshire.

The 23 class ships were ordered on 16 October, 1915, and work on No.23 started in February 1916. Basically, the 23 class was an enlarged No.9 with four 250hp Rolls-Royce Eagle I engines and a more Zeppelin-like shape. That is to say, like No.9, it was 53ft (16.2m) in diameter and had its main frames spaced 30ft (9.1m) apart. Also, like No.9, it had 17 longitudinals and the large external V keel, now attached only at the main frames. It had one more gas cell (making eighteen) and the capacity was greater at 997,640cu ft (28,250cu m). The biggest change was a retrograde step: the hull was made blunter at the stern so as to

increase its capacity within a given length. The bow radius (twice the diameter) was the same as No.1 and slightly greater than No.9 but the stern radius was much reduced, being only three times the diameter. The effect of this, combined with the three, rather lumpy gondolas and the prominent external V keel was to make these ships look even clumsier and more out-of-date than they really were. Not that they were anything but hopelessly outclassed by contemporary German developments by the time No.23 flew, for the first time, on 19 September, 1917. The next two ships in the class were completed in October and the last in March 1918.

The 23 class ships together flew over 900 hours and they must have accumulated more than half the total flying done by British rigid airships during the war. Their utility was seriously limited by their low speed, which was about the same as that of the L3 class which the Germans had at the start of the war. They were also deficient in disposable load and various modifications were introduced in not very successful attempts to improve this. The four ships built were used mainly for experimental purposes, particularly for mooring-mast experiments, although No.23 did make a test launching of a Sopwith Camel fighter over Great Yarmouth on 6 November, 1918, repeating an experiment made by the Germans nine months earlier. (*See* Note 17) The first hook-on of an aeroplane to an airship was not made until 1924, as will be recorded later. All four ships were scrapped in the latter part of 1919.

The next rigids in the British programme, R27 to 30, were originally ordered as 23 class ships. However, information from the wreckage of two L10 class Zeppelins, LZ77 and LZ85, shot down in 1916 at Révigny, in France, and at Salonika, in Greece, suggested that changes should be made to the later British ships to incorporate more re-

This view of Vickers No.23 shows to advantage the V-shaped keel, engine cars and tail surfaces. (Flight)

View looking aft showing the gunner's position atop a 23 class ship. (Pritchard collection)

No.23, which first flew in September 1917, was the first successful British rigid airship. (Vickers)

cent Zeppelin developments. In particular, evidence of the suppression of the external V keel, which had been such a prominent feature of earlier Zeppelins, led to the idea that the 23 class should also be modified in the same way.

The design of the improved 23 class, known as the 23X class, was undertaken by an Admiralty team under Constructor-Cdr C I R Campbell, which from 26 October, 1915, was made officially

Beardmore-built Sopwith 2F.1 Camel N6814 suspended beneath Vickers No.23, with the forward engine car on the right.
(Imperial War Museum)

The unpiloted 2F.1 Camel N6814 suspended beneath Vickers No.23 on 2 or 3 October, 1918, and seen from the airship's forward car.
(Courtesy Philip Jarrett)

The Beardmore-built No.24 (23 class) seen from the roof of the shed at Inchinnan on Clydeside and near the present Glasgow Airport.
(Pritchard collection)

Beardmore No. 24.

Armstrong Whitworth built No.25 first flew in October 1917.
(Flight)

Vickers-built R26.
(Pritchard collection)

This view of R26 shows how the keel was faired into the lower tail surfaces.
(Flight)

responsible for the design of all British rigid airships. The design of the 23X class was approved in June 1916.

Two 23X class ships were eventually completed: R27 by Beardmore and R29 by Armstrong Whitworth. Two other ships, R28, partly built by Beardmore and partly by Vickers, and R30, under construction by Armstrong Whitworth, were cancelled before completion.

The 23X class was surprisingly similar to the 23 class, considering the radical changes involved in replacing the external keel with an internal non-structural corridor. In the new design, all concentrated weights were attached directly to the main frames. The structure of the hull was strengthened to compensate for the loss of the keel by use of a stronger triangular girder, used with the apex outward.

The internal corridor caused some loss of gas volume because the bottoms of the cells had to be cut back to allow space for it. The loss was largely compensated

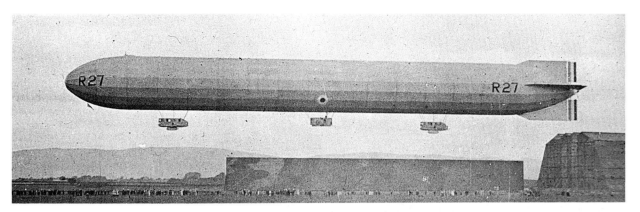

Beardmore-built R27 (23X class) airborne at Inchinnan, with the shed on the right and camouflaged windbreak.
(Pritchard collection)

The forward engine car of R27.

by a bluffer bow (with a radius $1^1/_2$ times the diameter, the same as the pre-war Zeppelins). Apart from this, the diameter of the hull and the number of gas cells were the same, while the length (539ft; 164.38m) was only slightly greater than 23 class. Gas capacity was rather less at 990,577cu ft (28,050cu m). As in 23 class ships, power was provided by four 300hp Rolls-Royce Eagle engines in three gondolas which were, however, now mounted closer to the hull. The gondolas at front and rear had single engines driving twin swivelling propellers. The third car – in the centre – had two engines, each driving a swivelling propeller. The changes made in the 23X ships partly achieved their objectives: disposable load was increased and drag was reduced so that the top speed rose slightly from 54.58mph (24.4m/s) to 55mph (24.6m/s).

Although the 23X class ships were reported to be rather flexible, they were significantly more practical than their predecessors and were claimed to be fully equal in performance and behaviour to pre-war Zeppelins. R27 and R29 were even used for some operational flying. R29 took part in a successful attack on the German U-boat UB 115 on 29 September, 1918. She flew over 400 hours before being broken up on

Part of the control car of R28 which was never completed.

24 October, 1919. R27 was accidentally destroyed with three blimps in a hangar fire at Howden on 16 August, 1918.

The last British rigid completed before the end of the war was the first of two wooden airships of the 31 class which were built by Short Brothers at a new construction facility at Cardington, near Bedford.

Early in 1916, details of some of the latest Schütte-Lanz designs of wooden rigid airships reached Britain. It appears that these were basically of the S.L.6 class, the first of which had flown in September 1915. However, there may also have been some information on the S.L.8 class, which had flown for the first time in March 1916.

R29 being walked from the shed.
(Flight)

23X class R29 was built by Armstrong Whitworth.

R32, built by Short Brothers, was not completed until September 1919.
(Pritchard collection)

R29 under construction with three of the eighteen gas cells installed. This photograph is dated January 1918 and the R29 made its first flight on 20 June that year.

R31, first of the two 31 class, was built at Cardington by Short Brothers.
(Pritchard collection)

How this information came to Britain has never been completely explained. It may well have resulted from espionage activity, of which there was a great deal during the First World War directed at obtaining information about German airship developments. Certainly a former Swiss employee of the Schütte-Lanz com-pany, known as Hermann Müller, brought drawings and other data to England and helped with the design and construction of the 31 class. (*See* Note 19)

Regardless of how the information was obtained, the design of the 31 class ships seems to have been basically that of a stretched S.L.6, re-drawn in Imperial units

Air Commodore E M Maitland, CMG, DSO, AFC.
(Pritchard collection)

R32 over Amsterdam.
(Pritchard collection)

the area of the fins. In this form, she was quite successful and flew a total of 212hr 45min before being scrapped in 1921.

Other British rigids were being developed during the First World War, notably the 33 class modelled on the famous German L30 class. These ships, and later developments of them, were flown for the first time after the war and are discussed later.

Vickers No.23 (23 class)

Manufacturer: Vickers Ltd

First of type built at Walney Island, Barrow-in-Furness

Number built: four

Chief designer: H B Pratt

Main structural material: duralumin

Design began: August 1915

First flight of type: 19 September, 1917

Powerplant: four 250hp Rolls-Royce Eagle I twelve-cylinder vee engines. Later modified with three and with two engines

Gas capacity (100 per cent inflation): 997,640cu ft (28,250cu m)

Overall length: 535ft (163.1m)

Maximum diameter: 53ft (16.2m)

Spacing of main frames: 30ft (9.1m)

Fineness ratio: 10.07

Number of gas cells: 18

Number of main longitudinals: 17

and with six instead of four engines. Compared with the S.L.6 class, the British ships were longer by two 12m (39ft 4¹/₃in) bays, giving a total of twenty gas cells. The diameter was unchanged at 19.75m (64ft 9¹/₂in) but the greater length gave a capacity of 1,552,964cu ft (43,975cu m).

These ships were potentially the most effective rigids produced by the Allies during the First World War. They were quite fast, having a top speed of 71.13mph (31.8m/s). However, only one, R31, was completed and flown before the Armistice, in August 1918. Apparently, Scotch glue had been used in part of her construction because casein cement was not available in Britain when manufacture of R31 started. (The glue's formula

is believed to have only arrived with Müller.) Scotch glue gave trouble when the ship was allowed to get wet. Combined with the insufficiently strong tail surfaces this led to R31 being scrapped after only two flights. Her sister-ship, R32, was completed after the war. She had modifications suggested by the tests with R31, including removal of one engine and a reduction in

Production (23 class)

C/n		First flight	Last flight	Hours flown	Disposal
No.23	No.23	19.9.17	November, 1918	321hr 30min	Broken up, Pulham September, 1919
No.24	No.24	27.10.17	December, 1919	192hr 53min	Broken up, Pulham 1 December, 1919
No.25	No.25	14.10.17	November, 1918	225hr 5min	Broken up, Cranwell September, 1919
R26	R26	20.3.18	19.2.19	238hr 27min	Broken up, 10.3.19

Vickers No.23 (23 class)

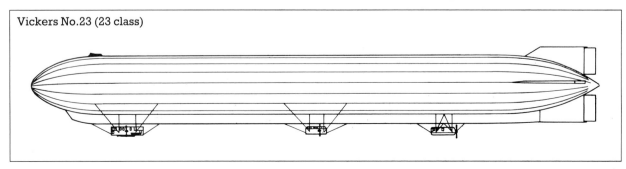

Beardmore R27 (Admiralty 23X class)

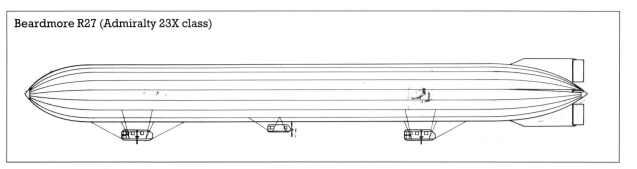

Empty weight: 59,525lb (27,000kg)
Typical gross lift: 67,880lb (30,790 kg) (1.09kg/cu m)
Typical disposable load: 3,790kg
Crew: 16
Maximum speed: 52mph (23.2m/s)
Maximum range: 1,895 miles (3,050 km)

Beardmore R27 (23X class)

Manufacturer: William Beardmore & Co Ltd
First of type built at Inchinnan near Glasgow; R29 built by Armstrong Whitworth at Barlow near Selby
Number built: two
Chief designer: C I R Campbell
Main structural material: duralumin
Design began: June 1916
First flight of type: 29 June, 1918
Powerplant: four 300hp Rolls-Royce Eagle III or VI twelve-cylinder vee engines
Gas capacity (100 per cent inflation): 990,577cu ft (28,050cu m)
Overall length: 539ft (164.28m)
Maximum diameter: 53ft (16.2m)
Spacing of main frames: 30ft (9.1m)
Fineness ratio: 10.14
Number of gas cells: 18
Number of main longitudinals: 17
Empty weight: 55,115lb (25,000kg)
Typical gross lift: 67,406lb (30,575 kg) (1.09kg/cu m)
Typical disposable load: 5,575kg
Crew: 16
Maximum speed: 55mph (24.6m/s)

Production (23X class)

C/n		First flight	Last flight	Hours flown	Disposal
R27	R27	29.6.18	16.8.18?	89hr 40min	Burned in shed at Howden 16.8.18
R28	R28	Not completed; cancelled August 1917			
R29	R29	20.6.18	June, 1919	437hr 58min	Broken up, 24.10.19 at East Fortune
R30	R30	Not completed; cancelled, early 1917			

Maximum range: 1,056 miles (1,700 km)

Short R31 (31 class)

Manufacturer: Short Brothers (Rochester & Bedford) Ltd
Built at Cardington near Bedford
Number of type built: two
Chief designers: C I R Campbell and C P T Lipscombe
Main structural material: wood
Design began: May 1916
First flight of type: 1 August, 1918
Powerplant: six 300hp Rolls-Royce Eagle III or IV twelve-cylinder vee engines (R31); five 300hp Rolls-Royce Eagle III or IV twelve-cylinder vee engines (R32)
Gas capacity (100 per cent inflation): 1,553,000cu ft (43,975cu m)
Overall length: 614ft 6in (187.3m)
Maximum diameter: 66ft (20.1m)
Spacing of main frames: 39ft $4^1/_3$in (12.0m)
Fineness ratio: 9.32
Number of gas cells: 20
Number of main longitudinals: 20
Empty weight: 68,784lb (31,200kg)
Typical gross lift: 105,680lb (47,936 kg) (1.09kg/cu m)
Typical disposable load: 16,730kg
Crew: 21
Maximum speed: 71.3mph (31.8 m/s)
Maximum range: 2,000 miles (3,200 km)

Production (31 class)

C/n		First flight	Last flight	Hours flown	Disposal
R31	R31	1.8.18	6.11.18	8hr 55min	Broken up, Howden July 1919
R32	R32	3.9.19	October 1920	212hr 45min	Broken up, Howden 27 April, 1921

Short R31 (Admiralty 31 class)

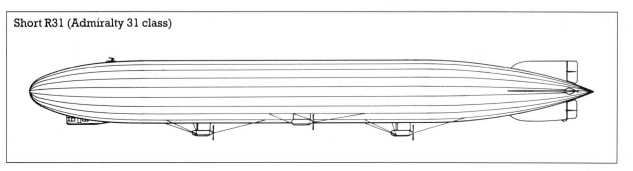

The Armstrong Whitworth built R33.
(H B Wyn Evans)

R33 leaving its camouflaged shed at Barlow near Selby on 6 March, 1919, before its first flight.
(H B Wyn Evans)

Across the Atlantic – R33 and R34

On 24 September, 1916, the burnt but otherwise complete structure of the L30 class Zeppelin L33 fell into Allied hands when she was forced down at Little Wigborough in England. Just over a year later, on 20 October 1917, L49, an L48 'Height-climber' class ship, was forced down in France. These two

R33 nearing completion. This fine view of the stern and tail surfaces was taken in January 1919. The tail gun position with Scarff mounting can be seen on the extreme left.
(H B Wyn Evans)

The navigation car of R33. The badge on the bow has the title HM R33, surmounted by a crown.
(H B Wyn Evans)

events had a profound effect on rigid airship development in both Britain and the United States.

Largely at the instigation of Cdr R B B Colmore at the Admiralty, a team from the Ordnance Survey in co-operation with Constructor-Cdr C I R Campbell and draughtsmen from the Admiralty Air Department were put on to the job of preparing detailed drawings of L33 as the wreckage was dismantled. The French made similar complete and careful drawings of L49.

The L33 data clearly offered an opportunity to catch up with German airship development and in November 1916 the Cabinet authorised the construction of

December 1917. More than a year passed between the decision to proceed and the start of actual construction. This period was spent adapting the design to British units and materials as well as incorporating certain additional information obtained by the French from the L49. R35 was going to be modified and would have differed in a number of features from R33 and R34 but she was cancelled following the Armistice on 11 November, 1918. Construction of R33 and R34 continued, however, and these ships were both flown by a test crew under Lt-Col W C Hicks (1890–1939) on 6 and 14 March 1919 respectively.

The 33 class ships, as they were known, followed the design of the L30 class very closely. Their diameter (78ft 9in/24m) is usually reported as slightly greater than the L30s, as was their capacity, but their length was slightly less. This occurred either because there were errors in the measurement of L33 or because of the need to adapt the drawings to British Standards. From every other point of view, the 33s and L30s were structurally identical. The engine arrangements, on the other hand, were influenced by the L49 data and the five 250hp Sunbeam Maoris were arranged in a manner similar to the engines in the L48 class. They gave the British ships a speed of 60mph

The control car of R33 seen in March 1919.
(H B Wyn Evans)

R33 with damaged bows after breaking away from the high mast at Pulham in April 1926.

three ships, R33, R34 and R35, to be built as replicas of the German design. R33 and R35 were ordered from Armstrong Whitworth, but R33 was not laid down at Barlow near Selby until June 1918. R34 was built by Beardmore who started work on her at Inchinnan on the Clyde in

(26.8m/s), seven miles an hour less than their German prototype.

Although they were too late for the war, R33 and R34 were the two most successful British rigids, if the amount of flying they did is taken as the yardstick. R33 was, in addition, the longest-lived British rigid and remained in intermittent use, depending on variations in British policy towards airships, until she was finally broken up in April 1928. She is believed to have been broken up then as a result of concern about fatigue in parts of the structure. Perhaps the most notable adventure of her career occurred while she was moored to the high mast at Pulham in a gale. On the morning of 16 April, 1926, she broke away with only a skeleton crew under Flight Lieut R S Booth on board and, with a smashed nose, was carried by the wind out over the North Sea before she could be gradually brought back to base under her own power. She was later repaired and returned to service.

The forward Sunbeam Maori, in the rear section of the navigation car of R33. This view is looking aft.
(H B Wyn Evans)

R33 moored to the high mast at Pulham.
(Flight)

R34 flying the White Ensign from the stern.
(Courtesy British Airways)

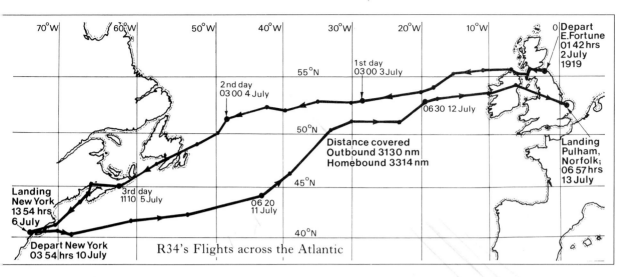

| 70°W | 60°W | 50°W | 40°W | 30°W | 20°W | 10°W | 0 |

Depart
E.Fortune
0142 hrs
2 July
1919

1st day
0300 3July

55°N

2nd day
0300 4 July

06 30 12 July

50°N

Distance covered
Outbound 3130 nm
Homebound 3314 nm

Landing
Pulham,
Norfolk;
06 57 hrs
13 July

45°N

Landing
New York
13 54 hrs
6 July

3rd day
1110 5 July

06 20
11 July

40°N

Depart New York
03 54 hrs 10 July

R34's Flights across the Atlantic

R34 had a shorter career because she accidentally flew into a hillside in Yorkshire on 28 January, 1921. She was lucky and did not catch fire, and was later flown back to her base at Howden in Yorkshire. However, she suffered further damage there and, not being considered worth repairing, was broken up. Before that, in July 1919, she had made her epic transatlantic return flight to the United States, winning for herself a place in history: the first aircraft to fly westward across the Atlantic and the first to make a return flight. The ship was commanded on this crossing by Maj G H Scott (1888–1930) and had Air Commodore E M Maitland (1880–1921), senior officer of the British Airship Service, on board. The outward flight was made in

The rear engine car of R34.

R34, the first airship to cross the North Atlantic. The non-rigid N.S.7 appears top right.
(Courtesy British Airways)

108hr 12min (a world endurance record which nearly caused the ship to run out of fuel before she reached New York) and the return in 75hr 3min.

Although certain desirable features of the later L48 class Zeppelins were incorporated in the 33 class ships they were fortunately too far along in design when the L48 data became available for them to be made into

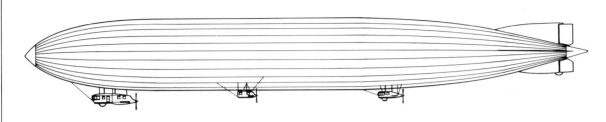

Armstrong Whitworth R33 (Admiralty 33 class)

Production

C/n		First flight	Last flight	Hours flown	Disposal
R33	R33 (G-FAAG)	6.3.19	23.11.26	735hr 1min	Broken up, April 1928
R34	R34	14.3.19	28.1.21	495hr 28min	Broken up, after being damaged, January 1921.
R35	R35		Not completed; cancelled early 1919		

complete replicas of the later design. This was a good thing because the basic L30 class was undoubtedly a better and stronger all-round airship, more durable for long life in peace-time and better able to stand up to rough

Major G H Scott AFC, Captain of R34.

handling than the later 'Height-climbers' which were lightened and weakened in efforts to gain the greatest possible operating height as a defence against aeroplane attack.

Thus, although R33 and R34 gave good service, later ships built by the Allies in more direct imitation of L49 (the British R36 and the United States ZR-1 *Shen-*

After the arrival of R34 at Mineola, Long Island, in July 1919. Left to right: Lieut-Cmdr Z Lansdowne, US Navy; 2nd Lieut R F Durrant (Wireless Officer) in borrowed tunic; Lieut Guy Harris (Meteorological Officer); Maj J E M Pritchard OBE (Special Duties); Brig-Gen E M Maitland CMG, DSO (Special Duties); 2nd Lieut H F Luck (Third Officer); and 2nd Lieut J D Shotter (Engineer Officer). The very badly retouched R34 in the background.
(Popperfoto)

andoah), had the germs of disaster in them from the start. It is an extraordinary fact that although the lightness and weakness of the structures of these ships were known to those who built them, they do not seem to have been able to impress this adequately upon those who flew them.

Armstrong Whitworth R33 (33 class)

Manufacturer: Sir W G Armstrong Whitworth & Co Ltd (R33); William Beardmore & Co Ltd (R34)

R33 built at Barlow near Selby, Yorkshire. R34 built at Inchinnan near Glasgow

Number of type built: two

Chief designer: C I R Campbell

Main structural material: duralumin

Design began: November 1916

First flight of type: 6 March, 1919

Powerplant: five 250hp Sunbeam Maori IV twelve-cylinder vee engines

Gas capacity (100 per cent inflation): 1,958,553cu ft (55,460cu m)

Overall length: 643ft (196.0m)

Maximum diameter: 78ft 9in (24.0m)

Spacing of main frames: 32ft 9^1/$_2$in (10.0m)

Fineness of ratio: 5.03

Number of gas cells: 19

Number of main longitudinals: 13

Number of intermediate longitudinals: 12

Empty weight: 81,350lb (36,900kg)

Typical gross lift: 133,269lb (60,450 kg) (1.09kg/cu m)

Typical disposable load: 23,550kg

Maximum fuel: 38,580lb (17,500kg)

Crew: 23

Maximum speed: 60mph (26.8 m/s)

Maximum range: 4,815 miles (7,750 km) at speed of 46mph (20.6m/s)

Static ceiling: 13,120ft (4,000m)

Cost: £350,000

R33 (G-FAAG) first flew 6.3.19, made last flight 23.11.26, flew 735hr 1min and was broken up April 1928

R34 first flew 14.3.19, made last flight 28.1.21, flew 495hr 48min and was broken up January 1921 after being damaged

R35 was not completed; cancelled early 1919

R38 built at Cardington was to have gone to the US Navy as ZR-2. It first flew in June 1921 and suffered inflight structural failure that August.
(Pritchard collection)

R38 and R80

Two more British airships were completed based on war-time Zeppelin designs. These were R36 discussed in the next chapter and R38 which was started by Short Brothers in November 1918 and taken over in 1919 by the Royal Airship Works at Cardington. She was completed for sale to the United States as ZR-2. Three sister-ships, R39, 40 and 41, were also ordered in September 1918 and the first two were laid down by Armstrong Whitworth at Barlow later in 1918. They were all cancelled soon after the end of the war, when about £1.8 million had already been spent on them.

R38 was started with the intention of producing an advance on the L70 class Zeppelins. The overall design was in the hands of C I R Campbell and his team at the Admiralty Airship Design Department. However, the detail design was largely the work of C T P Lipscomb of Short Brothers who, when the Royal Airship Works was set up in April 1919, stayed on at Cardington with

R38 in its shed. It bears the US Navy star beneath its bows. (Pritchard collection)

R38 being walked from its shed. (Pritchard collection)

about twenty draughtsmen until R38 was completed.

R38 was a much more ambitious extrapolation from German experience than was either R36 or the American ZR-1 *Shenandoah*. For a start, the designers went to a larger diameter. Zeppelin stayed with the L30 class diameter in all ships built up to the end of the war. A new type of Zeppelin, with increased diameter, was

under construction shortly before the Armistice but was not completed. R38 therefore represented a bold – events were to show too bold – step forward by the British designers from German experience.

R38 was the largest airship in the world when she was completed in 1921, and in fact remained the largest in terms of gross lift until R101 flew in 1929. Her diameter of 85ft 3½in (26m) was 2m up on the largest wartime Zeppelin, and her length of 695ft (211.8m) gave a capacity of 2,740,420cu ft (77,600cu m) in fourteen gas cells. In other re-

Commander L H Maxfield USN and part of the crew who would have flown R38 to the United States.
(Courtesy Philip Jarrett)

spects she followed L70 class practice quite closely, having 15m (49ft 2½in) bays with twelve intermediate longitudinals. The corridor keel was rectangular, instead of A-shaped, as in L70. All weights were carried on the main frames but there were no stirrup wires or intermediate frame stiffening as had been found necessary on the L70s.

A radical departure was made

C I R Campbell, designer of R38.

The wreckage of R38 in the Humber in August 1921.
(Courtesy Philip Jarrett)

Vickers-built R80. Chief designer, right, was Barnes Wallis and the ship first flew in July 1920. (Vickers)

in the gas cell wiring which replaced the wire-mesh and cord netting previously used. The lift of the gas cells was taken on circumferential wires and on catenary wires running fore and aft. The hull had a V bottom and main-frame trussing similar to that used later by the Zeppelin company on LZ126 (*See* page 138). The ship was powered by six 350hp Sunbeam Cossack engines.

R38 was first flown on 23 June, 1921. By then the American crew who had come to collect her had been training in England for some time on R32, R34 and R80, and some of them participated in the first flight tests. Fifteen of them were among the forty-four, out of a total complement of forty-nine, who lost their lives when the ship broke up and

caught fire during turning trials over the Humber on her fourth flight on 24 August. The airship showed serious control deficiencies and had suffered several minor structural failures on previous flights. In retrospect it seems clear that there was some over-confidence in the way in which the flight trials were conducted. The fact that no British rigid had previously suffered ca-

tastrophic structural failure in flight may have contributed to this. Amongst those who lost their lives were Air Commodore Maitland and C I R Campbell, the designer of the ship who had been made manager of the Royal Airship Works in 1920.

The British Government announced in May 1921 that it intended to close down airship operations unless commercial interests were prepared to take them over. Although a proposal was made in July for an Imperial Airship Company, the necessary financial interest was clearly not forthcoming and the loss of R38, and particularly of Air Commodore Maitland, the great airship protagonist, served to confirm the Government in its decision to stop airship activities.

One other British rigid airship was completed in the early post-war period before the shutdown in 1921. This was a Vickers design by B N Wallis, assisted by J E Temple, both of whom had been involved with Hartley Pratt

R80 under construction at Walney Island in October 1918. (Vickers)

in the design of No.9 and No.23. Known as R80, this new Vickers ship owed nothing to the Admiralty design team under Campbell and showed that the Vickers designers were beginning to acquire an independent rigid airship de- sign capability. The R80 design inevitably still owed much to ear- lier German airship practice, but this ship was not in any way a derivative of a previous design. For one thing, she was only the second metal rigid to have a hull of good streamlined form with no parallel section along its length (the first had been *Bodensee* which, although she flew much sooner was probably of later de- sign then R80). R80 did have 10m (32ft 9^1/$_2$in) bays on the Zeppelin pattern and had Zeppelin-type girders, but there were fewer longitudinals than in recent Zeppelins (eleven main and ten intermediate). The fifteen gas cells gave a capacity of 1,260,000cu ft (35,680cu m) which made her quite a small ship. She was, in fact, built in the old Walney shed which meant

The control car of R80. (Vickers)

that her length of 531ft 6in (162m) was actually less than that of the old 23 class. Power was provided by four 245hp Maybach Mb IVa engines.

R80 flew for the first time on 19 July, 1920. She had originally been ordered in November 1917 and her construction had started in April 1918, but progress was slow and was suspended for a time after the Armistice. A sister-ship, R81, was approved in March 1918 but was never or-

dered. R80 accumulated seventy-three hours' flying before being grounded in 1921 as a result of the shutdown of British airship operations. She was then stored at Pulham until the new airship programme began in 1924, when it was reported that she was to be reconditioned. For no very clear reason, this did not happen and she was dismantled. It was claimed at the time that this was for political, rather than for tech-nical, reasons, although it is clear

that with a top speed of only 60mph (26.8m/s), her perfor-mance was disappointing.

R80 suffered major structural failure on her first flight – eighty-three girders are said to have broken and the ship was so dis-torted that she was returned to her shed with only the greatest difficulty. After repairs and modifications, she flew until 20 September 1921, mainly training US crew for R38, and was finally broken up in 1925.

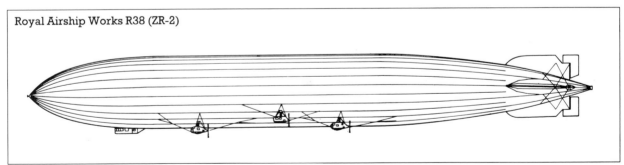

Royal Airship Works R38 (ZR-2)

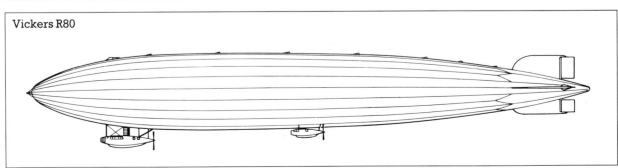

Vickers R80

Royal Airship Works R38, ZR-2

Manufacturer: Royal Airship Works

Built at Cardington near Bedford

Number of type built: one

Chief designer: C I R Campbell

Main structural material: duralumin

Design began: August 1918; (assembly began February 1919)

First flight: 23 June, 1921

Powerplant: six 350hp Sunbeam Cossack twelve-cylinder vee engines

Gas capacity (100 per cent inflation): 2,740,420cu ft (77,600cu m)

Overall length: 695ft (211.8m)

Maximum diameter: 85ft 3^1/$_2$in (26.0m)

Spacing of main frames: 49ft 2^1/$_2$in (15.0m)

Fineness ratio: 8.15

Number of gas cells: 14

Number of main longitudinals: 13

Number of intermediate longitudinals: 12

Empty weight: 80,910lb (36,700kg)

Typical gross lift: 186,475lb (84,584 kg) (1.09kg/cu m)

Typical disposable load: 47,884kg

Crew: 30

Maximum speed: 66mph (29.5m/s)

Maximum range: 6,525 miles (10,500km)

Cost: US$1,584,000

R38 crashed due to structural failure on 24 August, 1921, after 70hr 10min total flying time. The other three airships of this Admiralty A type (R39, R40 and R41) were cancelled in 1919 before completion.

Vickers R80

Manufacturer: Vickers Ltd

Built at Walney Island, Barrow-in-Furness

Number of type built: one

Chief designer: B N Wallis

Main structural material: duralumin

Design began: November 1917

First flight: 19 July, 1920

Powerplant: four 245hp Maybach Mb IVa six-cylinder inline engines.

Gas capacity (100 per cent inflation): 1,260,000cu ft (35,680cu m)

Overall length: 531ft 6in (162.0m)

Maximum diameter: 70ft (21.3m)

Spacing of main frames: 32ft 9^1/$_2$in (10.0m)

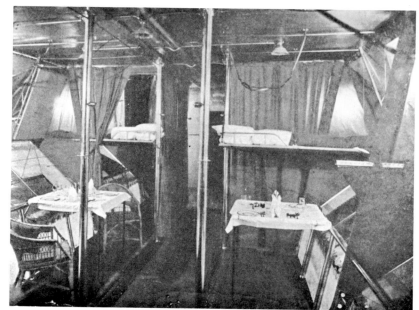

Part of the passenger accommodation aboard R36.

Fineness ratio: 7.61

Number of gas cells: 15

Number of main longitudinals: 11

Number of intermediate longitudinals: 10

Empty weight: 48,500lb (22,000 kg)

Typical gross lift: 85,738lb (38,890 kg) (1.09kg/cu m)

Typical disposable load: 16,890kg

Crew: 20

Maximum speed: 60mph (26.8 m/s)

Maximum range: 6,400 miles (10,300km)

Last flight on 20 September, 1921, after 73hr 12min flying time. Broken up in July 1925.

R36 and ZR-1 *Shenandoah*

The first airship directly patterned on L49 was the British rigid, R36. L49 was an L48 class Height-climber which had been captured by the French in October 1917. R36 had originally been ordered on 5 January, 1917, with a sister-ship (R37) which was later cancelled. These ships were intended to be simply straightforward 'stretches' of the 33 class. However, once the L49 data became available from the French in the autumn of 1917, the new Airship Design Department, formed at the Admiralty under C I R Campbell in November, used this information as the basis of its new ship. It was no doubt thought that L49 incorporated the latest rigid airship practice and must therefore be an advance on the L33. In fact she was probably less suitable for the wartime role in which the British intended to use her – maritime reconnaissance – and she was certainly less satisfactory for the peacetime role in which R36 was finally cast, that of low-level civil transport.

R36 was, in effect, an L48 class ship stretched by one 10m (32ft 9½in) bay to give a length of 672ft 6¾in (205m) but containing two more gas cells to give a capacity of 212,000cu ft (60,032cu m). The diameter (78ft 9in; 24m) was the same as 33 class. She was originally going to be fitted with four 350hp Sunbeam Cossack engines but in the event was completed with only three of these rather heavy units. The fourth was replaced by two power-cars, each containing a 245hp Maybach Mb IVa taken from the surrendered Zeppelin L71. These power-units

Beardmore-built R36 after the 50-passenger coach had been fitted. (Flight)

gave R36 a top speed of 65mph (29.1m/s).

Construction of R36 and R37 began in December 1917. Beardmore built the former at Inchinnan; Vickers started construction of the latter which was to have been erected in an enormous new shed under construction at Flookborough in Lancashire but was taken over by Short Brothers at Cardington. Work was suspended at the Armistice but was resumed early in 1919. R37 was cancelled but R36 was finally completed and flown for the first time on 1 April, 1921. By then she had been fitted with a 131ft (40m) passenger coach attached directly to the hull. This was intended to accommodate fifty people in two-berth cabins. R37

was taken over by the Royal Airship Works when Cardington was nationalised in 1919. Her structure was nearly complete when she was abandoned in February 1921 after £325,000 had been spent (£2.6 million in present-day values). She was finally broken up in the autumn of 1924. R36 cost £350,000 (£2.8 million), plus the unrecorded cost of the passenger coach modifications.

R36 did less than 100 hours of flying which was probably a good thing in view of the weakness of the structure. She had one narrow escape on an early flight on 5 April, 1921, when the upper fin and starboard tailplane failed in flight and the ship dived out of control from 6,000 to 3,000ft. On 21 June she was even more seri-

ZR-1 Shenandoah *built by the US Naval Aircraft Factory and first flown in September 1923.* (Science Museum)

Shenandoah, *with six engines and full US Navy markings, over the Hudson.* (Pritchard collection)

ously damaged while attempting to moor to the mast at Pulham. She was damaged still further while being put into the shed. This had been occupied by the surrendered L64 which had to be hurriedly smashed up so that the remains could be dragged clear to make room for the British ship. When a decision was taken soon afterwards to stop work on airships, R36 was stored in a damaged condition until 1924.

In 1924, when the new British

airship programme started, R36 was repaired at a cost of £13,800 (£110,000). She was to have been used for a flight to Egypt to gather meteorological and other data needed for the big new airships ordered in the programme. Work on R36 was completed in about August 1925 but she was not used for the proposed flight because she was, in fact, quite unsuitable. The passenger coach which had been added as an afterthought when she was built

weighed 37,000lb (16,780kg) and is reported to have reduced the disposable lift to only 35,900lb (16,284kg). R36 was not flown again and was broken up in June 1926.

The other ship derived from L49 was the American rigid ZR-1, later named *Shenandoah*. In the latter part of the war the United States authorities had been closely studying the possibilities of rigid airships and had concluded that they should build

one. Cdr Jerome C Hunsaker was charged with this project and a design team at the Naval Aircraft Factory under Starr Truscott was given the job. Truscott had been working for some time on rigid airship design for the joint Army/Navy Air Board and had obtained a set of the French drawings of L49 during a visit to France in 1918. These drawings were used as the basis of ZR-1's design.

The United States ship differed from the L48 class in much the same ways as R36. The hull was one 10m bay longer than the original German design but contained two more gas cells giving a capacity of 2,151,200cu ft (60,915cu m). The diameter at 78ft 9in (24m) was the same as the British copies of the L30 and L48 classes. The engines, originally six 300hp Packard 1A-1551, were later reduced to five. There were some detailed changes to the structure which, for example, incorporated provision for nose mooring to a mast on the British pattern, and there was a slight change in the length of the hull as compared with R36. However, basically, the German design was closely followed and it was claimed that ZR-1's structure was within five per cent of its design

weight, a comparable achievement to Zeppelin with LZ126 and LZ127.

Charles P Burgess (1888–1951), who was responsible for the stressing of ZR-1, later admitted that 'there was actually little more than a blind faith that an incalculable source of strength offset an equally incalculable source of strain' and it seems, in retrospect, that this was indeed the position in the case of all the adaptations by other designers at this time of the basic Zeppelin designs.

The US Naval Appropriations of July 1919 provided for one

The wreckage of the stern of Shenandoah *at Ava, Ohio, in September 1925.*
(Pritchard collection)

Lieut-Cmdr Jerome C Hunsaker USN was sent to Europe in 1913 to study naval aviation development, flew over Berlin in the Viktoria Luise, *and was long involved with the US naval airship programme.*
(US Navy)

rigid to be built in the United States (ZR-1) and for one to be purchased abroad; at this stage, the latter was presumably intended to be the Zeppelin LZ125 (*See* page 139).

Construction of the components of ZR-1 started at the Naval Aircraft Factory in Philadelphia in August 1919 and erection of a large assembly hangar was put in hand at Lakehurst, New Jersey. Assembly of the ship herself began at Lakehurst in April 1922. Inflated with helium (the first rigid to use this gas), she was flown for the first time on 4 September, 1923, the Americans having obtained the services of an experienced German Zeppelin captain, Anton Heinen, to help with the flying. (*Shenandoah*, as the ZR-1 was to be named, cost $2,200,000 (£3,960,000 in current values) and it was reported that a filling of helium cost $211,500 (£368,000).

Helium had been first detected spectrographically in the sun by Sir J Norman Lockyer in 1868. It was first identified on earth by Sir William Ramsay in 1895 and was first used in a pressure-airship, the US Army's C-7, on 5 December, 1921.

During the following two years, *Shenandoah* was flown quite intensively, accumulating a total of 740 hours in 57 flights. Much of her time was spent experimenting with mooring to high masts, of the type adopted from the British, but this caused its share of troubles, including a breakaway on 16 January, 1924, similar to that experienced fifteen months later by R33. As with R33, ZR-1 had a skeleton crew, under Heinen, on board at the time. A fin collapsed and the nose was crushed, but the damaged ship was able to return to base under her own power. She was repaired, put back into service and then proceeded to make a number of notable flights including one of some 9,000 miles (14,500km) in seven stages to San Diego and Seattle, and back to Lakehurst.

On 3 September, 1925, she was caught in a squall over Ava, Ohio, and broke up while being lifted uncontrollably in a 15m/s (2,950ft/min) up-draught. Reductions in the numbers of valves in the gas cells had been made to save weight and to help conserve the expensive helium and there were suggestions that this may have contributed to the structural failure. In any event, *Shenandoah* obviously inherited the deliberate weaknesses of the 'Height-climbers'. Inflated with helium, she did not catch fire and this reduced the fatalities to fourteen out of the forty-three on board.

Beardmore R36 (36 class)

Manufacturer: William Beardmore & Co Ltd

Built at Inchinnan near Glasgow

Number built: one

Chief designer: C I R Campbell

Main structural material: duralumin

Design began: January 1917

First flight: 1 April, 1921

Powerplant: three 350hp Sunbeam Cossack twelve-cylinder vee and two 245hp Maybach Mb IVa six-cylinder inline engines

Gas capacity (100 per cent inflation): 2,120,000cu ft (60,032cu m)

Overall length: 672ft 6³/₄in (205.0 m)

Maximum diameter: 78ft 9in (24.0m)

Spacing of main frames: 32ft 9¹/₂in (10.0m)

Fineness ratio: 8.54

Number of gas cells: 20

Number of main longitudinals: 13

Number of intermediate longitudinals: 12

Empty weight: 117,726lb (53,400 kg)

Typical gross lift: 144,255lb (65,433 kg) (1.09kg/cu m)

Typical disposable load: 12,033kg

Crew: 28

Passengers: 50

Maximum speed: 65mph (29.1 m/s)

Maximum range: 7,765 miles (12,500km)

Cost: £350,000

R36 (G-FAAF) probably made its last flight on 17 or 21 June, 1921, after a total of 97hr 5min flying time. She was broken up in June 1926. A second airship in this class (R37) was not completed, cancelled in February 1921.

Naval Aircraft Factory ZR-1 *Shenandoah*

Manufacturer: Naval Aircraft Factory, Philadelphia

Built at Lakehurst

Number built: one

Chief designer: S. Truscott

Main structural material: duralumin

Design began: August 1919

First flight: 4 September, 1923

Powerplant: six 300hp Packard 1A-1551 twelve-cylinder vee engines. Sixth engine later removed

Gas capacity (100 per cent inflation): 2,151,200cu ft (60,915cu m)

Overall length: 680ft 3in (207.3m)

Maximum diameter: 78ft 9in (24.0m)

Spacing of main frames: 32ft 9¹/₂in (10.0m)

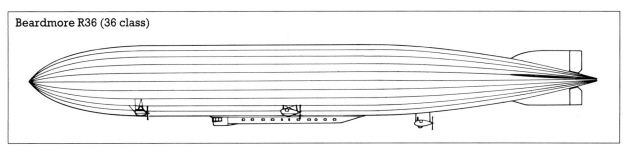

Beardmore R36 (36 class)

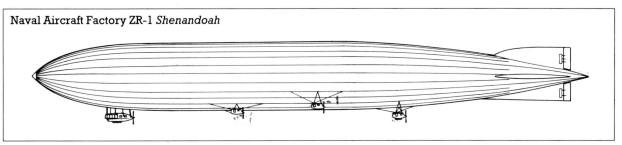

Naval Aircraft Factory ZR-1 *Shenandoah*

Fineness ratio: 8.64

Number of gas cells: 20

Number of main longitudinals: 13

Number of intermediate longitudinals: 12

Empty weight: 77,382lb (35,100kg)

Typical gross lift: 142,727lb (64,740kg) (helium) (1.079kg/cu m)

Typical disposable load: 29,640 kg

Maximum fuel: 14,550lb (6,600kg)

Crew: 23

Maximum speed: 62.63mph (28.0 m/s)

Maximum range: 2,610 miles (4,200km) at speed of 49.65mph (22.2m/s)

Cost: US$2,200,000

ZR-1 was rebuilt January–May 1924. After a total of 740 flying hours and 59 flights ZR-1 crashed as a result of structural failure on 3 September, 1925

Bodensee, Nordstern and Los Angeles

At the end of the First World War, Luftschiffbau Zeppelin had grown into a vast organisation employing 13,600 people at Friedrichshafen and Löwenthal, 4,700 at Staaken and 2,000 at Tempelhof, plus 2,500 in Maybach. The company was now making aeroplanes and other products but there were three more L70 class ships being built and work was in progress on a new, larger type of Zeppelin, the L100 class of 75,000cu m (2,648,600cu ft) capacity which had originally been ordered by the Navy in July 1918. The design of L100 was changed in September to one of 29.4m (96ft 6in) diameter and 108,000cu m (3,813,990cu ft) capacity. She was to have been powered by no fewer than ten 245 Maybach Mb IVa engines

Part of the passenger cabin in Bodensee. *A map of the Friedrichshafen—Berlin route is on the bulkhead.*
(Luftschiffbau Zeppelin)

LZ120 Bodensee *at Friedrichshafen.*
(Luftschiffbau Zeppelin)

LZ121 Nordstern *(DII)* *never went into DELAG service.*
(Luftschiffbau Zeppelin)

The passenger accommodation in LZ121 Nordstern, *with luggage racks,*
ceiling lights and opening windows.
(Luftschiffbau Zeppelin)

and would have been more than seventy per cent larger than the largest previous Zeppelin. However, she was cancelled in October 1918.

On 26 November, 1919, Alfred Colsman, who was still managing director of Luftschiffbau Zeppelin, had discussions with the Americans about the possible construction of an airship for sale to the United States. This ship, known as LZ125, would have been largely based on the L100 class and would have employed components already purchased or manufactured for the first L100 ships. By these means the Germans estimated that they could supply this large (100,000cu m; 3,531,470cu ft) ship for the ridiculously low price of 12 million devalued marks (probably equi-

LZ126 arriving at US Naval Air Station Lakehurst at the end of its transatlantic delivery flight. (Friedrich Moch collection)

LZ126, later ZR-3 Los Angeles, at Friedrichshafen in the summer of 1924. (Luftschiffbau Zeppelin)

LZ126 with US Navy markings as ZR-3 Los Angeles. (Pritchard collection)

(*Above and Below*) *Part of the accommodation in the* Los Angeles. (US Navy)

Star), was also built. LZ120 was of 18.7m (61ft 4½in) diameter and initially had had a capacity of only 20,000cu m (706,290cu ft), only slightly more than the pre-war *Hansa*, but she was lengthened by one 10m bay during the 1919–20 winter and her sister-ship was built from the beginning in lengthened form with a capacity of 22,550cu m (796,350cu ft). These ships were built of the smaller of two basic types of girder used in the L30 class and had main frames without kingposting. There was no axial wire. Four 245hp Maybach Mb IVa motors gave them the high top speed of 36.8m/s (82.3mph).

valent to about £760,000 in present-day values).

The other victorious Allies were not at all keen on the Americans placing this order because they wanted Germany's airship-building capability destroyed. Perhaps because of this the negotiations came to nothing. Shortly afterwards Colsman retired and Hugo Eckener succeeded him as head of the Zeppelin company, becoming general manager in 1922 and managing director in 1928.

Meanwhile, the works at Friedrichshafen had not been idle despite the Armistice and the Allies' ban on the construction of further military airships. At the end of the war, design work was immediately begun on a new class of small civil rigid suitable for use on short-range services such as DELAG had hoped to introduce before the war. The new design was finished in about three months and construction of the first ship, LZ120, later named *Bodensee* (*Lake Constance*), was started in January 1919. She was completed and flown for the first time on 20 August. In the latter part of 1919 DELAG used this ship to run a scheduled passenger service between Friedrichshafen and Berlin (*See* Appendix 2). Later, a second ship of the same type, LZ121 *Nordstern* (*North*

Dr Hugo Eckener.

The Allies objected to these activities by the Zeppelin company and eventually ruled that the two airships had to be handed over, one to Italy and the other to France, as war reparations in lieu of naval Zeppelins which had been destroyed by their crews to prevent them falling into Allied hands. LZ120 was handed over to Italy on 3 June, 1921 and – renamed *Esperia* – was based at Ciampino near Rome until she was broken up in July 1928. LZ121 – renamed *Méditerranée* – was delivered to the French on 18 July, 1921 and was based either at Rochefort or with the ill-fated L72 – *Dixmude* – at Cuers-Pierrefeu near Toulon in the south of France. She was finally broken up in September 1926. Both ships seem to have done quite of lot of flying in the hands of their new owners. LZ121 carried the French Air Minister, Laurent Eynac, on a visit to Rome in October 1923.

After the handing over of LZ120 and LZ121 in mid-1921, activity at the Zeppelin works reached a low ebb and it looked for a time as if this would be the end of the company. However, the Americans, although frustrated in their attempt to acquire LZ125, had not given up the idea of

This amazing photograph, taken at midday on 25 August, 1927, shows the Los Angeles *moored to the high mast at Lakehurst. The wind lifted the ship into the vertical attitude and swung it through 180 degrees. None of the 25 on board was hurt.*
(US Navy)

having the Zeppelin company build them a new airship. They planned to use this to gain rigid airship experience and as a pattern for new ships of their own which they might wish to develop in the future.

Early in 1921, the Luftschiffbau Zeppelin again raised the question with the Americans of an order for LZ125. Nothing came of this directly but discussions continued and eventually led to the signing, on 24 June, 1922, of a contract for an entirely new large Zeppelin, the LZ126. The Americans wanted a ship of 100,000cu m (3,531,470cu ft) but the Allies, through the London Protocol of 5 May, 1921, had put a ban on the Germans building airships larger than 30,000cu m (1,059,440cu ft). Eventually, after much negotiation, the other Allies agreed to the Americans buying a ship of 70,000cu m (2,472,030cu ft), rather larger than the largest size built during the war and the smallest which it was reckoned could be delivered safely across the Atlantic. She was also well inside the dimensions of Shed II at Friedrichshafen where she was built. The price agreed was three million gold marks (£1,540,000 in today's

values) of which 2.66 million marks (£1,360,000) was already due to the United States as their share of reparations. A US Navy inspection team of three, under Cdr Garland Fulton, USN, was stationed at Friedrichshafen throughout the manufacture of the airship. Work had begun speculatively on the design of this ship in September 1921, and she was planned for completion by the end of 1923.

LZ126, named *Los Angeles* after her delivery to the United States, proved notable in several respects. Not only did she provide work needed to keep the Zeppelin company alive but she was also a most successful ship and remained in commission for over fourteen years, the longest-lived of any rigid.

LZ126 was smaller in diameter (31.9m; 104ft 7³/₄in) than had been proposed for LZ125, and her length was shorter at 200m (656ft 2in) but she retained the 15m main frame spacing, with kingposted main frames and two intermediate frames, of the last wartime Zeppelins. An axial cable was re-introduced. There were thirteen gas cells and five 400hp Maybach VL1 engines, each in a separate engine-car. Although the

ship had been ordered for the US Navy, she was not armed or fitted out for military purposes. The structure represented a quite radical change from previous ships. In particular, the main girders were, for the first time, basically rectangular box sections instead of triangular, and one of the types used had plate webs. The main frame bracing was new, being in a diamond pattern.

Although the hull was completed in late 1923, there were delays in the development of the new twelve-cylinder engines and these held up the first flight until 27 August, 1924. Eckener then made a series of test flights culminating in a 3,500km (2,175 miles) round-trip to Malmö in Sweden with seventy-three people on board on 25 September. Finally, on 12 October, he left Friedrichshafen and safely delivered the ship to Lakehurst, New Jersey, on 15 October.

Thereafter, the *Los Angeles*, as she now became, was emptied of her hydrogen, re-filled with non-inflammable helium and put into commission in the US Navy. She flew some 4,180 hours during the next eight years and was kept inflated and used for mooring and other experiments for another six

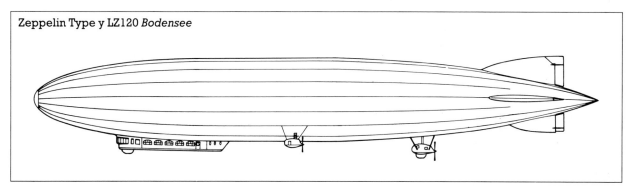

Zeppelin Type y LZ120 *Bodensee*

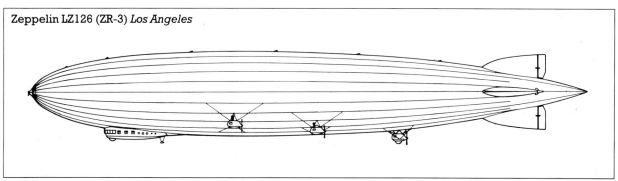

Zeppelin LZ126 (ZR-3) *Los Angeles*

Production

C/n	Name	First flight	Last flight	Hours flown	Disposal
LZ120	DI *Bodensee*	20.8.19	26.11.19	532+	Converted to LZ120A
LZ120A	DI *Bodensee*	early 1920	21.7.28		To Italy as *Esperia*, 3.6.21. Broken up July 1928
LZ121	DII *Nordstern*	8.6.21		25.8.26	To France as *Méditerranée.*, 18.7.21. Broken up Sept 1926

Bodensee enlarged to 22,550cu m capacity and *Nordstern* built to this capacity

years after that. Towards the end of her life she was used for various structural tests and was finally broken up in October 1939.

This long life was partly due to the way the Americans looked after her. Apart from being carefully and sensibly operated, she was given an extremely thorough overhaul in 1925. This included replacement of all the keel in particular, and a most comprehensive cleaning and protective varnishing of the whole of the rest of the structure. This had previously been completely unprotected against corrosion and was deteriorating rapidly. The ship was refilled with helium in March 1926.

Zeppelin LZ120 (Type y) *Bodensee*

Manufacturer: Luftschiffbau Zeppelin GmbH
Built at Friedrichshafen
Number built: two
Chief designer: L Dürr
Main structural material: duralumin
Design began: October 1918
First flight of type: 20 August, 1919
Powerplant: four 245hp Maybach Mb IVa six-cylinder inline engines
Gas capacity (100 per cent inflation): 20,000cu m, later 22,550cu m
Overall length: 120.8m, later 130.8m
Maximum diameter: 18.7m
Spacing of main frames: 10.0m
Fineness ratio: 6.46
Number of gas cells: 12, later 13
Empty weight: 13,200kg
Typical gross lift: 23,300kg (1.16kg/cu m)
Typical disposable load: 10,000kg
Maximum fuel: 2,400kg

Crew: 16
Passengers: 21
Maximum speed: 36.8m/s (82.3 mph)
Maximum range: 1,700km at speed of 26.4 m/s (59mph)
Static ceiling: 1,900m

Zeppelin LZ126 (ZR-3) *Los Angeles*

Manufacturer: Luftschiffbau Zeppelin GmbH
Built at Friedrichshafen
Number built: one
Chief designer: L Dürr
Main structural material: duralumin
Design began: July 1922
First flight: 27 August, 1924
Powerplant: five 400hp Maybach VL1 twelve-cylinder vee engines
Gas capacity (100 per cent inflation): 70,000cu m
Overall length: 200.0m
Maximum diameter: 31.9m
Spacing of main frames: 15.0m
Fineness ratio: 6.27
Number of gas cells: 13
Number of main longitudinals: 24
Empty weight: 42,200kg
Typical gross lift: 81,300kg (hydrogen) (1.16kg/cu m), 75,600kg (helium) (1.079kg/cu m)
Typical disposable load: 39,100kg
Maximum fuel: 17,100kg
Crew: 28
Passengers: 20
Maximum speed: 32.7m/s (73.14 mph)
Maximum range: 12,500km at speed of 27.8m/s (62.18mph)
Cost: US$863,332

LZ126 made her last flight on 30 June, 1932, after a total of 4,181¼ flying hours and 331 flights. She was not broken up until October 1939 being used for mooring and other experiments

Sheds and Mooring Masts for Rigid Airships

During her long career, *Los Angeles* was employed mainly for training although she made quite a few long-distance trips, took part in trial exercises with the fleet and was used extensively for experimental purposes. She was especially valuable in developing mooring and ground-handling techniques and equipment. This history has already made clear the major problems of handling rigid airships on and near the ground. The Germans have sometimes been accused of paying insufficient attention to this aspect of rigid airship operations. The criticism is not justified. The Germans had far more experience of flying rigids than all other countries taken together and probably did about 80 per cent of all rigid airship flying. While gaining this experience the Germans came to the conclusion that the best way to handle rigids on the ground was to use handling parties combined with special ground trolleys running on rails leading into fixed hangars. These were aligned as far as possible with the prevailing wind. They did try rotating-hangars on land, following the idea of Count Zeppelin's original floating sheds, but abandoned these because of their very high cost. (*See* Note 20) They were also vulnerable to snow and ice.

Alignment with the prevailing wind did not mean that the wind would not often be across a fixed shed's doors. To overcome this difficulty, the British made extensive use of giant windbreaks. These were supposed to provide shelter from the wind but, in practice generated unhelpful turbulence. Their use was finally abandoned.

View looking approximately northeast showing the three Friedrichshafen Zeppelin sheds in 1919. (Luftschiffbau Zeppelin)

Sheds for rigid airships were enormous structures – among the largest, cathedral-like buildings erected by man. The largest were up to 350m (1,150ft) long and 60m (200ft) high. The first purpose-designed airship shed was the so-called 'Hangar Y', completed in 1879 at the French aeronautical research establishment at Chalais-Meudon near Paris. It was built for the Renard and Krebs pioneer pressure-airship, *La France* of 1884. The building, whose design is attributed to Gustav Eiffel (1832–1922), still stands as a memorial to the first fully-controllable airship.

It was Count Zeppelin who first tackled the problem of the especially large sheds required for rigid airships which were usually themselves so much larger than contemporary pressure-airships. Zeppelin sited his first sheds at Manzell, 8km (5 miles) west of Friedrichshafen. The first floated on Lake Constance and was moored at one end only, so that the end-doors always faced exactly down-wind thus reducing the problems of exit and entry. Zeppelin's second shed was built on piles over the water, also at Manzell, and was intended for con-

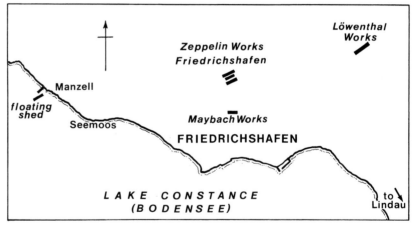

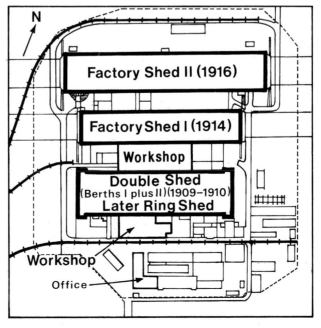

Zeppelin's first floating shed under construction at Manzell.

Zeppelin's second floating shed under construction at Manzell.

struction purposes only, particularly after a third shed – paid for by the Government – had been completed. The third shed also floated on the Lake, an arrangement which was not, however, repeated. All subsequent rigid airship construction sheds were built on land in Germany. Vickers in England copied Zeppelin's second shed, erecting HMA No.1 in a hangar, on piles, over Cavendish Dock.

The British spent a great deal of time and effort developing high mooring masts which had originally been suggested in Germany before 1910. *Mayfly* had been successfully moored, for three days, to a short mast in Cavendish Dock, when she was first brought out of her hangar in 1911, and a small pressure-airship, *Beta*, was moored to a mast at Farnborough in 1912. It was not until 1919 that the first, not very successful, experiments were made in mooring a rigid, No.23, to a high mast at Pulham; this was 120ft (36.5m) high. In 1921, further trials were made with R33 and R36, using a new type of masthead designed by Major G H Scott and the Royal Airship Works. These trials were more successful and the high mast (200ft; 60m high) was adopted for the 1924 British rigid airship programme.

The Germans, on the other hand, were never seriously attracted to high masts and the British soon found that they had major disadvantages. The most serious of these was that the ship had to be continuously 'flown' while at the mast. That is to say, all the problems of maintaining the ship in static and dynamic equilibrium continued while she was moored to a high mast, with the added complication introduced by the fact that the ship was anchored by her nose and was, therefore, subjected to additional large forces at that point. This was particularly critical in conditions of high or rapidly changing winds, changes in temperature or in a heavy precipitation. In addition there still remained the problem of handling when getting the ship into and out of her hangar, although – at least in theory – this needed to be done less frequently if a mast were also available. The Germans, for their part, usually preferred to put their ships in a shed.

The United States initially adopted the high mast from the British, and *Los Angeles* accordingly spent much time moored to, and on tests with, masts at Lakehurst and elsewhere, including one specially fitted to *USS Patoka*, a ship of the US Navy. An airship mast was even built on the top of a skyscraper (the Empire State Building) in New York City. During this period, on 25 August, 1927, *Los Angeles* had one spectacular and alarming experience when a sudden change of wind, combined with a particular static lift condition, made her do a sudden 'nose stand' on the Lakehurst mast. For a brief moment, the 200 metre-long (656ft 2in) airship stood absolutely vertical, anchored by her nose to the top of the mast. It says much for

her structural integrity that she suffered no serious damage.

The Americans eventually became disenchanted with high masts and stopped using them. *Los Angeles* played a major part in the development of new ground-handling equipment which represented a major step forward. The most important element of this was the travelling mast to which an airship could be moored

Vickers' shed at Walney Island photographed on 19 July, 1916.

The Zeppelin shed at Frankfurt-am-Main in 1912.
(Luftschiffbau Zeppelin)

A typical German wartime airship base – Borkum.

The rotating double shed at Nordholz.
(Pritchard collection)

Royal Airship Works and aerodrome, Cardington.

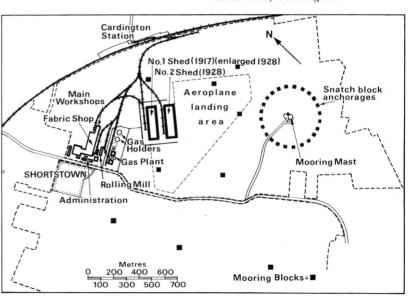

while the gondolas were close to, or in contact with, the ground. This type of mast could be used for mooring in the open when desired, but had the great advantage that, helped by other ground-handling devices, similar to those developed by the Germans, it could also tow an airship into and out of her shed.

In mid-1930, *Los Angeles* was taken into the hangar at Lakehurst, using the newly-developed equipment, with a ground-handling party of only about sixty men, while more than 200 other members of the normal handling party stood by. But, even with these new facilities, *Hindenburg* –

The Cardington mooring mast.

one of the last two rigids built — still required a normal ground-handling party of 230 men for her arrivals at and departures from Lakehurst while operating a scheduled service across the Atlantic in 1936–37. Without the new equipment, larger numbers had normally been required in the past to handle much smaller rigids on the ground.

For mooring out, the stub mast could be positioned away from all obstructions in the centre of a circular railway track on which a specially-designed car could travel and to which the airship's tail was attached by an appropriate structure. This so-called 'stern beam' would also allow the airship to be forced against the pressure of a cross-wind to align it with the shed's axis before it was towed inside by the travelling mast.

Among other experimental work undertaken by *Los Angeles* was the launching and hooking-on of aeroplanes while in flight. Although aeroplanes had been launched from rigids in Germany and the United Kingdom during the First World War, the first

Fixed short mooring mast at Staaken, Berlin, with LZ127 Graf Zeppelin.
(Lufthansa)

LZ127 moored to a German mobile mast.
(Lufthansa)

hook-on of an aeroplane to an airship (the US Army pressure-airship, TC-3) was made on 15 December, 1924, by First Lieut C V Finter in a Sperry Messenger. The first hook-on to a rigid (R33) was made on 15 October, 1925, by Sqn Ldr R A de Haga Haig, RAF, in a de Havilland D.H.53 ultra-light aeroplane. These were comparatively limited tests: *Los Angeles* was used for an extensive programme

of trials in the operation of aeroplanes from a rigid to prove its feasibility before this capability was built into the United States rigids, *Akron* and *Macon*. The first tests on *Los Angeles* were made by Lieut A W Gorton, USN, in a Vought UO-1 on 3 July, 1929. The former German fighter ace of the First World War, Ernst Udet, flying a Focke-Wulf Fw 44 Stieglitz trainer, made some hook-ons to and re-

The Goodyear-Zeppelin Airdock at Akron, Ohio.

leases from *Hindenburg* on 11 March, 1937.

Major features of rigid airship programmes were the enormous sheds required for the manufacture and operation of these vulnerable aircraft. Twenty-one construction bases were involved in the manufacture of 163 rigid

Rigid-Airship Assembly Sheds in Friedrichshafen Area

Shed	Type of Shed	Shed Dimensions; length, width, height (m)	Shed Started	Shed Completed	Shed Dismantled	First/last Airship built
Manzell (Old Shed I)	Floating shed (wood)	150 × 16 × 16	April 1899	June 1899	Nov 1900	LZ1 only
Manzell (Old Shed II)	Fixed single shed (wood)	140 × 26 × 25	June 1904	Jan 1905	Oct 1906	LZ2/LZ3
Manzell (Reichshalle)	Floating shed (steel)	150 × 25 × 23	March 1907	Sept 1907	1910	LZ4/LZ5
Friedrichshafen (Tent Hangar)	Single shed (wood & canvas)	141 × 20 × 19	April 1909	May 1909	July 1912	Storage
Ring Shed (Berth I)	Double shed (steel)	176 × 46 × 25	Jan 1909	Oct 1909	April 1929	LZ6/LZ39
Ring Shed (Berth II)	Double shed (steel)	176 × 46 × 25	Jan 1909	Feb 1910	April 1929	LZ10/LZ36
Factory Shed I	Single shed (steel)	192 × 32 × 28	Aug 1914	Nov 1914	1929	LZ38/LZ112
Factory Shed II	Single shed (steel)	232 × 35 × 28	July 1915	June 1916	1944	LZ80/LZ127
New Construction Shed	Single shed (steel)	250 × 50 × 46	1930	1932	1978	LZ129/LZ130
Friedrichshafen (moved from Löwenthal)	Single shed (steel)	270 × 46 × 49	1943	1943	1978	–
Löwenthal I	Single shed (steel)	232 × 35 × 28	Jan 1915	April 1915	1928	LZ41/LZ111
Löwenthal II (moved to Friedrichshafen)	Single shed (steel)	270 × 46 × 49	Jan 1931	Sept 1931	1943	–

Rigid-Airship Assembly Sheds outside Friedrichshafen Area

Germany

Shed	Length (m)	Width (m)	Height (m)	Started	Completed	First/Last Airship built)
Frankfurt (Rebstock)	160	30	25	1910	1911	LZ26 only
Potsdam (Wildpark)	165	30	55	1.1914	8.1914	LZ27/LZ73
Berlin (Staaken)						
North Shed	240	40	35	6.1915	4.1916	LZ77/LZ104
South Shed	240	40	35	6.1915	4.1916	
Mannheim (Rheinau)	137	26	25	1909	12.1909	S.L.1/S.L.22
Mannheim (Sandhofen)	184	35	28	–	1914	S.L.4 only
Berlin (Zeesen)	240	38	35	10.1915	4.1916	S.L.12/ S.L.21
Leipzig (Mockau)	184	60	39	1912	3.1915	S.L.6/S.L.18
Darmstadt	184	35	28	–	1914	S.L.5 only

Note: Schwarz No.2 was built at Berlin-Tempelhof but no shed details known

United Kingdom

Shed	Length (m)	Width (m)	Height (m)	Started	Completed	First/Last Airship built)
Barrow (Cavendish Dock)	161	65	29	11.1909	6.1910	No.1 only
Barrow (Walney Island)	164	45	33	1.1914	12.1914	No.9/R80
Glasgow (Inchinnan)	213	46.5	46.5	1.1916	7.1916	No.24/R36
Selby (Barlow)	213	46	30.5	–	1917	No.25/R33
Bedford (Cardington)						
Shed I	248	84	55	8.1916	4.1917	R31/R38
Shed II	248	84	55	5.1927	–	R101 only
Goole (Howden)	229	46	40	–	12.1916	R100 only

United States of America

Shed	Length (m)	Width (m)	Height (m)	Started	Completed	First/Last Airship built)
Lakehurst, New Jersey	278	85	59	10.1919	2.1922	ZR-1 only
Akron, Ohio	358	99	55	1929	1930	ZRS4/ZRS5
Grosse Ile, Detroit, Michigan	55	37	27	1927	1960	ZMC-2

France

Shed	Length (m)	Width (m)	Height (m)	Started	Completed	First/Last Airship built)
Saint-Cyr, Paris	160	25	24	9.1909	3.1911	Spiess only

Russia

Shed	Length (m)	Width (m)	Height (m)	Started	Completed	First/Last Airship built)
St Petersburg (Volhkov)	50	15	–	1892	9.1893	Schwarz No1. only

British 1924 Airship Programme – R100 and R101

airships in four countries: Germany, the United Kingdom, France and the United States. (*See* Note 21).

LZ127 taking on fuel and gas at Mines Field, Los Angeles, during its round-the-world flight in 1929.

An Imperial Conference, held in London in July 1921, discussed among other things the possibility of airship services to link different parts of the British Empire including a route to India and Australia. The view was still widely held at this time that the airship was superior to the aeroplane for long-distance services, particularly over water. Although the aeroplane was already significantly faster than the airship, it was still a short-range vehicle. Not until the late 1930s did aeroplanes begin to have enough range for regular intercontinental operations. No decision was reached at the Imperial Conference but in March 1922 Cdr Dennistoun Burney put forward proposals in association with Vickers and Shell for an Imperial Airship Scheme to take over all British airship assets and to operate Empire airship services. This was accepted in principle by the Government in mid-1923. Also in 1923 an alternative Anglo-German Airship Scheme was mooted but came to nothing. In December that year, the Airship Guarantee Company was formed with the backing of Vickers.

In May 1924, the Labour Government under Ramsay MacDonald, which had come to power in January, rejected the Burney scheme and adopted, instead, a plan for a part-Government, part-private enterprise three-year programme. A contract was signed with the Burney-Vickers Group for the private enterprise part of the programme on 1 November, 1924, its airship to be delivered by September 1927. The Government part of the new scheme involved a paral-

The R101 after lengthening. It is seen moored to the Cardington mast.
(Flight)

The R101 in its original form.
(Flight)

lel development at the Royal Airship Works at Cardington. Thus, the 1924 airship programme provided for the development of a new large rigid, R101, to be Government-built at Cardington, and the parallel development of a competitive, private enterprise ship, R100, by the Airship Guarantee Company at the former airship operating base at Howden in Yorkshire, which was taken over for the purpose.

A Conservative Government returned to power late in 1924 and took over the programme; thus development of the two airships went forward in parallel. The Conservative Government fell in the spring of 1929. Lord Thomson, who had been Air Minister in the 1924 Labour Government, returned to the Air Ministry, and once again became the minister responsible for the two airships. His involvement was to play a fatal part in the final outcome of the programme.

The story of the 1924 Airship Programme is a classic example of conflicting loyalties and interests in an enterprise already beset by formidable technical problems. Among the different influences impinging on the R101 at Cardington were the following:

1. Public versus private enterprise.
2. Aeroplanes versus airships.
3. The RAF versus the other Services, particularly the Navy (over the RAF's survival as a separate Service).
4. The politicians versus the Civil Service.
5. The Royal Airship Works versus the Air Ministry (over control of the airship programme).
6. The Royal Airship Works versus Vickers (in competition for future work).
7. The Aeronautical Inspection Directorate (AID) versus the Department of Civil Aviation (over certification of civil aircraft).

There were also important extraneous factors, such as the political aspiration of Lord Thomson who, when made a peer, had added Cardington to his title. He also had ambitions to become Viceroy of India and clearly thought a dramatic flight to the sub-continent would strengthen his prospects. Unwisely, as it turned out, he committed himself to making the trip before Parliament reassembled after the summer recess.

The programme had called for both airships to be completed within three years. As things turned out, the time-scale slipped badly: R101, the Government airship, flew for the first time on 14 October, 1929, two years late. R100, the private enterprise ship, flew two months later still on 16 December.

Both ships were extremely large, having roughly double the capacity of the *Graf Zeppelin*'s lifting cells (*See* page 163). It had been intended that the British airships would fly two years before the Zeppelin, in 1927. In the event, they took so long to develop that they flew

The R101, in original form, on the Cardington mast
(Vickers)

more than a year after the German ship.

R101 was designed by a team at Cardington headed by Vincent C Richmond. She had a capacity of 4,998,501cu ft (141,542cu m) and was 731ft 3in (222.88m) long with a maximum diameter of 131ft 6in (40m). Of good streamlined shape, she differed more from Zeppelin practice than any rigid built before or since. Her structure was mainly of steel (a 60 per cent content) and featured triangular longitudinal members of stainless steel strip and bracing pieces of duralumin. Components were manufactured by Boulton & Paul of Norwich. Major features of the design were the deep main frames which had no wire bracing and the so-called parachute wiring designed by F M Rope which restrained the sixteen gas cells. There were fifteen main and fifteen intermediate longitudinals. R101 was the only rigid built in which the spacing of the main frames was different in every bay. This was done to reduce the variations in gas cell capacity resulting from the marked changes in cross-section along the length.

Dining saloon in R101, photographed in October 1929. (Popperfoto)

The wreckage of R101 on the hillside near Beauvais on Sunday morning 5 October, 1930. (Science Museum)

R100 under construction at Howden. (Vickers)

Both ships were penalised by the sheer over-ambitiousness of the programme, but R101 in particular suffered from this. New, unproven ideas were to be incorporated which would provide a substantial technological advance. Inevitably, they also caused delays, shortfalls in performance and higher costs. Thus, both ships were originally intended to have seven 550hp engines running on a new Ricardo hydrogen-kerosene system which, in the event, proved unworkable.

Specially-developed Beardmore Tornado III diesel engines were substituted in R101 (there were five of them) but these turned out to be hopelessly heavy and gave a maximum power of only 585hp when 720hp was intended. Over-ambitious standards of accommodation and amenity for 100 passengers (originally) and unrealistic payload/range claims were further handicaps. Passenger accommodation arrangements were heavier than they need have been.

These factors contributed to the delays in the R101 programme. Additional causes were the lack of rigid airship experience of Richmond and most of his team and the very natural caution engendered by the report on the accident to R38 which had revealed inadequacies in previous design practices.

As completed and first flown, R101 did not approach her design targets. In fact, she fell so far short of them she could not achieve a worthwhile range even with a much reduced payload. This dilemma was resolved by lightening the ship, as far as possible, by letting out the gas cell wiring and, finally, by the classic method of inserting another bay which increased capacity to 5,509,753cu ft (156,020cu m). With these expedients, R101 was rashly judged ready to make a demonstration flight to India. As already mentioned, Lord Thomson had committed himself to the trip and felt morally unable to withdraw. After only one 17-hr test flight in her definitive form, R101 set out with Thomson and Sir Sefton Brancker, the Director of Civil Aviation, aboard. The passenger list also included a number of other senior civil aviation personalities, including R B B Colmore, the Director of Airship Development, and Richmond, the designer. They were all among the forty-

R100 dropping ballast. The elevators are up and the ship has right rudder.
(Vickers)

eight who lost their lives on 5 October, 1930, when the airship hit a hillside at Beauvais in northern France and burned.

The cause of the accident was never conclusively established. The official inquiry concluded that it was probably due to a large rent in the outer cover near the nose, causing collapse of one or more forward gas cells resulting in a major loss of gas. In an exhaustive analysis, Sir Peter Masefield concluded that the accident was due to a piloting error. However it seems quite possible that neither a material failure nor a misshandling of the controls was needed to cause an accident that dark, wet and windy night. Bucking a gusting 52mph (83km/hr) headwind and heavy with rain and loss of gas the R101 may simply have flown into the ridge as a result of a down-

draught or standing wave.

Technically, the private enterprise ship, R100, was superior to her competitor, as might have been expected with the design in the hands of Barnes Wallis who had had more experience of rigid airship design than any engineer outside Luftschiffbau Zeppelin. He was assisted by J E Temple and N S Norway (the author, Nevil Shute).

Sensibly, R100 was closer to Zeppelin practice than R101, the only differences being that there were no intermediate frames or longitudinals and that the longitudinal members of the triangular girders were made of tubes wound and riveted from duralumin strip. The lift wiring was also different, being helically wound from frame to frame. The main weakness in the design was that there were over-large unsup-

ported areas of outer cover. R100 also suffered the delays and some of the other penalties of her competitor, and for the same reasons.

Without the hydrogen-kerosene engines, and instead of the heavy diesels, R100 was powered by six 670hp conventional Rolls-Royce Condor IIIB petrol engines in three tractor/pusher engine-cars. By some curious twist of official reasoning, the petrol fuel was deemed to make her unacceptable for operation in the tropics because of the increased fire risk from petrol even though there were 5,156,000cu ft (146,000cu m) of highly inflammable hydrogen in her fifteen gas

A 1928 drawing by S W Clatworthy showing the accomodation aboard the R100
(The Sphere)

cells. For this reason, R100 was demonstrated on a flight to Canada and back, in July–August 1930, instead of on the United Kingdom–India–Australia route for which the programme had been launched originally. R100 was fast, 81mph (36.3m/s), and broadly met her guarantees, but it was clear that it was not possible to achieve with her what the protagonists of the 1924 programme had planned. After R101's accident, R100 was broken up and the British abandoned rigid airships.

Quite apart from the technical disappointments and inevitable failure of the 1924 programme, the entire episode illustrated the unfortunate consequences of excessive controversy, ill-directed competition and unbridled personal and partisan ambitions.

The lounge deck of R100 seen before much of the ship's outer covering was attached. (Science Museum)

R100 on the mast at St Hubert, Montreal, after its Atlantic crossing. (Vickers)

Royal Airship Works R101

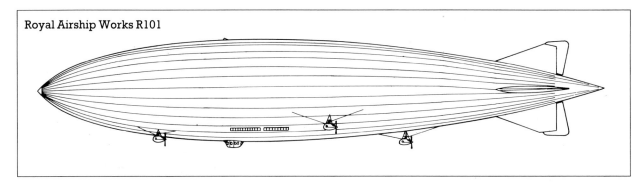

Airship Guarantee Company R100

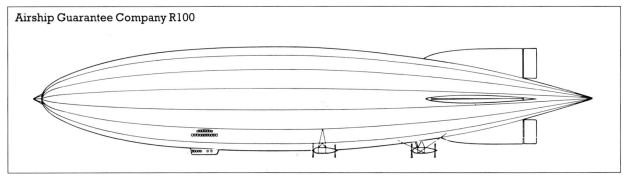

Production

C/n		First flight	Last flight	Hours flown	Disposal
R101	G-FAAW	14.10.29	28.6.30	102hr 56min	Lengthened
R101 (lengthened)	G-FAAW	1.10.30	5.10.30	24hr 24min	Wrecked near Beauvais 5.10.30

Royal Airship Works R101

Manufacturer: Royal Airship Works

Built at Cardington near Bedford

Number built: one

Chief designer: V C Richmond

Main structural material: steel and duralumin

Design began: November 1924

First flight: 14 October, 1929

Powerplant: five 585hp Beardmore Tornado III eight-cylinder inline diesels

Gas capacity (100 per cent inflation): 4,998,501cu ft (141,542cu m) (original), 5,509,093cu ft (156,000cu m) (lengthened)

Overall length: 719ft 9½in (219.19m) (original), 731ft 3in (222.88m) (lengthened)

Maximum diameter: 131ft 6in (40m)

Spacing of main frames: variable

Fineness ratio: 5.5

Number of gas cells: 16 (original), 17 (lengthened)

Number of main longitudinals: 15

Number of intermediate longitudinals: 15

Empty weight: 201,590lb (91,440 kg) (original), 235,189lb (106,680kg) (lengthened)

Typical gross lift: 340,129lb (154,280kg) (original), 374,874lb (170,040kg) (lengthened)

Typical disposable load: 62,840kg (original), 63,360kg (lengthened)

Maximum fuel: 65,036lb (29,500 kg) (79,366lb/36,000kg sometimes quoted)

Crew: 48

Passengers: 50

Maximum speed: 70mph (31.3m/s)

Maximum range: 5,345 miles (8,600km) at speed of 58mph (25.9m/s)

Cost: £527,000

Airship Guarantee Company R100

Manufacturer: Airship Guarantee Co Ltd

Built at Howden near Goole, Yorkshire

Number built: one

Chief designer: B N Wallis

Main structural material: duralumin

Design began: October 1924

First flight: 16 December, 1929

Powerplant: six 670hp Rolls-Royce Condor IIIB twelve-cylinder vee engines

Gas capacity (100 per cent inflation): 5,156cu ft (146,060cu m)

Overall length: 709ft (216.1m)

Maximum diameter: 133ft (40.53m)

Spacing of main frames: 40ft (12.2m)

Fineness ratio: 5.34

Number of gas cells: 15

Number of main longitudinals: 16

Empty weight: 235,012lb (106,600 kg)

Typical gross lift: 350,987lb (159,205 kg) (1.09kg/cu m)

Typical disposable load: 111,298kg

Maximum fuel: 77,382lb (35,100 kg)

Crew: 37

Passengers: 100

Maximum speed: 81mph (36.3m/s)

Maximum range: 6,338 miles (10,200 km) at speed of 68.6mph (30.7m/s)

Cost: £471,000

After a total of 296hr 57min flying time, R100 (G-FAAV) made its last flight on 16 August, 1930, and was broken up in November 1931

Most Famous Airship – LZ127 *Graf Zeppelin*

After the delivery of LZ126 in October 1924, Hugo Eckener realised that something would have to be done about financing a new airship if the Zeppelin works were to survive. His task was eased by the Locarno Treaty of 1925 which lifted all Allied restrictions on the building of airships in Germany. In the autumn of that year Eckener accordingly launched an appeal to the Ger-

Crew positions and passenger accommodation in the Graf Zeppelin.
(D Macpherson, courtesy The Sphere)

LZ127 Graf Zeppelin *with mooring lines suspended from the bow.*
(Lufthansa)

man public to subscribe to a fund (the Zeppelin-Eckener Spende), to pay for a new Zeppelin. Eckener and his colleagues toured the country lecturing on the possibilities and future of the rigid airship, and Eckener used all his considerable talents as a publicist to put the Zeppelin case before the general public and the authorities. This was not easy in a country still recovering from defeat but, by the end of 1926, over two million marks (£880,000) had been subscribed and to this amount the German Ministry of Transport added 1.1 million marks (£440,000) plus another 500,000 (£220,000) to cover test-flying and insurance. It is not clear where the remaining funds required to pay for LZ127's construction came from; partly, it is supposed, from further contributions to the Spende and partly from the German Government. The airship is reported to have cost a total of six million marks (£2.6 million).

Manufacture of the new Zeppelin was started in early 1927. On the nineteenth anniversary of the old Count's death, 8 July,

Graf Zeppelin *during a visit to Danzig.* (Science Museum)

Helpers ready to grab the Graf Zeppelin *when it landed at London Air Park, Hanworth, in August 1931.* (The Sphere)

1928, his daughter named the LZ127 *Graf Zeppelin* and the new ship made her first flight on 18 September – a 36hr endurance test. She was destined to become the most successful and the most famous airship ever built. During the following nine years she flew a total of 17,178 hours on 590 flights, an average utilisation of about 1,900 hours a year. This may seem a modest performance compared with modern transport aeroplanes which commonly average 3,000 or 4,000 hours a year and can remain in service for twenty years or more. (There are Douglas DC-3s in service today which were built forty-four years ago and which have flown up to 90,000 hours.) However, *Graf Zeppelin*'s performance was highly creditable for the time, comparing well with contemporary aeroplanes.

This airship was remarkable, not just for her distinguished career. She was also technically unique as the only rigid to operate on a gaseous fuel. The hull had a total capacity of 105,000cu m (3,708,043cu ft) but 30,000cu m (1,059,440cu ft) of this was

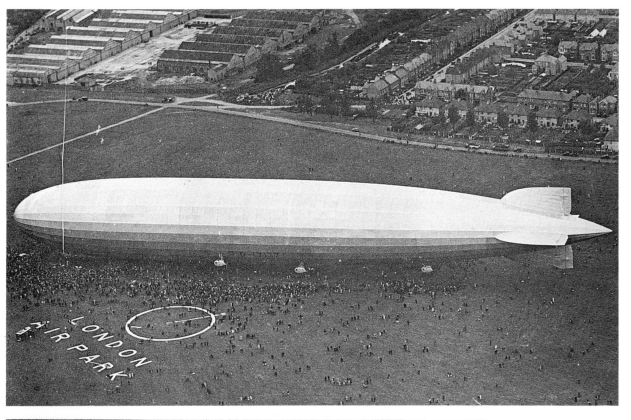

The Graf Zeppelin *at Hanworth.*
(Science Museum)

The control cabin of LZ127 with pitch control left and rudder control right.
(Lufthansa)

Part of Graf Zeppelin's *dining saloon.*
(Luftschiffbau Zeppelin)

LZ127 Graf Zeppelin *at Recife, Brazil.*
(Lufthansa)

filled with Blaugas (a fuel mixture of propylene, methane, acethane, acetylene, butylene and hydrogen) which was only about nine per cent heavier than air. Its consumption, therefore, had little effect on the ship's disposable lift. The Blaugas gaseous fuel was contained in separate gas cells in the lower part of the hull, with the hydrogen cells above. A triangular axial girder, instead of the

axial cable in LZ126, ran between the two types of cell and provided a corridor along the centre of the ship. The five engines, again in separate power-cars, were a developed 530hp version, known as the VL2, of the Maybachs fitted to the *Los Angeles.* Like the earlier engine, they were reversible. They could also operate on either petrol or Blaugas. The ship was 30.5m (100ft 0¾in) in diameter and had a 15m frame spacing with seventeen hydrogen cells. Her length of 236.6m (776ft 3in) and other dimensions were dictated by the size of the 1916 shed at Friedrichshafen in which she was built. Her structure was basically similar to that of her predecessor except that an improved type of duralumin was used (reported to be twenty per cent stronger). Passengers, 20–24 of them, were accommodated in a long gondola, integral with the control car and attached to the exterior of the hull.

Graf Zeppelin seems to have been faster (35.6m/s; 79.6mph) than *Los Angeles* (32.7m/s; 73.14mph), but after her first Atlantic crossing in October 1928,

Eckener went on record as saying that she was still not fast enough for a route such as the North Atlantic. Nevertheless, after several trial flights, *Graf Zeppelin* operated a regular service each summer season from 1932 to 1937 to South America. (*See* Appendices 3 and 8)

After her first North Atlantic return flight which turned out to be a highly profitable enterprise, paid for by revenue earned from press concessions, a special airmail and a few passengers at premium fares, *Graf Zeppelin* was used for a series of other special flights planned by Eckener to pay for themselves and, at the same time, give maximum publicity to rigid airships. These flights included a number to South America (before the scheduled service was started), flights around Spain and to other parts of Europe, one to the Middle East, an extended cruise in the Arctic, and a trip round the world with stops at Tokyo, Los Angeles and Lakehurst.

Altogether, *Graf Zeppelin* became a familiar sight around the world in the later 1920s and early 1930s, either in the headlines or actually flying overhead. She was withdrawn from service in June 1937 after the *Hindenburg* disaster had convinced the Zeppelin company that scheduled passenger services should not continue without non-inflammable helium. The *Graf Zeppelin* was not designed for the safer gas, even if it had been available to Germany, which it was not. (Helium could only be extracted from natural gas in the United States, and the Americans for strategic reasons were not prepared to export it.)

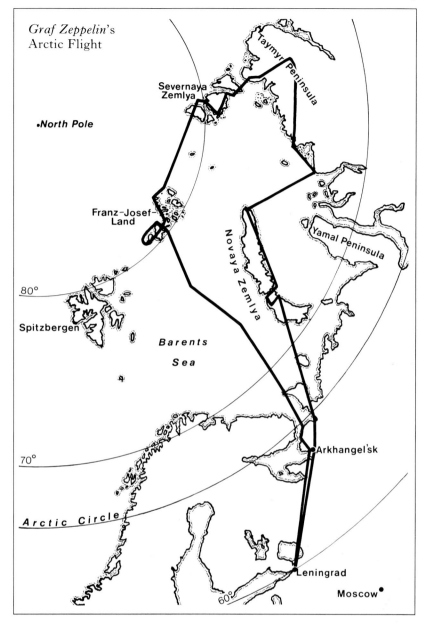

Graf Zeppelin's Arctic Flight

Therefore *Graf Zeppelin* was honourably retired and was finally broken up in May 1940 in the operating hangar at Frankfurt-am-Main which had been used by *Hindenburg* for the North Atlantic service. *Graf Zeppelin*, which was registered D-LZ127 and operated with the radio call sign D-ENNE, flew well over a million miles and made 144 ocean crossings.

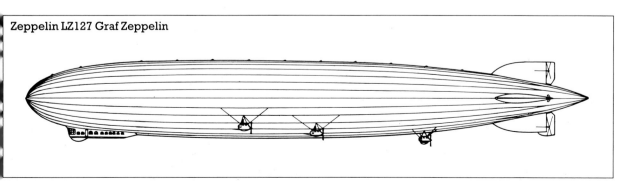

Zeppelin LZ127 Graf Zeppelin

Graf Zeppelin's Round-the-World Flight

Maximum speed: 35.6m/s (79.6 mph)

Maximum range: 10,000km at speed of 32.5m/s (72.7mph)

Cost: DM6,000,000

LZ127 made her last flight on 19 June, 1937, after accumulating a total of 17,178 flying hours. She was broken up in May 1940

Knud Eckener, son of the famous Zeppelin commander, climbing from an engine car of Graf Zeppelin *when a fuel tank had to be repaired off Madeira in October 1928 on the ship's first Atlantic crossing.* (The Sphere)

Zeppelin LZ127 *Graf Zeppelin*

Manufacturer: Luftschiffbau Zeppelin GmbH

Built at Friedrichshafen

Number built: one

Chief designer: L Dürr

Main structural material: duralumin

Design began: January 1927

First flight : 18 September, 1928

Powerplant: five 530hp Maybach VL2 twelve-cylinder vee engines

Gas capacity (100 per cent inflation): 75,000cu m (hydrogen) and 30,000cu m (Blaugas)

Overall length: 236.6m

Maximum diameter: 30.5m

Spacing of main frames: 15.0m

Fineness ratio: 7.25

Number of gas cells: 16

Number of main longitudinals: 17

Number of intermediate longitudinals: 11

Empty weight: 67,100kg

Typical gross lift: 87,000kg (1.16kg/cu m)

Typical disposable load: 19,900kg

Maximum fuel: 8,000kg (petrol) and 30,000cu m (Blaugas)

Crew: 36

Passengers: 20

Last American Rigids – *Akron* and *Macon*

After R101's accident in October 1930, R100 was scrapped and British official interest in airships ended. Meanwhile, the Americans were also embarking on a final fling with large rigid airships. In 1923, following the American order for LZ126, the Goodyear Company entered into negotiations with Luftschiffbau Zeppelin to acquire design information on rigid airships that would enable it to develop new large rigids to meet the requirements of the United States Government. An agreement was finalised in the autumn of 1923 whereby a team of Zeppelin design engineers, under Dr Karl Arnstein, went to the United States to work for a new joint American-German company which was named the Goodyear-Zeppelin Corporation. Arnstein had been chief designer at Zeppelin under Dürr, from 1915, and in this capacity had been responsible for the design of seventy Zeppelins. Negotiations with the United States Government during the later 1920s, including a design competition, led to a contract being signed on 6 October, 1928, for the development by Goodyear-Zeppelin of two new 6,850,000cu ft (193,970cu m) rigids for the Navy. These ships were to be built in a large new construction hangar specially erected in Akron, Ohio, in 1929.

In October 1928 work began on the first of the two ships, ZRS4, later named *Akron*. She was completed within three years and was first flown on 25 September 1931, about a year after termination of the British airship programme.

ZRS4 benefitted enormously from her Zeppelin background. Combined with the fact that she was designed in the sure knowledge that she would be inflated with helium, this made possible a number of radical innovations in design which, unlike some of those tried in the British ships, were firmly based on an adequate background of overall rigid airship design experience.

Perhaps the most important of these was the installation of the eight 570hp German Maybach VL2 engines within the hull structure and the use of swivell-

The US Navy's ZRS4 USS Akron.
(US Navy)

The first gas cell of Akron *being tested in the airship's first section of framework on 26 June, 1930. The balloon on the right was used by Goodyear-Zeppelin pilot Ward T Van Orman to win several races for the James Gordan Bennet cup.*

ing propellers which were remotely driven by shafts. By enclosing the engines within the hull, Arnstein was able to save weight and cut external excrescences to a minimum; they were reduced in effect to a small control-car, to the propeller mountings and to the semi-cantilever tail surfaces. The Zeppelin engineers had studied internal engine installations, as well as supercharged engines and variable-pitch propellers, towards the end of the First World War but had not adopted them then because of weight penalties associated with

fire precautions, essential if engines were to be permitted within a hull filled with hydrogen. Later, Zeppelin did not introduce internal engines in *Hindenburg* or *Graf Zeppelin II*, even though both these ships were intended to use helium, because there was always some doubt about the availability of the gas. Without helium, had these ships had internal engines, major re-design and re-construction would have been necessary, since the Americans did, in the event, refuse to supply the gas.

Like R101, the two big American ships had deep main frames without wire bracing, the gas cells being restrained in the plane of the frames by 'elastic' bulkheads. These ships therefore represented a radical departure by Arnstein and his colleagues from classic Zeppelin practice. There were twelve gas cells made of cot-

ton with a gelatine-latex elastomer. *Akron* had half her cells and *Macon* all of hers in the new material. The eleven main frames were spaced 74ft (22.5m) apart over a major part of the length with shorter bays at bow and stern. There were three intermediate frames in each bay. No less than thirty-six longitudinals gave the cotton cloth outer cover a good shape. Finally, the fins were attached to two main frames at the tail without the carried-through cruciform girder previously used.

Use of swivelling propellers was one of the most interesting and, perhaps, the most unexpected of the American innovations. As already recorded, the British tried them on their earliest rigids and had then abandoned them. Zeppelin never used them at any time, although they must obviously have studied them. Presumably their adoption for the new American ships indicates that the United States' experience with *Shenandoah* and *Los Angeles* had persuaded the US Navy that swivelling propellers could offer something of their undoubted theoretical advantages. This must have been confirmed by early flying experience with ZRS4, otherwise this

ZRS5 USS Macon *being moored to a short mast.*
(Goodyear-Zeppelin)

feature would not have been repeated in her sister-ship, ZRS5, later named *Macon*, first flown on 21 April, 1933, less than three weeks after her sister-ship was lost.

These last two United States rigids each survived in service for less than two years. *Akron* was lost on 4 April, 1933, in weather conditions apparently not greatly different from those which caused the loss of a number of earlier rigids. She was driven uncontrollably into a rough sea in stormy weather and all but three of her crew of seventy-six lost

their lives. *Macon* suffered structural failure on 12 February, 1935, and also came down in the open sea but, in her case, only two lives were lost. The cause of the accident was apparently a design defect in the tail unit, a surprising cause when her Zeppelin background of good structural integrity is remembered.

Akron and *Macon* were the fastest rigids ever built (84mph; 37.6m/s) and were intended to operate with the fleet in the open Atlantic and Pacific. They did, in fact, take part, with limited suc-

A Curtiss F9C-2 Sparrowhawk about to hook on to the USS Macon. *Eight Sparrowhawks were built for these experiments and one is now on display at the National Air and Space Museum in Washington.*
(US National Archives)

Dr Karl Arnstein joined Luftschiffbau Zeppelin in 1915, emigrated to the United States in 1924 and was responsible for the design of Akron *and* Macon.
(Goodyear)

cess, in a number of exercises during their short careers.

A major new tactical concept was involved in the use of these two ships. They were employed as aircraft carriers, as had first been suggested by H G Wells in his 1907 novel, *The War in the Air*. For this purpose they had small hangars within their hulls, capable of housing three or four fighter aircraft each. The equipment and techniques to make this possible derived from the earlier tests with *Los Angeles* and proved to be entirely satisfactory. The aeroplanes were used primarily for reconnaissance but could also have made dive-bombing attacks on surface forces. They would, if necessary have been able to defend their parent ship against air attack.

In the end, these interesting tactical possibilities never came to anything because of the loss of both airships. They were, in any case, overtaken by events. Even had *Akron* and *Macon* survived, it is unlikely that they would have been of any use in the Second World War in the role proposed. The capabilities of carrier-based and long-range shore-based aeroplanes increased so enormously as the war progressed that large rigid airships, even with a few defensive fighters, could not have long survived anywhere near a hostile surface aircraft carrier or within reach of long-range shore-based aeroplanes. Small pressure-airships were a more economical solution to the inshore patrol requirements for the North Ameri-

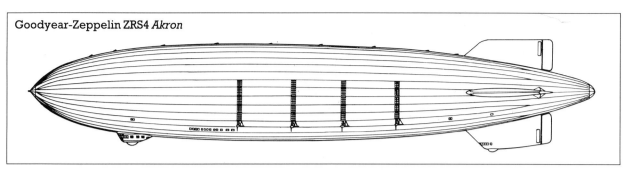

Goodyear-Zeppelin ZRS4 *Akron*

can continent and there was therefore no suggestion that further rigids should be built for the latter purpose.

Thus the later 1930s saw the majestic rigid finally pass from the scene. For military as for peaceful purposes her day was done. As Count Zeppelin had foreseen in 1917, the aeroplane controlled the air.

A footnote to the story of *Macon* was added in the first half of 1990 when US Navy scientists in a small deep-diving submarine located the wreck of the airship at a depth of about 1,500ft off Point Sur about 100 miles south of San Francisco. At least two of the *Macon*'s four fighter aeroplanes were found to be intact.

Goodyear-Zeppelin ZRS4 *Akron*

Manufacturer: Goodyear-Zeppelin Corporation

Built at Akron, Ohio

Number built: two

Chief designer: K Arnstein

Main structural material: duralumin

Design began: October 1928

First flight of type: 25 September, 1931

Powerplant: eight 570hp Maybach VL2 twelve-cylinder vee engines

Gas capacity (100 per cent inflation): 6,850,000cu ft (193,970cu m)

Overall length: 785ft (239.3m)

Maximum diameter: 132ft 11in (40.5m)

Spacing of main frames: 74ft (22.5m)

Fineness ratio: 5.9

Number of gas cells: 12

Number of main longitudinals: 36

Number of main frames: 11

Empty weight: 244,713lb (111,000kg)

Typical gross lift: 461,207lb (209,200kg) (helium) (1.079kg/cu m)

Admiral William A Moffett USN, played a major role in United States airship development, was three times Chief of the Bureau of Aeronautics, and was killed in the Akron *crash.*
(Goodyear)

Typical disposable load: 98,200kg

Maximum fuel: 124,010lb (56,250kg)

Crew: 60

Maximum speed: 84mph (37.6m/s)

Vice Admiral Charles E Rosendahl USN (1892–1977), one of the great names in United States airship history. As Lieut Cmdr, Rosendahl was the senior officer on the Shenandoah *when its bow section free ballooned for about 2hr after the ship crashed. He was commander of the* Los Angeles *and was commander at Lakehurst on the night the* Hindenburg *was destroyed.*
(Goodyear)

Maximum range: 8,990–11,000km at speed of 53.23mph (23.8m/s)

Cost: US$5,375,000 (ZRS4), US$2,450,000 (ZRS5)

Production

C/n	First flight	Last flight	Hours flown	Disposal
ZRS4 *Akron*	25.9.31	4.4.33	1,695	Wrecked at sea
ZRS5 *Macon*	21.4.33	12.2.35	1,798	Wrecked at sea: structural failure

The Last Zeppelins – LZ129 *Hindenburg* and LZ130 *Graf Zeppelin II*

Not long after the completion of the original *Graf Zeppelin* in September 1928, Luftschiffbau Zeppelin started work on a second airship to supplement her in scheduled service on whichever routes were finally selected as the most suitable. The new ship, named LZ128, was to have had a capacity of 155,000cu m (5,473,778cu ft) with a diameter

of 39m (127ft 11½in) and a length of 232m (761ft). Eight 500hp Maybach VL2 engines in four gondolas were to have run on Blaugas. They would have given a speed of 35.8m/s (80mph). Accommodation was to have been provided for thirty to thirty-four passengers in two groups of cabins within the hull.

After the disaster to the British rigid R101 at Beauvais on 5 October, 1930, the Germans decided that their new ship must be inflated with helium and should have diesel engines running on heavy oil which is less inflammable than petrol. Assembly of LZ128 was delayed, awaiting completion of a new, larger assembly hangar which was under construction at Friedrichshafen in 1930–31. (The old 1916 shed, used for LZ127, was too small for LZ128). A new airship design, LZ129, was therefore decided upon in 1931 and construction of this revised ship began in the

LZ129 Hindenburg *bearing the registration D-LZ129 and the Olympic Games symbol – they were held in Berlin.*
(Luftschiffbau Zeppelin)

new building as soon as it was completed. The new shed had been paid for, partly by the State of Württemberg and partly by the German Government which is also thought to have put up the DM9 million (£3.4 million) which the ship herself cost.

LZ129 was designed initially for helium in the hope that the United States, which had a complete monopoly of the gas at the time, would make it available. In the event they refused to supply it, believing – probably justifiably – that it was of strategic value and could be used for military purposes. LZ129 had, therefore, to revert to hydrogen, with fatal results, the design being adapted to this lifting agent from an early

View from the rear of LZ129 under construction. Part of the tailplane spar can be seen on the right, the tail cone stands vertically on the left, with work in progress on the rudder post in the foreground. With the complexity of the structure, the close attention being shown to the drawings is not surprising. (Luftschiffbau Zeppelin)

Phot.: Luftschiffbau Zeppelin.

stage. New diesel engines, the 1,200hp Maybach L-O-F6 (which were later known as the Daimler-Benz DB 602), were specially developed for the ship and, in due course, proved highly successful, offering a significant saving in fuel weight and cost.

Although substantially larger, originally to allow for the lower lifting power of helium, LZ129 inherited many features from LZ128. Diameter was increased to 41.2m (135ft 2in) and length to 245m (803ft 9½in), raising the capacity to 200,000cu m (7,062,900cu ft), but the main frame spacing remained at 15m, divided by two intermediate frames as it had been ever since the war. The usual triangular girders had corner booms of omega-section instead of the previous open channels. The hull was of good streamlined shape, un-marred by the passenger accommodation (now for fifty) which was kept within the hull. A small

The size of LZ129 is apparent in this view of the ship under construction. (Luftschiffbau Zeppelin)

Dining saloon of LZ129. Dr Hugo Eckener is indicated by the arrow. (Popperfoto)

control car, four engine-gondolas and the cruciform tail unit were the only major external excrescences. The appearance of the hull was improved by the use of a larger number of longitudinals than in previous Zeppelins, a change previously introduced by Goodyear-Zeppelin in the last American rigids. LZ129 had no less than thirty-six main and intermediate longitudinals compared with twenty-eight in *Graf Zeppelin*. Other features included a central corridor keel and two side corridors level with the engine-cars. There was also a corridor in the axial girder which passed through the centre of the gas cells. The sixteen cells were made of a new material, a gelatin-oid film, which was claimed to be superior to skinned fabric.

Hindenburg, as LZ129* was named, when she made her first flight on 4 March, 1936, proved to be fast: 37.5m/s (83.88mph). Filled with hydrogen, she had a formidable range: 14,000km (8,700 miles) in still air with 19,000kg (41,888lb) of payload and 10,000kg (22,046lb) of ballast. In 1936 she operated successfully on both the South Atlantic route, alongside the old *Graf Zeppelin*, and on the North Atlantic. She had only just resumed the service for the 1937 season when she was destroyed in a disastrous hydrogen fire while

* It was registered D-LZ129 and used radio call sign D-EKKA

landing at Lakehurst on 6 May, 1937. This was dramatically filmed by a news-reel camerman who happened to be reporting on her arrival.

There has been much speculation about the cause of the fire which was probably due to a static discharge. However, speculation is pointless. There was already ample evidence, from 40 years of operations with rigids, that hydrogen was too dangerous to be trusted. If *Hindenburg* and her almost identical sister-ship,

LZ129 Hindenburg *leaving the shed at Frankfurt-am-Main. The site was within the boundaries of the present airport.*
(Lufthansa)

GAS BAG
AWAY LAT
TO SHOW
AIR SHA

LENGTH OF
ONE
GAS BAG

ENGINE
NACELLE

DO
I
HU

WIRE MESH
BETWEEN
GAS BAGS &
OUTER ENVELOPE

RUDDER

DOOR
IN
HULL

CAT-WALK
LEADING FROM
KEEL CAT-WALK
TO NACELLE

FUEL &
WATER
TANKS

ELEVATOR

FUEL &
WATER
TANKS

ENGINE
NACELLE

ENGINE
NACELLE

CAT-WALK TO
NACELLE
FROM KEEL
CAT-WALK

MAIN
LOWER
CAT-WALK

RUDDER

CREW'S
SLEEPING
QUARTERS

FIN

SWIVELLING
TAIL WHEEL

Partly sectioned drawing of the LZ129/130 type with perspective of accommodation
(Max Millar courtesy of Flight)

MILLAR
RIEDRICHSHAFEN.

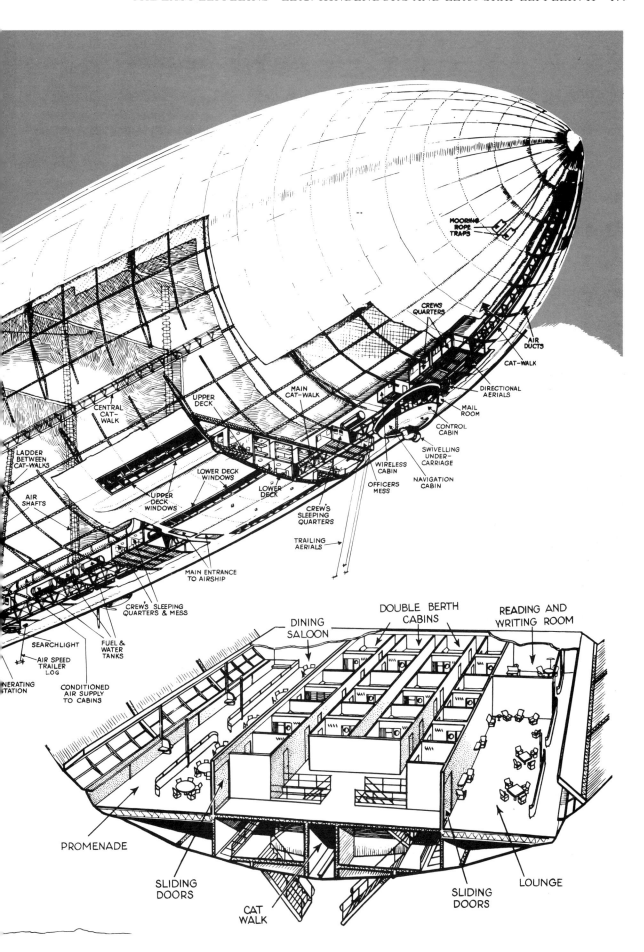

MOORING ROPE TRAPS

CREWS QUARTERS

AIR DUCTS

CAT-WALK

DIRECTIONAL AERIALS

MAIL ROOM

CONTROL CABIN

SWIVELLING UNDER-CARRIAGE

NAVIGATION CABIN

WIRELESS CABIN

OFFICERS MESS

UPPER DECK

MAIN CAT-WALK

CENTRAL CAT-WALK

LADDER BETWEEN CAT-WALKS

LOWER DECK WINDOWS

UPPER DECK WINDOWS

LOWER DECK

AIR SHAFTS

CREW'S SLEEPING QUARTERS

TRAILING AERIALS

MAIN ENTRANCE TO AIRSHIP

CREW'S SLEEPING QUARTERS & MESS

SEARCHLIGHT

AIR SPEED TRAILER LOG

FUEL & WATER TANKS

NERATING STATION

CONDITIONED AIR SUPPLY TO CABINS

DINING SALOON

DOUBLE BERTH CABINS

READING AND WRITING ROOM

PROMENADE

SLIDING DOORS

CAT WALK

SLIDING DOORS

LOUNGE

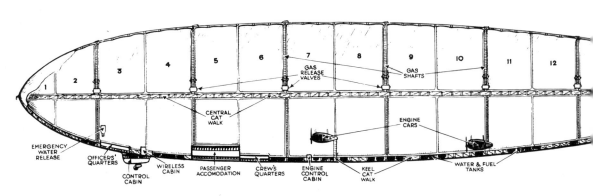

AIR
DUCT

FUEL AND
WATER TANKS

CAT
WALK

**OFFICERS'
QUARTERS**

D/F.LOOP
AERIAL

**CONTROL
CABIN**

**CHART
ROOM**

**NAVIGATION
CABIN**

SWIVELLING
UNDERCARRIAGE

BAGGAGE
ACCOMODATION

**WIRELESS CABIN
ABOVE
CONTROL CAR**

FUEL AND
OIL TANKS

CAT WALK

RETRACTABLE
TRAILING
AERIALS

EMERGENCY
WATER
RELEASE

AIR
SHAFTS

PASSENGERS'
DOOR
(RETRACTED)

**MAIN
PASSENGER CABINS,
DINING ROOM, LOUNGE, ETC.**

SEARCHLIGHT

**CREW'S
QUARTERS**

1   2   3   4   5   6   7   8   9   10   11   12

GAS
RELEASE
VALVES

GAS
SHAFTS

CENTRAL
CAT
WALK

ENGINE
CARS

EMERGENCY
WATER
RELEASE

OFFICERS'
QUARTERS

CONTROL
CABIN

WIRELESS
CABIN

PASSENGER
ACCOMODATION

CREW'S
QUARTERS

ENGINE
CONTROL
CABIN

KEEL
CAT
WALK

WATER & FUEL
TANKS

COPYRIGHT

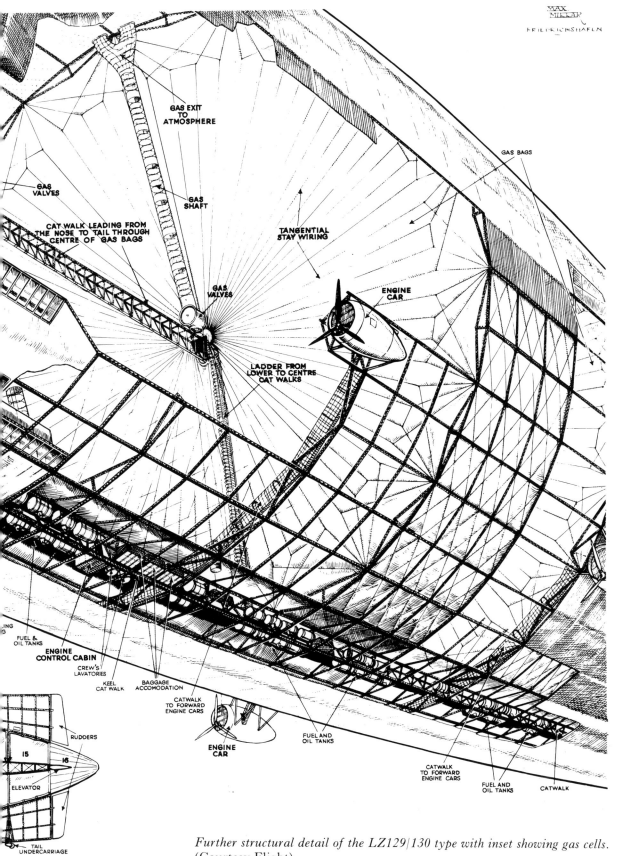

MAX
MILLAR
FRIEDRICHSHAFEN

GAS EXIT
TO
ATMOSPHERE

GAS BAGS

GAS
VALVES

GAS
SHAFT

CAT WALK LEADING FROM
THE NOSE TO TAIL THROUGH
CENTRE OF GAS BAGS

TANGENTIAL
STAY WIRING

ENGINE
CAR

GAS
VALVES

LADDER FROM
LOWER TO CENTRE
CAT WALKS

ING

FUEL &
OIL TANKS

ENGINE
CONTROL CABIN

CREW'S
LAVATORIES

KEEL
CAT WALK

BAGGAGE
ACCOMODATION

CATWALK
TO FORWARD
ENGINE CARS

ENGINE
CAR

FUEL AND
OIL TANKS

CATWALK
TO FORWARD
ENGINE CARS

FUEL AND
OIL TANKS

CATWALK

RUDDERS

15

16

ELEVATOR

TAIL
UNDERCARRIAGE

Further structural detail of the LZ129/130 type with inset showing gas cells.
(Courtesy Flight)

Graf Zeppelin II, had been able to operate as intended, with helium, they would probably have continued to fly safely, if less economically, until the outbreak of the Second World War. But that would have made little difference. The day of the rigid airship was already passing. Use of helium would have made the Zeppelins safer but would have gravely prejudiced their economy of operation. (*See* Note 22). It would not have affected their survival against the aeroplane in any wartime role.

Hindenburg was probably able to operate without losing money because of the high fares and load factors prevailing on the North

The noise level in an LZ129 engine car is dramatically emphasized in this picture.
(Luftschiffbau Zeppelin)

The end of the rigid airship. The destruction by fire of the Hindenburg *at Lakehurst on the first crossing of the 1937 season.*
(Popperfoto)

Atlantic, particularly after she had been modified to carry seventy-two passengers during her second season (*See* Appendix 2). However, neither she, nor indeed any later rigid, could hope to compete much longer with the rapidly developing aeroplane. By the end of the Second World War, the rigid's day had gone for ever.

LZ130, named *Graf Zeppelin II*, flew for the first time on 14 September, 1938, more than a year after the *Hindenburg* disaster. She was closely similar to her predecessor, the most obvious difference being that the four Daimler-Benz DB 602 diesels were arranged to drive tractor airscrews instead of pushers. Lightened by several tons, compared with *Hindenburg*, the expectation was that, filled with helium, she would be able to carry forty passengers across the Atlantic. This was not to be. With only a year to go before war would again engulf Europe, *Graf Zeppelin II* was taken over by the German authorities for experimental purposes. Nine of the

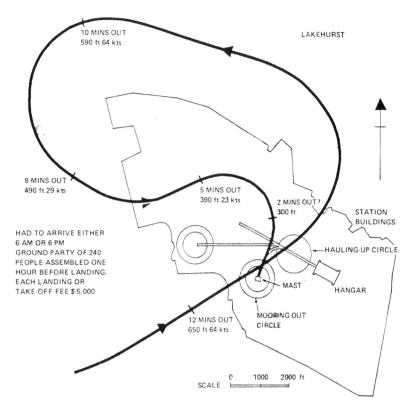

The Hindenburg*'s track on its landing approach to Lakehurst on 6 May, 1937 (local time), 7 May (GMT).*

LZ130 (D-LZ130) Graf Zeppelin (II) leaving its shed. (Lufthansa)

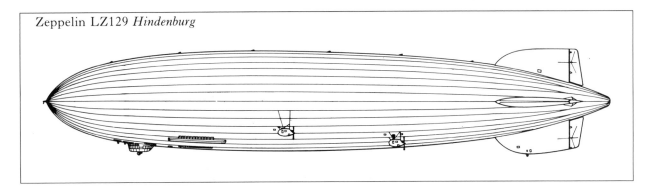

Zeppelin LZ129 *Hindenburg*

thirty flights she made during her brief career were on what would now be called electronic reconnaissance, probing the pioneer radar defences of the British Isles in which the Germans had good reason to be interested.

Like her older and more famous namesake, *Graf Zeppelin II* was broken up in the Frankfurt hangar in May 1940. She thus passed into history – the last of a famous line.

Zeppelin LZ129 *Hindenburg*

Manufacturer: Luftschiffbau Zeppelin GmbH

Built at Friedrichshafen

Number built: two

Chief designer: L Dürr

Main structural material: duralumin

Design began: October 1931

First flight of type: 4 March, 1936

Powerplant: four 1,050hp Daimler-Benz DB 602 sixteen-cylinder vee diesel engines

Gas capacity (100 per cent inflation): 200,000cu m

Overall length: 245.0m

Maximum diameter: 41.2m

Number of frames: 48, including 16 main frames

Spacing of main frames: 15.0m

Fineness ratio: 6.02

Number of gas cells: 16

Number of main longitudinals: 32

Empty weight: 130,000kg

Typical gross lift: 232,000kg (hydrogen) (1.16kg/cu m)

Typical disposable load: 102,000kg

Maximum fuel: 65,000kg

Crew: 40

Passengers 50, later 72

Maximum speed: 37.5m/s (83.88 mph)

Maximum range: 16,500km at speed of 34.7m/s (77.62mph)

Cost: DM9,000,000

Production

C/n		First flight	Last flight	Hours flown/ flights	Disposal
LZ129	*Hindenburg*	4.3.36	6.5.37	3,088hr	Burned, landing at Lakehurst
LZ130	*Graf Zeppelin II*	14.9.38	20.8.39	30 flights	Broken up, May 1940

The last Zeppelin – LZ130 Graf Zeppelin (II) *in 1938.* (Luftschiffbau Zeppelin)

Notes

Note 1

In order to provide an approximate indication of the relative worth of the money values quoted, these are first given in then contemporary values in the appropriate local currency followed by a computed, approximate present-day equivalent, in brackets. The latter have been calculated by converting first into sterling, at the then prevailing rate of exchange and then correcting for the present-day purchasing power of the pound.

Note 1A

The typical gross lift given for each airship in the data tables derives from its gas capacity. In Germany, a thousand cubic metres of hydrogen was assumed to lift 1,160kg. In the United Kingdom, this figure was 1,090kg, while in the United States 1,000cu m of helium was assumed to lift 1,079kg. As an example of how this worked in practice, the 31,900cu m gas capacity of the German naval airship L10 gave a gross lift of 31,800 multiplied by $^{1160}/_{1000}$ or 37,000kg. As L10 had an empty weight of 20,800kg, its disposable lift was 37,000 minus 20,800kg, in other words 16,200kg. Of this, the fuel for maximum range weighed 4,800kg, leaving sufficient lift for 11,400kg of payload and ballast (typically assumed to be about four per cent of the gross lift).

Note 2

First balloon ascents (*See* page 10)

Note 3

It was the brothers, Anne-Jean (1758–1820) and Marie-Noel Robert, who devised the balloon envelope material. The Roberts were suppliers of scientific equipment and apparently ran a discreet but lucrative sideline in the then illegal manufacture of contraceptives. It seems that the material used for their product, rubberised silk, known as lawn, lutestring or lustring, proved to be the solution to the previously intractable envelope problem. This impermeable material, developed by an artisan named Bernard, was said to be produced by impregnating a sturdy taffeta (a plain-weave, silk fabric) with a solution of rubber in turpentine, a gomme élastique or india rubber.

Similar, but heavier, material was already in use for umbrellas but another thirty-five years were to pass before Syme and Mackintosh introduced even heavier rubberised cloth for waterproof garments.

The Roberts' part in the invention of the hydrogen balloon is an interesting illustration of the factors which can influence recorded history. Their involvement was played down in contemporary accounts and there is even uncertainty about which of the two brothers accompanied Charles on the historic first flight. Perhaps the Roberts were not given due recognition at the time because of the nature of their illegal and indelicate business. No doubt their inferior social status as tradesmen also counted against them. Today their unique technical contribution is clear.

Note 4

Goldbeaters' skins are normally quite small, varying in size from 22cm (8$^1/_2$in) by 28cm (11in) to 100cm (39$^1/_3$in) by 25cm (10in). However, with the right process they can be over-lapped in one or more thicknesses so that they 'grow' together to form a homogeneous envelope material that is remarkably gas-tight.

Note 5

The British Army's adoption in 1883 of goldbeaters' skin for its balloon envelopes resulted from an initiative taken by Captain (later Colonel) James L B Templer who was then in charge of the Army Balloon Factory at Chatham. The factory later moved to Aldershot and then to Farnborough where it provided the origins of the Royal Aircraft Factory (later Royal Aircraft Establishment and, now, Royal Aerospace Establishment).

Goldbeaters' skin derives from the interior membrane of the caecum or blind gut (cul-de-sac) in the large intestine of the ox and had been used for some years for toy balloons and as contraceptive sheaths. Attempts had been made during the nineteenth century to use the skins to make full-size balloon or airship envelopes. To do this effectively, however, a process was needed whereby the small skins could be stuck together, thus providing a sufficiently strong and light material which was also exceptionally impervious to hydrogen.

In 1881, Walter Powell, Conservative Member of Parliament for Malmesbury in Wiltshire, discovered an Alsatian family, named Weinling, in the East End of London who specialised in processing goldbeaters' skins and, in particular, knew a secret technique of sticking together one or more layers to form a single homogeneous sheet.

Powell was a friend of Templer and, like him, an enthusiastic balloonist. Powell financed the manufacture, by the Weinlings of a goldbeaters' skin balloon for the Army. It was to be named *Heron* and was to have a capacity of 10,000cu ft (283cu m). The project ran into difficulties in December 1881 when Powell was swept out to sea and drowned while on a balloon trip with Templer from Bath. Templer then obtained the War Office's permission to take over the balloon's manufacture and to complete its erection in an old, covered-in ball-court in St Mary's Barracks in Chatham.

Further delay occurred when the elder Weinling was jailed for three months for assaulting the local police. His mother, who apparently ran the family business, was most reluctant to allow two sappers to take over the work in his absence because they would learn the secret process. In the end, the Government resolved the difficulty by bringing the Weinlings into their own employ and moving the final assembly of the balloon to Chatham. The work was completed by the end of 1883 and *Heron* proved such a success that the Army standardised on goldbeaters' skin balloons two years later. Italian hemp was selected at the same time for nets and rigging. These developments meant that British military balloons, although much more expensive, were stronger, smaller, lighter and less subject to loss of gas than their equivalents abroad. A diminishing team of Weinlings – there had originally been seven – continued to be employed in the manufacture of goldbeaters' skin envelopes at the Balloon Factory for the following thirty years.

In 1888, five years after the above events, Templer was court-martialled, but acquitted, for allegedly having leaked the secrets of goldbeaters' skin balloons to the French. Undaunted, he continued to be the leading figure in British military aeronautics until his retirement eighteen years later.

Note 6
Caquot kite-balloons, designed by the Frenchman Albert Caquot (1881–1976), or similar types, were universally adopted by all belligerents from 1916. Caquot balloons could be flown satisfactorily in winds of up to 30m/s (67mph) whereas the earlier Drachen was acceptable as a stable observation platform only in winds of up to 8m/s (18mph). It was however claimed that a spherical captive balloon could be used, although with great difficulty, in winds as high as 13m/s (29mph).

Note 7
The two fatal airship accidents over – or near – Paris in 1902 involved Augusto Severo in the *Pax* on 12 May and Ottokarde Bradsky on 13 October.

Note 8
The low cruising speeds of pressure-airships – 15.6 to 20.1m/s (35 to 45mph) – are inadequate for cross-country flying because of high average wind speeds experienced world-wide. For example, at low levels over the North Atlantic, the incidence of high winds is as follows:

Per cent of occasions	Wind exceeds
50	11.2m/s (25mph)
20	17.7m/s (40mph)
2½	25.7m/s (57mph)

Thus, on an average of six days a month, the wind speed will exceed 17.7m/s (40mph). This means that the airship will be unable, on those days, to make any significant progress to windward. As another example, over the North Sea on average:

3 days in 4 (75 per cent), the wind exceeds 5.1m/s (11.4mph)

1 day in 3 (33 per cent), the wind exceeds 10.3m/s (23mph)
1 days in 8 (13 per cent), the wind exceeds 15.4m/s (34.5mph)
1 day in 50 (2 per cent), the wind exceeds 20.5m/s (45.85mph)

Winds over land are less strong than over the sea but not sufficiently so to invalidate the above conclusions. For example, wind speeds at ground level in Paris have been measured as follows:

Days in the year	Possibility of wind exceeding
248 (68 per cent)	5m/s (11.18mph)
109 (30 per cent)	10m/s (22.36mph)
42 (11 per cent)	15m/s (33.5mph)
15 (4 per cent)	20m/s (44.73mph)
7 (2 per cent)	25m/s (55.92mph)
2 (0.5 per cent)	30m/s (67.1mph)

At the top of the Eiffel Tower (315m, 1,033ft) winds are, on average, four times those at the base

Sources: L S Sazerac de Forge, *La Conquête de l'Air*.
A Hildebrandt, *Airships Past, Present and Future*.
A Berget, *Conquest of the Air*.

Note 9
The term gas bag was usually used in England.

Note 10
Count Zeppelin made his first ascent in a (captive) spherical balloon while at Fort Snelling in St Paul, Minnesota, on 18 August, 1863. At the time he was on a visit to the United States as a foreign military observer during the American Civil War.

Note 11
Schwarz is believed to have built his two airships out of un-alloyed aluminium components, supplied by Carl Berg, the aluminium manufacturer. It is however possible that he used a 'Viktoria' alloy of unknown composition. Zeppelin, on the other hand, probably on the advice of Berg, adopted a zinc-aluminium alloy which was sometimes referred to as 'hard aluminium'. Zeppelin apparently continued with this material until 1914 when he changed to duralumin, an age-hardened alloy of aluminium which had been discovered by Alfred

Wilm in Germany in 1908 and which became commercially available late in 1909. At that time duralumin was between two-and-a-half and five times as strong as aluminium for the same weight. It was adopted by Vickers for *Mayfly* in 1910 despite the fact that it was difficult to manufacture in the sections required for airship girders and had been initially rejected by Zeppelin for this reason. By 1914 acceptable duralumin components were available and proved superior to magnesium alloys which were considered as alternatives. Duralumin, in improved forms, continued to be used for rigid airships although wolfranium, an aluminium-tungsten alloy, which had similar characteristics to duralumin, was thought to be a possible alternative at one stage in the early 1920s.

Note 12
The *City of Glendale* was built by the Slate Aircraft Company of Glendale, California, between 1927 and 1931. It was a metal-clad airship, more than half as large again as the ZMC-2. Capacity was 330,000cu ft (9,345cu m) and length 212ft (64.6m). It was flown briefly as a tethered balloon without its steam powerplant in 1929 and 1931.

Note 13
Because of the limitation imposed on airships flying from a base at high elevation, it is remarkable that the most important development of the rigid should have been at Manzell and Friedrichshafen which are at about 400m (1,300ft) above sea level. The lift of an airship is governed by its pressure height, the height at which its gas containers are completely distended (as height or temperature increases) and above which a loss of gas occurs. It is, of course, possible to leave the ground with cells full, but gas will blow off as the ship ascends to its chosen operating height. Loss of gas means loss of lift when the airship returns below the greatest height reached. This can be compensated by various factors, such as consumption of fuel, use of dynamic lift, superheating of the gas, changes in barometric pressure or discharge of ballast. But, on average, these also bring penalties. For this

reason, to obtain maximum pay-load/range (and lowest operating cost) it is usually important to operate airships as low down as possible, and it was normal practice in all flying where greater heights could be avoided to try to keep below a pressure height of, say, 200 or 300m (650–1,000ft). Operating from Lake Constance at 400m, the Zeppelins suffered an unavoidable penalty in their payload/range capabilities because their pressure heights had to be that much higher than if they had been taking off at sea level.

Note 14

Apparently, before the new girder in zinc-aluminium alloy was incorporated in *Deutschland*, the Zeppelin engineers had done a good deal of work studying alternatives. Press reports in 1909 spoke of a new magnesium alloy called Elektron or Elektrometall but there is no evidence that it was ever used by Zeppelin. When the zinc-aluminium alloy was abandoned, it was replaced by an early type of duralumin.

Note 15

Barnes Wallis seems to have got the idea of his geodetic aeroplane structures from a French designer of the early 1920s, rather than from an airship precedent such as the Schütte-Lanz S.L.I or the MacMechan. The fuselage structure of the Latécoère 6 bomber (exhibited at the 1921 Paris Salon) had a metal skin over a metal geodetic framework making it obviously too heavy. Wallis dispensed with the metal skin and substituted fabric for the covering as suggested by C G Grey, editor of *Jane's All the World's Aircraft* in the 1923 issue of that annual. A greatly improved metal framework then carried all the loads. This proved quite effective in the Vickers Wellington bomber of the Second World War, of which more than 11,000 were built. However, there was less 'learning' in this form of manufacture so that the production manhours of the Wellington remained higher than an equivalent conventional stressed-skin all-metal structure. This fact was clearly not appreciated by the Vickers directors when they decided to build the Wellington incorporating Wallis's geode-

tics. If a conventional structure had been used, more aircraft could have been produced for fewer manhours.

Note 16

Types of ammunition used by the Royal Flying Corps, Royal Naval Air Service and Royal Air Force.

SPK Mk.7T (Sparklet) – approved for RFC, 7/16. Tracer ammunition used one to three ordinary bullets.

Buckingham incendiary. Invented by J F Buckingham. Patented, 1/15. First adopted by RNAS, 12/15; then RFC, 4/16.

Buckingham Mk.7 produced in 6/16.

Buckingham (with flat nose) – widely used until end of War.

Brock incendiary. Invented by Cdr F A Brock. First delivered in 12.16. Use suspended by RFC early in 1917 but used by RNAS to end of War.

Pomeroy or P.S.A. incendiary. First produced, 5/16. Home Defence units of the RFC usually used a mixture of Buckingham, Brock and Pomeroy bullets. Invented by J Pomeroy.

RTS incendiary and explosive bullet. First produced 11/17. Used overseas from 9/18.

SPG Mk.7G. Superseded Mk.7T in about 6/17. Developed by Royal Laboratory and Dr S Smiles. Also used by France, USA and Italy.

PSA Mk.II – Approved 2/17 and superseded Mk.I.

RTT explosive version of RTS.

Sources: H A Jones, Vol 3, App V. *Air Stories*, Vol 4, p 60.

Note 17

Airships as Aircraft Carriers: A Chronology of Hook-on Operations.

25 January, 1918	German Naval Airship Division investigates the problem
26 January, 1918	Albatross DIII fighter successfully dropped from L35 Zeppelin rigid airship operating from Juterbog experimental unit. Programme terminated 23 February, 1918
June 1918	A Sopwith Camel

fighter dropped without pilot from No.23 rigid. Another drop made from No.23 with Lieut R E Keys as pilot. Aircraft lands safely.

6 November, 1918	Two piloted Sopwith Camels dropped from No.23. Lieut Keys, and same two pilots made second drop.
November 1918	Lieut G Crompton, US Army, designs hook-on and release mechanism for an aeroplane lifted by an airship.
12 December, 1918	Curtiss JN-4, piloted by Lieut A W Bradfield, lifted to 2,600ft by C-2 pressure-airship from Rockaway Beach, near New York, and successfully dropped.
May 1920	Sopwith Camel without pilot dropped from R33 rigid to test crash-proof fuel tanks. Did not burn.
September 1921	Lawrence B Sperry advocates hook-on as well as drop to US Army at Bolling Field.
17 July, 1922	Lawrence Sperry flies a Sperry Messenger biplane in close proximity to C-2 pressure-airship to determine possible hook-on problems.
18 September, 1923	Lieut R K Stoner, US Army, tries unsuccessfully to hook on to D-3 pressure-airship.
3 October, 1924	US Army TC-5 pressure-airship from Scott Field drops Sperry Messenger flown by Lieut C V Finter.
15 December, 1924	Finter hooks onto TC-3 at third attempt. This was the first successful hook-on.
Spring 1925	US Navy first shows interest in hook-ons when experiments with *Shenandoah* proposed.

15 October, 1925	Sqn Ldr R de Haga Haig in de Havilland D.H.53 drops from R33 rigid at 3,000ft. Tries unsuccessfully to hook-on again.
4 December, 1925	Flt Lieut Janor successfully hooks D.H.53 onto R33 rigid. First hook-on to a rigid airship.
21 October, 1926	Gloster Grebes flown by Fl Off C Mackenzie-Richards and Fl Off R L Ragg dropped by R33 rigid.
23 November, 1926	Two more Gloster Grebes successfully dropped from R33.
11 June, 1927	Lieut de Long Mills in Vought UO-1 makes six approaches to the *Los Angeles* to investigate turbulence problems.
December 1928	Trapeze fitted to *Los Angeles*.
1 July, 1929	Ground-testing of trapeze on *Los Angeles* completed.
3 July, 1929	First hook-on tests by Lieut A W Gorton with Vought UO-1 onto *Los Angeles*. These are not successful.
15 August, 1929	Lieut-Cdr L C Stevens tries unsuccessfully to pick up a trailing wire while flying a Vought O2U Corsair.
20 August, 1929	Gorton achieves a successful hook-on to the *Los Angeles* trapeze with UO-1 in three out of four approaches.
21 August, 1929	Gorton makes successful hook-on at 40kt. Lieut-Cdr C A Nicholson makes two out of four hook-ons followed by Stevens with one good hook-on.
24 August, 1929/ 2 September, 1929	Public announcement and demonstrations at National Air Races held in Cleveland.

	Lieut C M Bolster is first to leave an airship and travel to the ground in the UO-1.
10 October, 1929	Hook-on development programme starts.
31 January, 1930	Lieut R S Barnaby in Prüfling glider dropped from *Los Angeles*.
20 May, 1930	Nicholson takes off from aircraft carrier, *USS Lexington*, and then hooks-on *Los Angeles* trapeze.
25 August, 1930	Trapeze removed from *Los Angeles*.
February 1931	Lieut D W Harrington reports to Lakehurst for hook-on training. Others follow him.
26 May, 1931	Trapeze re-installed on *Los Angeles*. Training takes place using six Consolidated N2Y biplanes.
29 August, 1931	First night hook-ons made by Lieuts H L Young and Harrigan.
23 September, 1931	*Akron* makes its first flight.
23 October, 1931	Curtiss XF9C-1 ready with Skyhook and first *Los Angeles* hook-ons made by Harrington and Young.
18 December, 1931	Last hook-on *Los Angeles* trapeze.
7 February, 1932	Trapeze sent to Lakehurst for *Akron*.
3 May, 1932	Young and Harrigan make first hook-ons on *Akron*, first with N2Ys and then with XF9C-1.
Autumn 1932	HTA Unit in *Akron* work up their search procedures.
4 April, 1933	Akron lost.
21 April, 1933	*Macon* makes first flight. Waco XJW-1 takes over from N2Ys as 'running boats'.
6 July, 1933	First hook-ons on *Macon*
12 October, 1933	Macon flies to West Coast. During this period there is some hook-on training of

	HTA Unit pilots on the Curtiss F9C-2.
15 November/ 16 November, 1933	*Macon* uses the F9C-2 in an exercise with the Fleet. This is repeated during subsequent exercises.
12 February, 1935	*Macon* lost.
11 March, 1937	Hook-ons attempted by Ernst Udet with Focke-Wulf Stieglitz on *Hindenburg*.
22 April, 1937	Udet makes four successful hook-ons out of six tries, there being difficulties with turbulence.

Note 18
Vickers built the first two rigid airship hangars in the United Kingdom. The first was in the Cavendish Dock in Barrow-in-Furness for No.1 *Mayfly* and the second on Walney Island nearby for the No.9.

Note 19
A former Schütte-Lanz engineer, Hermann Müller, come to England early in 1916 with comprehensive wooden airship data (*See* page 117). Another German aeronautical expert, Bernard Schrieb-Muller, was reported on board L32 when she was shot down later in 1916. Several airship crewmen survived after being shot down in flames – Alfred Muhler in LZ37 being probably the first. Possibly Schreib-Muller or one of the other survivors also brought airship information to the Allies.

Note 20
The Germans built two rotating sheds, one at Blisdorf near Berlin in 1910 and a second at the Nordholz naval base in 1913.

Note 21
[See tables on pages 152-153]

Note 22
Today the case for the use of helium in airships is irresistible. The risks of fire with hydrogen have been made clear to all. However, there was a time in the 1920s and 1930s when airship protagonists outside the United States argued that the advant-

ages of hydrogen over helium were so great that the risk of a hydrogen fire was acceptable. With the United States refusing to export helium, use of hydrogen was, in any case, the only way airships could be operated.

The pro-hydrogen arguments ran roughly as follows:

(1) Only a small number of rigid airships had been destroyed by fire compared to the large numbers of HTA (Heavier-than-Air) fire accidents. (This conclusion ignored the fact that there had been incomparably more airship than HTA fires in proportion to the numbers of the two types flying.)

(2) At the time, helium was at least forty times as expensive as hydrogen and was unobtainable, except from the United States which had a monopoly of supplies and was not prepared to export the gas. (This monopoly no longer exists: The Soviet Union is believed to have helium in commercial quantities today.)

(3) Helium provided $7^1/_2$ per cent less lift than hydrogen.

(4) This meant that a helium airship had to be as much as 20 per cent larger if it were to have the same payload/range capabilities.

(5) For the same reason, a helium airship had about a third less range than an equivalent hydrogen airship.

(6) Manufacturing and operating costs of the smaller hydrogen airship were proportionately lower.

Appendices

Appendix 1
Fixed and Movable Control Surfaces of Early Zeppelins

The early development of the Zeppelin airship was particularly characterised by the evolution of its fixed and control surfaces, mainly mounted on the aft end of the hull. Several different forms of fixed tailplane were tried on successive airships over a four-year period, use also being made of the ideas of other experimenters such as Renard and Hervé at Chalais-Meudon near Paris who, in 1903, proposed tail surfaces attached directly to an airship's hull. As a result, the simple cruciform tail was evolved and ap-peared in its final form on Zeppelins on LZ25 in July 1914. It is clear that this final design was also influenced to an important extent by the Schütte-Lanz wooden rigids which introduced the simplified tail earlier on S.L.II in February 1914.

LZ1 (Type a), the first Zeppelin, had a weight which could be shifted fore and aft by a cable which ran on pulleys attached at bow and stern. This method of control in pitch was sup-plemented by a single monoplane elevator attached under the hull aft. Control in the yawing plane was by two similar units beneath and above the hull, also aft. The early aerodynamic controls were too small to be effective. Stability was also inadequate.

Nine steps in the subsequent development of the Zeppelin tails are illustrated here. The arrange-ments selected are not definitive but give a good idea of the pro-gression from multiple small con-trol surfaces to two interconnected, large elevators (one each side of the centreline) and two large rud-ders of similar coinfiguration.

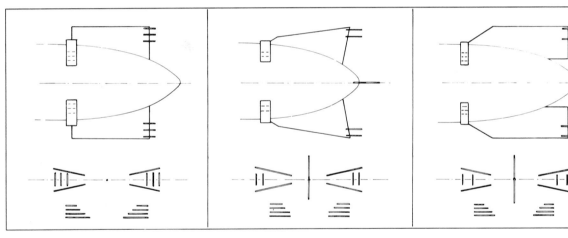

LZ2/3 (Type b): The second and third Zeppelins were the first to provide some measure of con-trol in both pitch and yaw. Large rectangular fixed tailplane sur-faces – two with dihedral and two with anhedral – considerably im-proved stability in both pitch and yaw. Triple box rudders were mounted each side between the tailplane tips. Two sets of quad-ruplane 'diving planes' (as they were known in Britain) were mounted fore and aft for pitch control.

LZ4/5 (type c): The third type of Zeppelin – of which two were built – had near-triangular fixed tailplane surfaces with twin double-box rudders again mounted at the tips of the tail-planes. The quadruple 'diving planes' remained unchanged. A rectangular rudder was mounted on the centreline on the aft end of the hull. This was later re-placed by a much larger oval rud-der in the same position. At about the same time a large fixed fin was mounted on the top of the hull and, later, a similar sur-face beneath the underside also.

LZ6 (Type d): This airship had the same basic tail configura-tion as LZ4/5, differing mainly in the area and plan form of the tailplanes which, however, re-tained their dihedral/anhedral ar-rangement. 'Diving planes' were also retained.

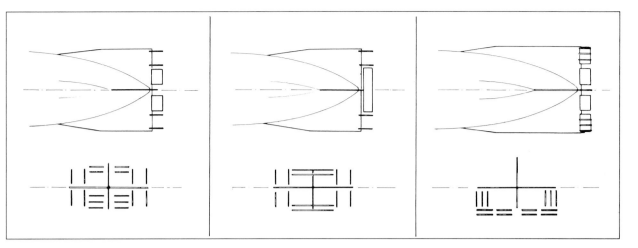

LZ9 (type f): The big change in the design of this airship's tail unit resulted from a re-arrangement of the tailplanes and central fin. Instead of the dihedral and anhedral on the tailpanes, these were now horizontally mounted with eight rudders and ten elevators attached in part directly to the main fixed surfaces and partly to a special framework. 'Diving planes' were omitted for the first time.

LZ10/12 (Type f): Basically similar to LZ9, the tail unit of this airship differed in having eight small elevators and eight rudders. There were no 'Diving planes'.

LZ14-17/19/20 (Type h): These airships had horizontal monoplane tailplanes and vertical fins as extensions of the hull. There were six small rudders and eight elevators attached to the fixed main surfaces by a box framework.

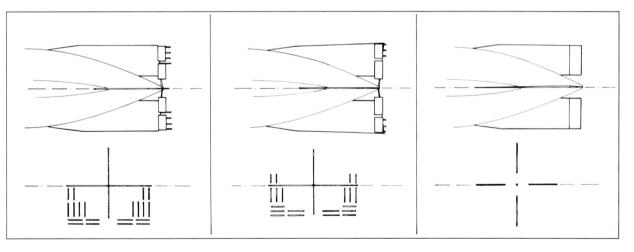

LZ18 (Type i): In this case the tail unit was cruciform with the control surfaces attached below the large main fixed surfaces. There were twelve rudders and eight elevators.

LZ24 (Type m): With a similar overall arrangement this airship's tail had the number of rudders reduced to ten and that of the elevators increased to the same number.

LZ25 (Type m2): This was the first Zeppelin to incorporate the basic cruciform tail unit with two rudders mounted on two fins and two elevators attached to two tailplanes. This became the standard design thereafter.

Appendix 2 Commercial Operations with Rigid Airships

Between 1910 and 1937 German Zeppelins were used for four different sustained commercial operations:

    1 Seasonal pleasure flying in Germany, 1910–1914.

    2 Scheduled service between Friedrichshafen and Berlin, 1919.

    3 Seasonal scheduled service between Friedrichshafen and South America, 1932–37.

    4 Seasonal scheduled service between Frankfurt-am-Main and Lakehurst, New Jersey, 1936–37.

In addition Zeppelins were used for quite a number of special charter flights. Baron R G Rothschild chartered LZ6A in September 1910 for a series of joy-rides at 2,000 marks for the first two hours plus 1,000 marks for each additional hour. The 2,000 marks were approximately equivalent to £1,700 today – all sterling values similarly computed are given in brackets (*See* Note 1). In August 1929 LZ127 *Graf Zeppelin* was chartered for a round-the-world flight, one of Hugo Eckener's most successful publicity ventures. The American newspaper proprietor, William Randolph Hearst, put up part of the money – $100,000 (£186,000 in today's terms) for the exclusive story rights. Other funding came from carriage of a special mail which yielded $112,500 (£208,000) in stamps and covers; the fares of special passengers which totalled $40,000 (£74,400); and a press concession to three German publishers which raised $12,500 (£23,000). The total cost of the flight came to $225,000 (£416,000), yielding a profit of $40,000 (£74,400).

The DELAG seasonal pleasure flying in 1910–14 was undertaken with seven different airships, four of which were destroyed in accidents. A total of 10,197 revenue passengers were carried on 1,588 flights in 3,176 hours, representing a rate of utilisation for each of the seven ships while they were in service of about 620 hours per annum. The total operating costs, between 22 June, 1910, and 31 July, 1914, have been estimated at about 4,260,000 marks (£3.6 million), against which a total commercial revenue of about 2,020,000 marks (£1,720,000) was earned (47.4 per cent of the expenditure). In addition, a subvention was received from the German Government for the training given to naval and military crews by DELAG during commercial flights. It is probable that this subvention more than covered the above loss.

The US Navy and Goodyear made a similar arrangement in the 1950s when the training of naval reserve crews on the Goodyear advertising blimps also made these operations commercially viable. Once this source of revenue was removed the advertising blimps ceased to be a commercial proposition and were operated primarily as an advertisement for Goodyear itself together with a limited amount of pleasure flying.

The DELAG scheduled service operated with the LZ120 *Bodensee* between Friedrichshafen and Berlin from 24 August to 5 December, 1919 (with an intermediate stop at Munich up until 4 October). It was operated at a substantial loss despite a load factor of 100 per cent – that is twenty-two passengers on each of the seventy-eight commercial flights, northbound one day, southbound the next. The one-way fare for the 600km (370 miles), flown in about seven hours, was 575 marks (£40.50). Altogether a total of 103 flights were made in 104 consecutive days. It is difficult to interpret the commercial implications of this operation because of the gal-

loping inflation from which Germany suffered as an aftermath of the war. A reported loss of nearly $40,000 (£61,400) was incurred, probably about 40 per cent of the direct operational costs. A total of 2,253 passengers were carried in 532 hours of flying, which represented a utilisation rate of about 1,850 hours per annum.

The Zeppelin service between Germany and South America was operated from March 1935 by DZR (Deutsche Zeppelin-Reederei), the German Zeppelin airline which was founded on 22 March and again had affiliations with the Hamburg-Amerika shipping line and Deutsche Lufthansa, the German flag airline. An experimental flight to South America with the LZ127 *Graf Zeppelin* was made in 1930, followed by three proving return flights in 1931. From 1932 a regular seasonal service which ran every other week from April to October was started. There were nine return flights that year and again in 1933; twelve in 1934 and sixteen in 1935.

The *Graf Zeppelin* flew another twelve in 1936 and a further seven were flown by the new LZ129 *Hindenburg*, making a total for that season of nineteen, or one a week. The service was discontinued in 1937 after the *Hindenburg* was destroyed at Lakehurst. Up to the end of 1935 the service normally terminated at Recife (Brazil), either nonstop from Friedrichshafen or with one stop at Seville in Spain. The Brazilian Government agreed to provide a terminal, including a shed, at its own expense (variously reported as $750,000 to $1 million) near Rio de Janeiro and this opened at Santa Cruz at the end of 1935. The 1936 and 1937 flights went right through to Rio de Janeiro.

No complete information on the South American service has been published but there is no doubt that it was extremely popular with the Brazilians and was of great prestige value to the Germans. Despite the seasonal nature of the service, the small number of trips and the limited accommodation (twenty passengers in ten two-berth cabins), a thousand passengers were carried in 1936 (in both directions) at a one-way fare of $461 (£930). Loads were good; the passenger load factor was reported to have averaged 92.9 per cent for 1935 and 1936, but not all the passengers paid full fares – a large number were officials or other people travelling free or at reduced rates.

The financial results of the service are not known; it was not subsidised by the Brazilian Government (other than the provision of the Rio de Janeiro base) but it clearly must have been by the Germans although to what extent is difficult to estimate.

In 1932, during early operations on the route, it was said that the loss per trip averaged about $3,100 (£6,240). An average of eleven revenue passengers (a 55 per cent passenger load factor) was being carried each way at that time, yielding $5,070 (£10,200) per trip. $11,330 (£22,800) of mail revenue was received per trip but it is not clear to what extent, if any, this contained an element of subsidy. The total income per trip was thus $16,400 (£33,000) to set against a total expenditure of $19,500 (£39,200). It would seem that, in 1932, revenue covered 84 per cent of cost at an average revenue passenger load factor of 55 per cent. The breakeven load factor would therefore have been just under 90 per cent, assuming the same mail revenue.

Southbound trips were scheduled to take seventy-two hours and actually averaged sixty-eight in 1932, while northbound the schedule was ninety-six hours and actually averaged ninety. If the above cost figures are correct, the Graf Zeppelin cost $243 (£490) per hour and could have been operated profitably on this route at a passenger revenue load factor of about 90 per cent providing that the mail payments, totalling well over double the 1932 passenger revenue, were maintained at the 1932 level.

Although the Graf Zeppelin made a number of flights across the North Atlantic it was always clear that she had insufficient speed for this route. Eckener made a statement to this effect soon after his first crossing of the Atlantic in Graf Zeppelin in 1928. LZ129 Hindenburg, on the other hand, was intended for that route and it was thought that she would have sufficient performance to be operable on it for about nine months of the year. Her top speed was, in fact, only 1.9 m/s (under 5mph) faster that the Graf Zeppelin although her cruising speed seems to have been a higher percentage of her top speed.

During her first, 1936, season on the route, Hindenburg made the first crossing on 6 May, returning on 12 May. Thereafter she completed fifteen round trips that year, during which 1,081 revenue passengers were carried at a load factor of 89.3 per cent. The average journey time was 64$\frac{1}{2}$ hours westbound and 52 hours eastbound. The fares charged in 1936 were $400 single and $700 return but these were increased by 12$\frac{1}{2}$ per cent for 1937. The latter were somewhat higher than those charged on the first flying-boat service initiated by Pan American Airways in 1939.

Again, only incomplete information is available about the economics of the operation. It appears that the total aircraft costs of a round trip, Frankfurt–Lakehurst–Frankfurt, averaged about $70,000 (£139,000) or some $600 (£1,186) per hour, about half of which were direct costs.

As originally built, and as used

for the 1936 season, the airship was fitted with fifty passenger berths in double cabins although additional passengers were occasionally carried in the officers' accommodation. For the 1937 season, passenger accommodation was increased to seventy-two berths. In 1936 the passenger revenue apparently averaged about $40,000 per round trip and the mail and express revenue is said to have made the total income sufficient to cover all operating costs. Whether the mail payments included an element of subsidy is not clear. If these figures are correct, with seventy-two berths, Hindenburg should, in 1937, have been able to cover her costs at a 98 per cent passenger load factor on passenger revenue alone. Taking account of mail and express, it is probable that Hindenburg was just about operating profitably on the difficult North Atlantic route when her career was cut short by the disaster at Lakehurst.

The somewhat speculative cost figures discussed in this appendix are summarised and tabulated here. Total costs of LZ120 are assumed in this comparison to have been twice the direct operating costs.

Comparative typical total operating costs per seat/statute mile in Europe for transport aeroplanes in scheduled airline service would be as follows (also given in 1990 values). The years indicated are those in which each type entered airline service.

De Havilland D.H.4A	(1919)	91.6p
Fokker F.VIIa-3m	(1926)	38.2p
Junkers-Ju 52/3m	(1933)	23.0p
Douglas DC-3	(1936)	11.6p

Airship	Year	Total Operating Costs (1990 values)		
		Cost per hr	Cost/ aircraft statute mile	Cost/ seat statute mile
DELAG (average)	1910–14	£1,142	£33.70	138.6p
LZ120	1919	£576	£8.16	43.6p
LZ127	1932	£490	£8.00	40.0p
LZ129 (50 berths)	1936	£1,186	£17.50	35.0p
LZ129 (72 berths)	1937	£1,186	£17.50	24.2p

In comparing the above airship and aeroplane costs it should be remembered that those for the last two airships (LZ127 and LZ129) were achieved over long stages – several thousand miles – whereas those of the aeroplanes of the period applied to much shorter ranges of, at most, 500/1,000 miles.

Appendix 3
Operating Statistics of Rigid Airships

Hours Flown by Rigid Airships (*estimated*)

		Hours	
1900–14	3 Zeppelins		
	12 Army		
	3 Navy		
	2 Schütte-Lanz	2,000	(approx)
	7 DELAG	3,200	
1914–18	65 Navy } Zeppelins		
	35 Army }	27,500	
	9 Navy } Schütte-Lanz		
	10 Army }	5,000	(approx)
1918–39	LZ120–121		
	Other Zeppelins	2,000	(approx)
	17 British Rigids	3,900	
	4 US Rigids (ZR-1, ZR-3, ZRS4, ZRS5)	9,600	
	ZMC-2	2,300	
	LZ127/129–130	21,000	
	Total	76,500	
	Possibly	80,000	

Rigid Airship Accidents Analysis

	Ships lost
Burned in shed	13
	—
Handling and flying accidents	
coming out of shed	3
burned on ground	3
landing	15
burned in flight	7
failed structurally in flight	3
lost in storms, at sea, etc	16
	—
	47
	—
War casualties	
shot down by anti-aircraft fire	20
shot down by aircraft	15
bombed in sheds	4
	—
	39
	—
Ships which met violent ends	99
Broken up (including two after flying accidents)	63
Ships launched	162
Ships converted to new configuration	16
Total number of configurations launched	178

Rigid Airships Destroyed in Fatal Accidents
(excluding war risk losses)

Airship	Date lost	Type of accident	Fatalities
LZ14(L1)	9.9.13	Storm at sea	14
LZ18(L2)	17.10.13	Burned in flight (design defect)	28
LZ27(L4)	17.2.15	Blew away after forced landing	4
LZ40(L10)	3.9.15	Struck by lightning. Burned in flight	19
LZ44(LZ74)	8.10.15	Hit ground in cloud	3?
LZ54(L19)	2.2.16	Ditched (engine failure)	16
S.L.4	30.3.16	Storm at sea	20?
S.L.X	28.7.16	Storm at sea	20?
LZ56(LZ86)	5.9.16	Landing accident	8
S.L.9	30.3.17	Struck by lightning. Burned in flight	23
LZ89(L50)	20.10.17	Blew away after forced landing	4
LZ104(L59)	7.4.18	Burned in flight	23
LZ107(L62)	10.5.18	Burned in flight (structural failure?)	20?
R38(ZR-2)	24.8.21	Broke in flight	44
LZ114(L72)	21.12.23	Burned in flight (structural failure)	50
ZR-1	3.9.25	Broke in flight	14
R101	5.10.30	Hit ground, burned	48
ZRS4	4.4.33	Storm at sea	73
ZRS5	12.2.35	Broke in flight	2
LZ129	6.5.37	Burned in flight (static discharge?)	35
		Approximate total fatalities	468

Rigid Airship Safety Statistics

Five-year period	Approximate hours flown	Airships lost in accidents	Hours flown per ship lost in accident	Airships lost in fatal accidents	Hours flown per fatal accident
1906–10	400	5	80	0	
1911–15	10,600	17 (+15 from enemy action)	624 (461)*	5 (+3 from enemy action)	2,120 (1,768)*
1916–20	29,000	31 (+24 from enemy action)	936 (725)*	8 (+17 from enemy action)	3,625 (2,070)*
1921–25	6,200	3	2,066	3	2,066
1926–30	11,800	1	11,800	1	11,800
1931–35	14,000	2	7,000	2	7,000
1936–40	4,500	1	4,500	1	4,500
1906–40	76,500	60 (+39 from enemy action)	1,275	20 (+20 from enemy action)	3,825

* approximate correction for ships lost by enemy action on the assumption that ships destroyed by the enemy would have suffered a comparable accident rate to other airships.

For comparison with the above estimates, aeroplanes have achieved the following typical hours flown per fatal accident over the years:

1910	100 hours	1939	5,000 hours (US general aviation)	1970	35,000 hours (US general aviation)
1914	140 hours	1940	125,000 hours (US domestic airlines)	1970	330,000 hours (ICAO airlines, Five-year average)
1918	2,000 hours (training)			1980s	1,000,000 hours (major jet airlines)

DELAG Operations in Germany, 1910–14

(Statistics for period 22 June, 1910, to 31 July, 1914)

Airship	Operating life	Utilisation rate pa	DELAG flights	DELAG hours	DELAG km	People* carried	Revenue passengers
LZ7	1 week	1,066 hours	7	20.5	1,035	220	142
LZ6A	3 weeks	1,144 hours	34	66	3,132	1,100	726
LZ8	5 weeks	489 hours	22	47	2,379	458	129
LZ10	52 weeks	479 hours	218	479.5	27,321	4,354	1,553
LZ11	124 weeks	411 hours	489	981.3	54,312	9,738	2,995
LZ13	104 weeks	424 hours	399	840.7	44,437	8,321	2,187
LZ17	112 weeks	344 hours	419	741	39,919	9,837	2,465
DELAG Fleet		622 hours	1,588	3,176	172,535	34,028	10,197

* Includes crews, supernumeries and crews under training

DELAG Operations in Germany, 1919

(Statistics for period 24 August to 5 December, 1919)

One airship (LZ120) operated, flown by three pilots:
Dr H Eckener, H C Fleming and A Heinen.
During an elapsed time of 98 days, flew on 88 days and made 103 flights
totalling 532 hours in which 51,258km (32,300 miles) were covered.
There were 78 commercial flights:
Friedrichshafen–Staaken or Staaken–Friedrichshafen.
Sometimes with a stop at Munich.
Average block time of 7 hr for the 600km (370 miles).
Carried 4,050 people, including 2,253 passengers plus
5,000kg (11,000lb) of mail and 3,000kg (6,600lb) of other cargo.
Average of 22 passengers per flight (100 per cent load factor)
at an average fare of about 575 marks (£40.5)

DELAG and DZR Statistics

Airship	Hours flown	Km flown	Number of flights	People carried†	Passengers carried	Mail carried (kg)	Freight carried (kg)
LZ120 Bodensee	532	51,258	103	4,050	2,253	5,000	3,000
LZ127 Graf Zeppelin	17,177	1,695,272	590	34,000	13,110	39,219	30,442
LZ129 Hindenburg	3,088	337,129	63	7,305	3,059	8,869	9,758
Totals	20,797	2,083,659	756	45,355	18,422	53,088	43,200
DELAG 1910–14	3,176	172,535	1,588	34,028	10,197	–	–
Totals	23,973	2,256,194	2,344	79,383†	28,619	53,088	43,200

† Includes crews, supernumeries and crews under training

Appendix 4
Manufacture of Rigid Airships

Rigid airships were the first large, relatively complex aircraft and the first metal aircraft to be made in production quantities. Their manufacture, particularly in Germany just before and during the First World War, revealed many of the technical, organisational, industrial and financial problems that were later to become familiar in the development and production of aeroplanes.

Before the First World War the design and manufacture of the first of a new type of rigid airship required up to three years from the start of the project to first flight. This was reduced to a six-month to two-year period during the war. Later, between the wars, the time required increased again to a two- to five-year period.

These development times compare with the two or three months it took to design, build and fly most new types of aeroplane up to the end of the First World War, although a few of the larger and more advanced designs of that era did require eight to twelve months. Thereafter, the time required to develop the average aeroplane increased steadily until, by the 1930s, with the introduction of all-metal aeroplanes, it rose markedly: one to two years was normally required, still significantly less than that for rigid airships even though the design effort required was now comparable. The difference in time was due to the fact that the aeroplane manufacturers were able to use larger design teams.

Since the Second World War, development times for most types of aircraft have increased even further. Today between three and five years to first flight are commonly required, a time comparable to that of the rigids of the 1930s. The difference is that incomparably larger design teams, aided by computers, are now employed. A large, modern aeroplane may have four or five million direct design manhours expended on it to first flight, a figure perhaps twenty times greater than was required for the last rigid airships.

So far as production is concerned, the rigid airship again required a much larger effort per unit produced than contemporary aeroplanes. Thus, before the First World War, from 100,000 to 300,000 manhours of direct shop-labour were required for the first airship of a new type. This figure increased to 800,000/1,000,000 manhours for the larger airships of the First World War period. During the between-wars years, direct shop-labour hours for the first of a new design increased still further so that as much as two to three million manhours, or even more, were needed. These totals are comparable to the effort required to manufacture the airframe and install the equipment in the first example of a modern wide-body transport aircraft such as the McDonnell Douglas MD-11 or Lockheed TriStar. The cost, and therefore the labour content, of the bought-out equipment installed in a large modern aeroplane is, however, much greater.

From such information as is still available it appears that experience in the several factories which manufactured Zeppelins during the First World War must have given some of the earliest indications in aircraft manufacture of the reductions in manhours per unit which occur in the quantity production of complex articles. This process, which later came to be known as the 'learning curve' effect, had originally been observed, though not quantified, in the mass production of rifles during the American Civil War. The effect also appears to have been known to aeroplane manufacturers, at least in France, from before the First World War but was understood and fully exploited only from the 1930s. From that time, manufacture of aircraft came to be planned on the assumption of the 'learning effect' along about an 80 per cent curve: in other words, for every doubling of the numbers made, the manhours required per unit are reduced by 20 per cent.

The learning effect means that the average man hours required to manufacture a quantity of even the largest and most advanced type of aircraft is greatly reduced from that expended on the first machine of the type, providing a reasonable number of that type is made. Thus the average hours required to make each of 100 aircraft will be only about one-third of those required for the first aircraft and for 250 aircraft only about one-quarter. The economies manifested themselves in the manufacture of rigid airships even before the First World War. Their importance was limited by the small numbers made. Nevertheless, estimates suggest that the manhours needed for the nine L3 class Zeppelins built in the Ring Shed at Friedrichshafen were reduced along an approximate 80 per cent curve.

The costs of manufacturing aeroplanes are, of course, incomparably higher today than they were fifty years ago. The same would be true for rigid airships, were they still being built. Jigging and tooling costs are greater under modern conditions for a given rate of production, and investment in plant and machinery has to be much higher. Investment in 'work in progress' peaks at much higher levels today because of higher costs of labour, materials and bought-out parts.

The American Goodyear Aerospace Company, which was absorbed into the Loral Systems Group in 1987, was one of the last manufacturers of rigid airships. In competition with the British company, Airship Industries, (formed in 1980), it is still

Goodyear Study of Pressure-Airship Manufacturing Costs, 1967

Size of airship (gas capacity)	42,475cu m (1.5m cu ft)	283,170cu m (10.0m cu ft)
Design engineering costs	$37.7m (£15.7m)	$52.5m (£21.9m)
Prototype airship	$14.9m (£6.2m)	$40.0m (£16.7m)
Production airships (each)	$5.85m (£2.44m)	$18.0m (£7.5m)

(Figures in brackets are sterling equivalents at the then current rate of exchange.)

building pressure-airships – or was until recently.

In 1967 Goodyear undertook a study for the US Government of the likely costs of developing and producing pressure- and rigid airships. Although 1967 costs have roughly trebled in 1990, they do provide some indication of what airship development and manufacture might cost under modern conditions. The study concluded that rigid airships would cost roughly twice as much today as pressure-airships for a given capacity. These figures suggest that, while in 1933 dollars *Akron* and *Macon* cost $8 million, under modern conditions they would cost well over $600 million. Nor does this take into account the effect on expenditure of the 25 to 30 year advance in related technologies. A modern aeroplane of comparable weight would have development and tooling costs of between 500 and 1,000 million dollars (equivalent to £650 to £1,300 million today).

Looking back over the history of airship development, estimates suggest that something over £6,000 million (in today's values) has been spent on airships during the past ninety years. This figure includes all aircraft and base costs but excludes those of personnel in the armed forces engaged in operating airships. It compares with, for example, something over £1,600 million (again in today's values) spent by Britain and France during the first ten years of the development of supersonic air transport.

Probably nearly half the airship expenditure was American, the greater part of this on pressure-airships during and after the Second World War. More than a third was German, mainly on rigids before and during the First World War and between the wars. The British, French and Italians together contributed almost all the remainder.

An estimated 60 per cent of the total was spent on research and development and probably about half went on rigid airships. However, allowing for the fact that all rigid airship development and manufacture occurred in the first forty years of this century (when labour costs were relatively low), the rigid airship share must have been much larger in man-hour terms.

The governments which invested all this effort on rigid airships can only have concluded in the end that the practical returns obtained were grossly inadequate.

Appendix 5
Characteristics of
Rigid Airships

The main characteristics of each
type of airship are detailed, on
the following pages, as far as
possible in a standardised tabular
form. This can be summarised as:
Airship by number or class
and, where applicable, type letter;
date of first flight; gas capacity
(100 per cent inflation); engine/s
and total maximum power;
dimensions; spacing of main
frames; number of gas cells;
empty weight; typical gross lift;
empty weight as a percentage
of gross lift; maximum speed
(metres/second); maximum range;
number of crew and passengers;
main constructional material; and
number built.

Appendix 5
Characteristics of Rigid Airships

Airship	Type	First flight	Gas capacity (cu m)	Gas capacity later (cu m)	Engines	Total max power (cv)	Length (m)
Schwarz No.2		3.11.97	3,700	–	1 Daimler P1896	12	47.5
Zeppelin LZ1	a	2.7.00	11,300		2 Daimler N1899	28	128.0
Zeppelin LZ2	b	17.1.06	10,400	12,200	2 Daimler H4L	160	128.0
Zeppelin LZ4	c	20.6.08	15,000	–	2 Daimler J4	210	136.0
Zeppelin LZ6	d	25.8.09	15,000	16,000	2 Daimler J4L	230	136.0
Zeppelin LZ7 Deutschland	e	19.6.10	19,300	–	3 Daimler J4F	360	148.0
Vickers No.1		(22.5.11)ø	18,800		2 Wolseley	320	156.0
Zeppelin LZ10 Schwaben	f	26.6.11	17,800	16,550	3 Maybach A-Z	435	140.0
Schütte-Lanz S.L.1	'a'	17.10.11	20,500	–	2 Daimler J8L	480	131.0
Zeppelin LZ11 Viktoria-Luise	g	14.2.12	18,700	–	3 Maybach B-Y	450	148.0
Zeppelin LZ14 (L1)	h	7.10.12	22,470	19,500	3 Maybach B-Y	540	158.0
Zodiac 13 Spiess		4.13	12,800	16,400	2 Chenu	420	113.0
Zeppelin LZ18 (L2)	i	9.9.13	27,000	–	4 Maybach C-X	840	158.0
Zeppelin LZ21 (ZVI)	k	10.11.13	20,870	–	3 Maybach C-X	540	148.0
Zeppelin LZ22 (ZVII)	l	8.1.14	22,140	–	3 Maybach C-X	540	156.0
Schütte-Lanz S.L.2 (S.L.II)	'b'	28.2.14	25,000	27,000	4 Maybach C-X	720	144.0
Zeppelin LZ24 (L3)	m	11.5.14	22,470	–	3 Maybach C-X	540	158.0
Zeppelin LZ26 (ZXII)	n	14.12.14	25,000	–	3 Maybach C-X	540	161.2
Schütte-Lanz S.L.3	'c'	4.2.15	32,410	–	4 Maybach C-X	840	153.1
Zeppelin LZ36 (L9)	o	8.3.15	24,900	–	3 Maybach C-X	540	161.4
Zeppelin LZ38 (L10)	p	3.4.15	31,900	35,800	4 Maybach C-X	720	163.5
Schütte-Lanz S.L.6	'd'	19.9.15	35,130	–	4 Maybach C-X	840	162.1
Zeppelin LZ59 (L20)	q	21.12.15	35,800	–	4 Maybach H-S-Lu	960	178.5
Schütte-Lanz S.L.8	'e'	30.3.16	35,130	38,780	4 Maybach H-S-Lu	960	174.0
Zeppelin LZ62 (L30)	r	28.5.16	55,000	55,200	6 Maybach H-S-Lu	1440	198.0
Vickers No.9		27.11.16	25,180	–	4 Maybach C-X	600	161.5
Zeppelin LZ91 (L42)	s	22.2.17	55,500	–	5 Maybach H-S-Lu	1200	196.5
Zeppelin LZ93 (L44)	t	1.4.17	55,800	–	5 Maybach H-S-Lu	1200	196.5
Zeppelin LZ95 (L48)	u	22.5.17	55,800	–	5 Maybach H-S-Lu	1200	196.5
Zeppelin LZ100 (L53)	v	8.8.17	56,000	–	5 Maybach H-S-Lu	1200	196.5
Schütte-Lanz S.L.20	'f'	10.9.17	56,000	–	5 Maybach H-S-Lu	1200	198.3
Vickers No.23		19.9.17	28,250	–	4 Rolls-Royce Eagle	1000	163.1
Zeppelin LZ102 (L57)	w	26.9.17	68,500	–	5 Maybach H-S-Lu	1200	226.5
Admiralty R27 (23X class)		29.6.18	28,050	–	4 Rolls-Royce Eagle	1200	164.3
Zeppelin LZ112 (L70)	x	1.7.18	62,200	68,500	7 Maybach Mb IVa	1715	211.1
Admiralty R31		1.8.18	43,975	–	6 Rolls-Royce Eagle	1800	187.3
Admiralty R33		6.3.19	55,460	–	5 Sunbeam Maori IV	1250	196.0
Zeppelin LZ120 Bodensee	y	20.8.19	20,000	22,550	4 Maybach Mb IVa	980	120.8
Vickers R80		19.7.20	35,680	–	4 Maybach Mb IVa	980	162.0
Admiralty R36		1.4.21	60,030	–	5 3 Sunbeam Cossack and 2 Maybach Mb IVa	1540	205.0
RAW R38 (ZR-2)		23.6.21	77,600	–	6 Sunbeam Cossack	2100	211.8
NAF ZR-1 Shenandoah		4.9.23	60,915	–	6 Packard 1A-1551	1800	207.3
Zeppelin LZ126 Los Angeles		27.8.24	70,000	–	5 Maybach VL1	2000	200.0
Zeppelin LZ127 Graf Zeppelin		18.9.28	75,000	–	5 Maybach VL2	2650	236.6
Metalclad ZMC-2		19.8.29	5,720	–	2 Wright J-5 Whirlwind	440	45.5
RAW R101		14.10.29	141,540	156,000	5 Beardmore Tornado III	2925	222.9
AGC R100		16.12.29	146,060	–	6 Rolls-Royce Condor IIIB	4020	216.1
Goodyear-Zeppelin ZRS4 Akron		25.9.31	193,970	–	8 Maybach VL2	4560	239.3
Zeppelin LZ129 Hindenburg		4.3.36	200,000	–	4 Daimler-Benz DB 602	4200	245.0

* Oval section: 14 m by 12 m
ø Did not fly. Date of leaving shed
† Helium

NOTES

1 Most published data on airships are unreliable and often contradictory. The figures in the above table are taken from what appears to be the most reliable source in each case and, as far as possible, are mutually consistent.

2 The capacities quoted are intended to be for 100 per cent inflation of the lifting gas cells. However there are usually wide discrepancies in recorded figures for gas capacities. This is because of confusion with 'nominal capac (usually 95 per cent of full) and with the air ume of the hull. There are also frequent er of conversion to and from metric units.

3 'Typical gross lift' is a notional figure der from gas capacity in each case. It is calculated the assumption of 1,160 kg of lift per 1,000 c of hydrogen or 1,070 kg of lift per 1,000 cu r helium, as the case may be.

4 Sometimes there were quite important ferences between individual airships in one c

main frames (m)	Gas cells	Empty weight (kg)	Typical gross lift (kg)	Empty weight as percentage of gross lift	Maximum speed (m/s)	Maximum range (km)	Crew/passengers	Main structural material	Number built	Remarks
3.5	1	3,560	4,300	82.8	7.5		1	Aluminium	1	Crashed on first flight
8.0	17	10,300	13,100	78.6	7.8	280	5	Zn-Al Alloy	1	
8.0	16	9,250	12,050	76.6	11.0	1,100	7	Zn-Al Alloy	2	
8.0	17	12,750	17,400	73.3	13.5	1,450	11/14	Zn-Al Alloy	2	
8.0	17	13,550	17,400	77.9	13.5	2,000	7/10	Zn-Al Alloy	1	Later 3 engines
8.0	18	15,600	22,400	69.6	16.7	1,600	8/20	Zn-Al Alloy	2	
'ar	17	19,900	20,500	91.3	(18.8)	(1,750)	22/-	Duralumin	1	Did not fly
8.0	17	13,600	20,650	65.9	21.0	1,450	8/20	Zn-Al Alloy	3	
2.0	7	19,300	23,800	81.1	19.7	1,060	12/-	Wood	1	
8.0	18	15,150	21,700	69.8	21.0	1,100	8/25	Zn-Al Alloy	2	
8.0	18	17,900	26,100	68.5	21.2	2,300	20/-	Zn-Al Alloy	6	
9.0	14		12,875		18.0	1,560	7/-	Wood	1	At first 1 engine
8.0	18	20,250	31,350	64.6	21.0	2,100	23/-	Zn-Al Alloy	1	
8.0	17	15,450	24,250	63.6	20.5	1,900	18/-	Zn-Al Alloy	1	
8.0	18	16,850	25,700	65.5	20.0	1,900	18/-	Zn-Al Alloy	2	
2.0	15	21,000	29,000	72.4	24.5	2,100	19/-	Wood	1	
8.0	18	16,900	26,100	64.7	23.4	2,200	16/-	Zn-Al Alloy	12	
0.0	15	16,800	29,000	57.9	22.5	3,300	18/-	Duralumin	1	
0.0	17	24,400	37,600	64.9	23.5	2,500	19/-	Wood	3	
0.0	15	17,800	28,900	61.6	23.6	3,300	16/-	Duralumin	2	
0.0	15	20,800	37,000	56.3	26.7	4,300	18/-	Duralumin	22	
0.0	18	24,900	40,700	61.2	25.8		16/-	Wood	2	
0.0	18	23,650	41,550	57.0	26.5	4,300	16/-	Duralumin	12	
0.0	18	22,000	40,750	54.1	26.9		16/-	Wood	10/12	
0.0	19	31,400	63,800	49.1	28.7	7,400	17/-	Duralumin	17	
0.1	17	27,100	27,470	92.8	20.1	2,600	14/-	Duralumin	1	Later 3 engines
0.0	18	28,100	64,500	43.6	27.7	10,400	23/-	Duralumin	2	
0.0	18	26,900	64,750	41.6	28.9	11,500	23/-	Duralumin	2	
0.0	18	25,750	64,750	39.8	29.9		19/-	Duralumin	5	
5.0	14	25,000	65,000	38.5	29.9	13,500	19/-	Duralumin	10	
0.0	19	27,100	65,000	41.7	28.5		16/-	Wood	3	
0.1	18	27,000	30,790	82.3	23.2	3,050	16/-	Duralumin	4	Later 3 engines
5.0	18	27,400	79,500	34.5	28.6	16,000	22/-	Duralumin	2	
0.1	18	25,000	30,575	76.6	24.6	1,700	16/-	Duralumin	2	
5.0	15	24,700	72,200	34.2	36.4	12,000	30/-	Duralumin	3	Later 6 engines
2.0	20	31,200	47,935	61.1	31.8	3,200	21/-	Wood	2	Later 5 engines
0.0	19	36,900	64,450	57.3	26.8	7,750	23/-	Duralumin	2	
0.0	12	13,200	23,200	56.9	36.8	1,700	16/21	Duralumin	2	
0.0	15	22,000	38,890	53.1	26.8	10,300	20/-	Duralumin	1	
0.0	20	53,400	65,430	76.6	29.1	12,500	28/50	Duralumin	1	With passenger cabin
5.0	14	36,700	84,585	40.8	29.5	10.500	30/-	Duralumin	1	
5.0	20	35,100	64,740†	53.4	28.0	4,200	23/-	Duralumin	1	Later 5 engines
5.0	13	42,200	81,300	52.0	32.7	12,500	28/20	Duralumin	1	Later helium-filled
5.0	16	67,100	87,000	77.1	35.6	10,000	36/20	Duralumin	1	Blaugas fuel
	1	4,135	6,175†	67.1	27.7	1,100	3/-	Dural and Alclad	1	
'ar	16	91,440	154,280	67.8	31.3	8,600	48/50	Dural and Steel	1	
2.2	15	106,600	159,205	62.8	36.3	10,200	37/100	Duralumin	1	
2.5	12	111,000	209,200†	53.1	37.6	11,000	60/-	Duralumin	2	
5.0	16	130,000	232,000	56.1	37.5	16,500	40/50	Duralumin	2	

general the table gives details of the first air- in each class only. Alternative gas capacities quoted for cases where 'stretched' or 'cut-n' variants are known to have existed, either riginally built or produced by modification. The figures for maximum range in the table unfortunately, almost certainly not all comable. This is partly because figures were often ted for fuel tankages which included fuel car- in ballast tanks, which was not a normally eptable operating practice.

6 Performance and load-carrying capabilities of airships are more sensitive to operating conditions, pilot technique, weather and climate than are heavier-than-air craft. Thus, for example, the disposable lift of R101 would have been reduced from its average value in Britain by no less than 11 tons (30 per cent) in the summer months in India. There were different operating philosophies in relation to the use of dynamic lift. Zeppelin pilots apparently tended to keep their ships more in static equilibrium than some others; that is to say they made less use of the upward or downward force resulting from flying nose up or nose down. Use of dynamic lift had a serious adverse effect on speed.

Appendix 6
Key to Rigid Airship Designations

Germany: Zeppelin

Design Type	Class	Works Number	Designation Army	Navy	Name/ remarks	Built at	
a	–	LZ1	–	–	–	Manzell	
b	–	LZ2	–	–	–	,,	
b	–	LZ3	–	–	–	,,	
b	–	LZ3A	Z I	–	–	,,	
c	–	LZ4	–	–	'Z II'	,,	
c	–	LZ5	Z II	–	–	,,	
d	–	LZ6	–	–	'Z III'	Friedrichshafen	
d	–	LZ6A	–	–	–	,,	
e	–	LZ7	–	–	Deutschland	,,	
e	–	LZ8	–	–	Ersatz Deutschland	,,	
f	Schwaben class	LZ9	Ersatz Z II	–	–	,,	
f	Schwaben class	LZ9A	Ersatz Z II	–	–	,,	
f	Schwaben class	LZ10	–	–	Schwaben	,,	
g	Schwaben class	LZ11	–	–	Viktoria Luise	,,	
f	Schwaben class	LZ12	Z III	–	–	,,	
g	Schwaben class	LZ13	–	–	Hansa	,,	
h	L1 class (Improved Schwaben)	LZ14	–	L1	–	,,	
h	(Improved Schwaben)	LZ15	Ersatz Z I	–	–	,,	
h	(Improved Schwaben)	LZ16	Z IV	–	–	,,	
h	(Improved Schwaben)	LZ17	–	–	Sachsen	,,	
h	(Improved Schwaben)	LZ17A	–	–	Sachsen	,,	
i	(Improved Schwaben)	LZ18	–	L2	–	,,	
h	L1 class	LZ19	Desatz Z I	–	–	,,	
h	L1 class	LZ20	Z V	–	–	,,	
h	L1 class	LZ20A	Z V	–	–	,,	
k	Improved L1 class	LZ21	Z VI	–	–	,,	
l	Improved L1 class	LZ22	Z VII	–	–	,,	
l	Improved L1 class	LZ23	Z VIII	–	–	,,	
m	L3 class	LZ24	–	L3	–	,,	
m2	L3 class	LZ25	Z IX	–	–	,,	
n	Z XII class	LZ26	Z XII	–	–	Frankfurt	
m2	L3 class	LZ27	–	L4	–	Friedrichshafen	
m2	L3 class	LZ28	–	L5	–	,,	
m2	L3 class	LZ29	Z X	–	–	,,	
m2	L3 class	LZ30	Z XI	–	–	Potsdam	
m2	L3 class	LZ31	–	L6	–	Friedrichshafen	
m2	L3 class	LZ32	–	L7	–	,,	
m2	L3 class	LZ33	–	L8	–	,,	
m2	L3 class	LZ34	LZ34	–	–	Potsdam	
m2	L3 class	LZ35	LZ35	–	–	Friedrichshafen	
o	Z XII class	LZ36	–	L9	–	,,	
m2	L3 class	LZ37	LZ37	–	–	Potsdam	
p	L10 class	LZ38	LZ38	–	(Million cu ft)	Friedrichshafen	
o	Z XII class	LZ39	LZ39	–	–	,,	
p	L10 class	LZ40	–	L10	(Million cu ft)	,,	
p	L10 class	LZ41	–	L11	–	,,	(Löwenthal)
p	L10 class	LZ42	LZ72	–	–	Potsdam	
p	L10 class	LZ43	–	L12	–	Friedrichshafen	
p	L10 class	LZ44	LZ74	–	–	,,	(Löwenthal)
p	L10 class	LZ45	–	L13	–	,,	
p	L10 class	LZ46	–	L14	–	,,	(Löwenthal)
p	L10 class	LZ47	LZ77	–	–	,,	
p	L10 class	LZ48	–	L15	–	,,	(Löwenthal)
p	L10 class	LZ49	LZ79	–	–	Potsdam	
p	L10 class	LZ50	–	L16	–	Friedrichshafen	
p	L10 class	LZ51	LZ81	–	–	,,	(Löwenthal)
p	L10 class	LZ51A	LZ81	–	–	,,	,,

Design Type	Class	Works Number	Designation Army	Navy	Name/ remarks	Built at	
p	L10 class	LZ52	–	L18		Friedrichshafen	(Löwenthal)
p	L10 class	LZ53	–	L17		,,	
p	L10 class	LZ54	–	L19		,,	
p	L10 class	LZ55	LZ85	–		Potsdam	
p	L10 class	LZ56	LZ86	–		,,	
p	L10 class	LZ56A	LZ86	–		,,	
p	L10 class	LZ57	LZ87	–		Friedrichshafen	(Löwenthal)
p	L10 class	LZ57A	LZ87	–		,,	,,
p	L10 class	LZ58	LZ88	–		Potsdam	
p	L10 class	LZ58A	LZ88	L25		,,	
q	L20 class	LZ59	–	L20	–	Friedrichshafen	
p	L10 class	LZ60	LZ90	–	(Million cu ft)	Potsdam	
p	L10 class	LZ60A	LZ90	–		,,	
q	L20 class	LZ61	–	L21	–	Friedrichshafen	(Löwenthal)
r	L30 class	LZ62	–	L30	(Super-Zeppelin)	,,	
p	L10 class	LZ63	LZ93	–	(Million cu ft)	Potsdam	
p	L10 class	LZ63A	LZ93	–		,,	
q	L20 class	LZ64	–	L22	–	Friedrichshafen	(Löwenthal)
q	L20 class	LZ65	LZ95	–	–	,,	
q	L20 class	LZ66	–	L23	–	Potsdam	
q	L20 class	LZ67	LZ97	–	–	Friedrichshafen	(Löwenthal)
q	L20 class	LZ68	LZ98	–	–	,,	,,
q	L20 class	LZ69	–	L24	–	Potsdam	
q	L20 class	LZ70	Not completed	L26	–	–	
q	L20 class	LZ71	LZ101	–	–	Potsdam	
r	L30 class	LZ72	–	L31	(Super-Zeppelin)	Friedrichshafen	(Löwenthal)
q	L20 class	LZ73	LZ103	–	–	Potsdam	
r	L30 class	LZ74	–	L32	(Super-Zeppelin)	Friedrichshafen	
r	L30 class	LZ75	–	L37		Staaken	
r	L30 class	LZ76	–	L33		Friedrichshafen	
q	L20 class	LZ77	LZ107	–	–	Potsdam	
r	L30 class	LZ78	–	L34	(Super-Zeppelin)	Friedrichshafen	(Löwenthal)
r	L30 class	LZ79	–	L41		Staaken	
r	L30 class	LZ80	–	L35		Friedrichshafen	
q	L20 class	LZ81	LZ111	–	–	Potsdam	
r	L30 class	LZ82	–	L36	(Super-Zeppelin)	Friedrichshafen	
r	L30 class	LZ83	LZ113	–		Staaken	
r	L30 class	LZ84	–	L38		Friedrichshafen	(Löwenthal)
r	L30 class	LZ85	–	L45		Staaken	
r	L30 class	LZ86	–	L39		Friedrichshafen	
r	L30 class	LZ87	–	L47		Staaken	
r	L30 class	LZ88	–	L40		Friedrichshafen	
r	L30 class	LZ89	–	L50		Staaken	
r	L30 class	LZ90	LZ120	–	*Ausonia*	Friedrichshafen	(Löwenthal)
s	–	LZ91	–	L42	(Height-climber)	,,	
s	–	LZ92	–	L43		,,	
t	–	LZ93	–	L44		,,	(Löwenthal)
t	–	LZ94	–	L46		,,	
u	L48 class	LZ95	–	L48		,,	
u	L48 class	LZ96	–	L49		,,	(Löwenthal)
u	L48 class	LZ97	–	L51		,,	
u	L48 class	LZ98	–	L52		Staaken	
u	L48 class	LZ99	–	L54		,,	
v	L53 class	LZ100	–	L53		Friedrichshafen	
v	L53 class	LZ101	–	L55		,,	(Löwenthal)
w	–	LZ102	–	L57	Afrika-Zeppelin	,,	
v	L53 class	LZ103	–	L56	(Height-climber)	Staaken	
w	–	LZ104	–	L59	Afrika-Zeppelin	,,	
v	L53 class	LZ105	–	L58	(Height-climber)	Friedrichshafen	
v	L53 class	LZ106	–	L61		,,	
v	L53 class	LZ107	–	L62	*Italia*	,,	(Löwenthal)
v	L53 class	LZ108	–	L60		Staaken	
v	L53 class	LZ109	–	L64		,,	
v	L53 class	LZ110	–	L63		Friedrichshafen	
v	L53 class	LZ111	–	L65		,,	(Löwenthal)
x	L70 class	LZ112	–	L70	–	,,	
x	L70 class	LZ113	–	L71	–	,,	
x	L70 class	LZ113A	–	L71	–	,,	
x	L70 class	LZ114	–	L72	*Dixmude*	,,	(Löwenthal)
–	L100 class	LZ115	Not built	L100	–		
x	L70 class	LZ116	Not completed	L73	–		
x	L70 class	LZ117	Not completed	L74	–		

Design Type	Class	Works Number	Designation Army	Navy	Name/ remarks	Built at
x	L70 class	LZ118	Not completed	L75	–	
–	L100 class (?)	LZ119	Not built	–	–	
y	–	LZ120	–	–	Bodensee	Friedrichshafen
y	–	LZ120A	–	–	Bodensee/ Méditerranée	,,
y	–	LZ121	–	–	Nordstern/Esperia	,,
–	–	LZ122	Not built	–	–	
–	–	LZ123	Not built	–	–	
–	–	LZ124	Not built	–	–	
–	–	LZ125	Not built	–	'Hensley Airship'	
–	–	LZ126	–	ZR-3	Los Angeles	Friedrichshafen
–	–	LZ127	–	–	Graf Zeppelin	,,
–	–	LZ128	Not built	–	–	
–	–	LZ129	–	–	Hindenburg	,,
–	–	LZ130	–	–	Graf Zeppelin II	,,
–	–	LZ131	Not built			

NOTE: Suffix A has been shown on some Zeppelin Works Numbers to indicate airships with lengthened hulls. At the time, the suffix was not always used.

Germany: Schütte-Lanz

Design Type	Class	Works Number	Designation Army	Navy	Remarks	Built at
'a'	–	S.L.1	–	–	–	Rheinau (Mannheim)
'b'	–	S.L.2	S.L. II	–	–	,,
'b'	–	S.L.2*	S.L. II	–	–	,,
'c'1	S.L.3 class	S.L.3	–	S.L.3	(Million cu ft)	,,
'c'2	S.L.3 class	S.L.4	–	S.L.4		Sandhofen (Mannheim)
'c'3	S.L.3 class	S.L.5	S.L. V	–		Darmstadt
'd'1	S.L.6 class	S.L.6	–	S.L.6	–	Mockau (Leipzig)
'd'2	S.L.6 class	S.L.7	S.L. VII	–	–	Rheinau
'e'1	S.L.8 class	S.L.8	–	S.L.8	–	Mockau
'e'2	S.L.8 class	S.L.9	–	S.L.9	–	,,
'e'3	S.L.8 class	S.L.10	S.L. X	–	–	Rheinau
'e'4	S.L.8 class	S.L.11	S.L. XI	–	–	Mockau
'e'5	S.L.8 class	S.L.12	–	S.L.12	–	Zeesen
'e'6	S.L.8 class	S.L.13	S.L. XIII	–	–	Mockau
'e'7	S.L.8 class	S.L.14	–	S.L.14	–	Rheinau
'e'8	S.L.8 class	S.L.15	S.L. XV	–	–	,,
'e'9	S.L.8 class	S.L.16	S.L. XVI	–	–	Mockau
'e'10	S.L.8 class	S.L.17	S.L. XVII	–	–	Zeesen
'e'11	S.L.8 class	S.L.18	S.L. XVIII	–	Not completed	
'e'12	S.L.8 class	S.L.19	S.L. XIX	–	Not completed	
'f '1	S.L.20 class	S.L.20	–	S.L.20	(Two million cu ft)	Rheinau
'f '2	S.L.20 class	S.L.21	S.L. XXI	–		Zeesen
'f '3	S.L.20 class	S.L.22	–	S.L.22		Rheinau
'g'1	–	S.L.23	Design only	–	–	
'g'2	–	S.L.24	Not completed	–	–	
'h'	–	S.L.25(?)	Project only	–	Atlantic	

* Lengthened

Germany: Schwarz

Type	Built at	Remarks
No.1	Volkhov, near St Petersburg	Did not fly
No.2	Tempelhof, Berlin	Crashed on first flight

France: Zodiac

Type	Built at	Remarks
13 Spiess	Saint-Cyr, Paris	
13A Spiess		Type 13 lengthened

United Kingdom

Manufacturer	Class	Designation	Name/Registration	Built at
Vickers	–	No.1	*Mayfly*	Barrow-in-Furness
Vickers	9 class	No.9	–	,,
Armstrong Whitworth		No.14	Not built	
Armstrong Whitworth		No.15	Not built	
Vickers	23 class	No.23	–	Barrow-in-Furness
Beardmore	23 class	No.24	–	Inchinnan
Armstrong Whitworth	23 class	No.25	–	Selby
Vickers	23 class	R26	–	Barrow-in-Furness
Beardmore	23X class	R27	–	Inchinnan
Beardmore/Vickers	23X class	R28	Not completed	
Armstrong Whitworth		R29	–	Selby
Armstrong Whitworth		R30	Not completed	
Short Brothers	31 class	R31	–	Cardington
Short Brothers	31 class	R32	–	,,
Armstrong Whitworth	33 class	R33	G-FAAG	Selby
Beardmore	33 class	R34	–	Inchinnan
Armstrong Whitworth		R35	Not completed	
Beardmore	36 class	R36	G-FAAF	Inchinnan
Short Brothers/Royal Airship Works		R37	Not completed	
Royal Airship Works	38 class	R38	ZR-2	Cardington
Armstrong Whitworth		R39	Not completed	
Armstrong Whitworth		R40	Not completed	
Beardmore		R41	Not built	
Vickers	80 class	R80	–	Barrow-in-Furness
Vickers		R81	Not built	
Airship Guarantee Co	–	R100	G-FAAV	Howden
Royal Airship Works	–	R101	G-FAAW	Cardington
Royal Airship Works	–	R101*	G-FAAW	,,
Royal Airship Works	–	R102	Project only	

* Lengthened

United States of America

Manufacturer	Works Number	USN Designation	Name	Built at
Naval Aircraft Factory	–	ZR-1	*Shenandoah*	Lakehurst
Royal Airship Works	R38	ZR-2	–	Cardington
Zeppelin	LZ126	ZR-3	*Los Angeles*	Friedrichshafen
Goodyear-Zeppelin	GZ-1	ZRS4	*Akron*	Akron
Goodyear-Zeppelin	GZ-2	ZRS5	*Macon*	,,
Metalclad	A8282	ZMC-2	*'Tin Ship'*	Detroit

Appendix 7 Rigid Airship Projects

This book is concerned with the approximately fifty different types of rigid airship which were built and flown between 1893 and 1940. Account has not been taken of the numerous designs which were projected or partly built in the years before 1893. In addition no mention has been made of projects which appeared alongside the successful programmes but which failed themselves to achieve success. Nor has attention been given to the relatively insignificant projects which have appeared since 1940.

Early Proposals

Ideas for the construction of controllable lighter-than-air vessels began to appear soon after the first practical balloons were successfully demonstrated in 1783. Envelopes of better aerodynamic shape than the spherical balloon were the obvious first step (Meusnier, 1784). A stiffened (semi-rigid) envelope (Lippich, 1812) was another. Numerous projects up to the end of the Nineteenth Century proposed large, often cylindrical, metal hulls with conical ends (Prosper Mellor, 1851, Ganswindt, 1883 and Boyman, 1886). The idea of a metal envelope covered in sheet copper (Dupuis-Delcourt, 1843) or other metal was a popular formula although it seemed impractical for reasons of weight until the suggested use of aluminium (Schwarz, 1884 and Stedman, 1888). A number of pioneers proposed a sectional envelope (Cayley, 1837) or one containing numerous separate gas cells (Vanaisse, 1863 and Spiess, 1873). Other useful ideas, later incorporated in many successful airships, were the rigid attachment of car to envelope (Kramp, 1785) and the mounting of propellers on the sides of the hull (Yon, 1865).

The establishment in the 1870s of government committees in several countries to study the military possibilities of aeronautics provided a significant impetus to more practical airship projects. Thus, in 1873, Count Zeppelin first began to think about airships and soon produced his initial 'flying-train' idea and his long, cylindrical configuration. Within ten years Schwarz was proposing his aluminium airship.

Uncompleted Projects

At the peak of rigid airship development during the First World War there were four design teams – Zeppelin, Schütte-Lanz, Vickers and the British Admiralty – active in Germany and Britain. In the early 1920s the Schütte-Lanz team was wound up. Its loss was compensated in the United States by the formation of a team at the Naval Aircraft Factory in Philadelphia and at Lakehurst. In Britain the team at the Admiralty was amalgamated with a small group from Short Brothers (which had designed the wooden R31 and R32) to form the Royal Airship Works drawing office at Cardington. The Vickers team was also in existence still and became the design office of the Airship Guarantee Company, a Vickers subsidiary, after the launching of the 1924–30 British rigid airship programme. After the R101 disaster in 1930 this programme was abandoned.

Zeppelin in Germany and Goodyear-Zeppelin in the United States survived but only until the end of the decade. All these organisations were primarily concerned with the designs described in this book. However, an important part of their effort was devoted to programmes which were never completed. Some of these are listed here.

Zeppelin: LZ115 (L66), LZ116 (L68), LZ117 (L73), LZ118 (L67), LZ119 (L69 or L100), LZ122, LZ123, LZ124, LZ125, 'Hensley Airship', LZ128, LZ175 (108,000 cu m), Zeppelin Types 1-5, LZ131, LZ132.

Schütte-Lanz: S.L. Type 'g'1, S.L. Type 'g'2, S.L. Atlantic.

Vickers: Mayfly successor, Nos.14 and 15, R28, R81, Vickers Types I–IV.

Admiralty: 'A' Design, 'Y' Class.

US Naval Aircraft Factory: US Navy JNAB design (1917), USN No.60, Burgess 'Ultimate Airship', Burgess ZRV.

Royal Airship Works: (out of Admiralty and Shorts). Short projects in 1916 and 1918, R102, R103, R104.

Airship Guarantee Company: (out of Vickers), R100 development, AGC Atlantic project.

Goodyear-Zeppelin: ZR-6, ZRN.

Appendix 8
Atlantic Zeppelin Service Schedules

The following pages are reproductions of schedules published in 1936 and 1937 by Deutsche Zeppelin-Reederei.
1. Europe–South America schedules published March 1936
2. Europe–South America schedules published June 1936
3. Note on *Hindenburg* sailings and timetable cover June 1936
4. Sailings to United States and South America published March 1937

South America Sailing Schedule of the Deutsche Zeppelin-Reederei 1936

		EUROPE — SOUTH AMERICA						SOUTH AMERICA — EUROPE					
		Service of the DEUTSCHE ZEPPELIN-REEDEREI			Airplane Connections maintained by SYNDICATO CONDOR Ltda. (3 motored Junkers planes type Ju 52)						Service of the DEUTSCHE ZEPPELIN-REEDEREI		
Sailing No.	Types of Air Mail carried: LC = first class mail, printed matter and parcels post; AOP = only printed matter and parcels post	Frankfort — Monday/Tuesday Leave	Recife (Pernambuco) — Thursday Arrive Leave	Rio de Janeiro — Friday Arrive	Rio de Janeiro — Sunday morning Leave	Montevideo Buenos Aires — Sunday afternoon Arrive	Santiago — Monday noon Arrive	Santiago — Wednesday morning Leave	Buenos Aires Montevideo — Thursday morning Leave	Rio de Janeiro — Thursday afternoon Arrive	Rio de Janeiro — Saturday evening Leave	Recife (Pernambuco) — Sunday/Monday Arrive Leave	Frankfort (or Friedrichshafen) — Thursday Friday Arrive
1	AOP	March 30/31¹)	April 2	April 3	April 5	April 5	April 6	April 1	April 2	April 2	April 5 (by exception Sunday)	April 6/7 (by exc. Monday/Tuesday)	April 9/10¹)
2	AOP	April 13/14	April 16	April 17	April 19	April 19	April 20	April 15	April 16	April 16	April 18	April 19/20	April 23/24
3	AOP	April 27/28	April 30	May 1	May 3	May 3	May 4	April 29	April 30	April 30	May 2	May 3/4	May 7/8
4	AOP	May 11/12	May 14	May 15	May 17	May 17	May 18	May 13	May 14	May 14	May 16	May 17/18	May 21/22¹)
5	AOP	May 25/26	—	May 29	May 31	May 31	June 1	May 27	May 28	May 28	May 30	—	June 4/5¹)
6	AOP	June 8/9	June 11	June 12	June 14	June 14	June 15	June 10	June 11	June 11	June 13	June 14/15	June 18/19
		Wednesday/Thursday Leave	Saturday Arrive Leave	Sunday Arrive	Probable dates for subsequent sailings, subject to change.						Wednesday evening or Thursday evening Leave	Thursday/Friday Arrive Leave	Monday Tuesday Arrive
7	LC	June 24/25	June 27	June 28							July 1	July 2/3	July 6/7
8	LC	July 8/9	July 11	July 12	Airplane connections on basis similar to that given above. Exact dates will be announced later.						July 15	July 16/17	July 20/21¹)
9 Olympic Sailing	AOP	July 20/21 (by exception Monday/Tuesday)	—	July 24 (by exception Friday)							July 25 (by exception Saturday)	—	July 30 (by exception Thursday)
10	LC	July 29/30	August 1	August 2							August 5	August 6/7	August 10/11
11	LC	August 12/13	August 15	August 16							August 19	August 20/21	August 24/25¹)
12	LC	August 26/27	—	August 30							September 3	—	September 7/8¹)
13	LC	September 9/10	Sept. 12	September 13							September 16	Sept. 17/18	September 21/22
14	LC	September 23/24	Sept. 26	September 27							September 30	October 1/2	October 5/6
15	LC	October 7/8	October 10	October 11							October 14	Oct. 15/16	October 19/20¹)

7 more trips to South America (No. 16—22) are to follow largely at weekly intervals according to a similar schedule; final dates will be announced later.

¹) Possibly Friedrichshafen instead of Frankfort

Airplane Connections in Europe: To and from Frankfort (airplane and Zeppelin airport) by the regular services operated by the Deutsche Lufthansa; in the case of arrival at Friedrichshafen special airplanes of the Deutsche Lufthansa are at disposal for connection to Stuttgart and Berlin.

Airship Service: The South America service is principally maintained by the "Graf Zeppelin", while the LZ 129 is also making a few trips to South America. Information can be obtained at the offices of the Deutsche Zeppelin-Reederei and at all travel bureaus.

The **airships depart** from the Airplane and Zeppelin Airport Rhine-Main near Frankfort o. M. in the case of trips No. 2 – 6 and No. 9 during the night from Monday to Tuesday, in the case of trips No. 7 – 8 and No. 10—22 during the night from Wednesday to Thursday (at about midnight). On the day of embarkation passengers assemble at the Hotel Frankfurter Hof in Frankfort at about 6 P.M.

Intermediate landings at Seville will only be made when necessary.

Fares (including meals and tips):
Frankfort – Pernambuco   RM 1400.—
Frankfort – Rio de Janeiro RM 1500.—

Rio de Janeiro–Montevideo (Airplane Connections) . RM 300.—
Rio de Janeiro–Buenos Aires (Airplane Connections) . RM 320.—
Rio de Janeiro–Santiago (Airplane Connections) . . RM 500.—

Round-Trip Fares: 20% reduction on return fare of round-trip tickets when purchased in advance. Round-trip tickets good for 12 months. This also applies to airplane connections.

Children's Rates: Children, if ordinary berth is not required, up to 6 years pay one quarter fare; up to 12 years half fare.

Baggage: 120 kilos (264 pounds) of baggage will be carried free on each ticket 20 k los (44 pounds) of this baggage allowance may be carried by the airship and the balance of 100 kilos by a German steamship.

Air Mail and Air Express: Use the Zeppelin service for your urgent printed matter and parcels post. Inquire at any post office. For Air Express rates and information ask for our special folder.

For special Zeppelin Trips to the United States see last page!

South America Sailing Schedule of the Deutsche Zeppelin-Reederei 1936

EUROPE — SOUTH AMERICA

Sailing No.	Types of Air Mail carried: LC = first class mail, printed matter and parcels post. AOP = only printed matter and parcels post	Service of the Deutsche Zeppelin-Reederei Frankfort (Wednesday/Thursday Leave)	Recife (Pernambuco) (Saturday Arrive Leave)	Rio de Janeiro (Sunday Arrive)	Airplane Connections maintained by Syndicato Condor Ltda. Rio de Janeiro (Monday Leave)	Porto Alegre (Monday Arrive)	Porto Alegre (Tuesday Leave)	Montevideo Buenos Aires (Tuesday Arrive)
7	LC	24/25 June	27 June	28 June	29 June	29 June	30 June	30 June
8	LC	8/9 July	11 July	12 July	13 July	13 July	14 July	14 July
9	AOP Olympic Sailing	20/21 July (by except. Monday/Tuesd.)	—	24 July (by exception Friday)	26 July	26 July (by exception Sunday)	26 July	26 July
10	LC	29/30 July	1 August	2 August	3 Aug.	3 Aug.	4 Aug.	4 Aug.
11	LC	12/13 August (by exception from Friedrichshafen)	15 August	16 August	17 Aug.	17 Aug.	18 Aug.	18 Aug.
12	LC	26/27 August	—	30 August	31 Aug.	31 Aug.	1 Sept.	1 Sept.
13	LC	9/10 Sept.	12 Sept.	13 September	14 Sept.	14 Sept.	15 Sept.	15 Sept.
14	LC	23/24 Sept.	26 Sept.	27 September	28 Sept.	28 Sept.	29 Sept.	29 Sept
15	LC	7/8 October	10 October	11 October	12 Oct.	12 Oct.	13 Oct.	13 Oct.
16	LC	21/22 October	—	25 October	26 Oct.	26 Oct.	27 Oct.	27 Oct.
17	LC	28/29 October	31 October	1 November	2 Nov.	2 Nov.	3 Nov.	3 Nov.
18	LC	4/5 November	—	8 November	9 Nov.	9 Nov.	10 Nov.	10 Nov.
19	LC	11/12 Nov.	14 Nov.	15 November	16 Nov.	16 Nov.	17 Nov.	17 Nov.
20	LC	18/19 Nov.	—	22 November	23 Nov.	23 Nov.	24 Nov.	24 Nov.
21	LC	25/26 Nov.	28 Nov.	29 November	30 Nov.	30 Nov.	1 Dec.	1 Dec.
22	LC	2/3 December	—	6 December	7 Dec.	7 Dec.	8 Dec.	8 Dec.

Subject to change without notice.

SOUTH AMERICA — EUROPE

Sailing No.	Airplane Connections maintained by Syndicato Condor Ltda. Buenos Aires Montevideo (Tuesday Leave)	Porto Alegre (Tuesday Arrive)	Porto Alegre (Wednesday Leave)	Rio de Janeiro (Wednesday Arrive)	Service of the Deutsche Zeppelin-Reederei Rio de Janeiro (Wednesday or Thursday Leave)	Recife (Pernambuco) (Thursday/Friday Arrive Leave)	Frankfort (Monday/Tuesday Arrive)
7	30 June	30 June	1 July	1 July	1 July	2/3 July	6/7 July
8	14 July	14 July	15 July	15 July	15 July	16/17 July	20/21 July
9	23 July	23 July (by exception Thursday)	23 July	23 July	25 July (by exception Saturday)	—	30 July (by exception Thursday)
10	4 Aug.	4 Aug.	5 Aug.	5 Aug.	5 August	6/7 August	10/11 August (by exception arr. Friedrichshafen)
11	18 Aug.	18 Aug.	19 Aug.	19 Aug.	19 August	20/21 Aug.	24/25 August
12	1 Sept.	1 Sept.	2 Sept.	2 Sept.	3 September	—	7/8 September
13	15 Sept.	15 Sept.	16 Sept.	16 Sept.	16 September	17/18 Sept.	21/22 Sept.
14	29 Sept	29 Sept	30 Sept.	30 Sept.	30 September	1/2 October	5/6 October
15	13 Oct.	13 Oct.	14 Oct.	14 Oct.	14 October	15/16 Oct.	19/20 October
16	27 Oct.	27 Oct.	28 Oct.	28 Oct.	29 October	—	2/3 Nov.
17	3 Nov.	3 Nov.	4 Nov.	4 Nov.	4 November	5/6 Nov.	9/10 Nov.
18	10 Nov.	10 Nov.	11 Nov.	11 Nov.	12 November	—	16/17 Nov.
19	17 Nov.	17 Nov.	18 Nov.	18 Nov.	18 November	19/20 Nov.	23/24 Nov.
20	24 Nov.	24 Nov.	25 Nov.	25 Nov.	26 November	—	30 Nov./1 Dec
21	1 Dec.	1 Dec.	2 Dec.	2 Dec.	2 December	3/4 Dec.	7/8 Dec.
22	8 Dec.	8 Dec.	9 Dec.	9 Dec.	10 December	—	14/15 Dec.

Subject to change without notice.

Airship Service: The South America service is principally maintained by the LZ 127 "Graf Zeppelin", while the LZ 129 "Hindenburg" will probably make trips No. 9, 12, 16, 18, 20, 22. Information can be obtained at the offices of the Deutsche Zeppelin-Reederei and at all travel bureaus.

The airships depart from the Airplane and Zeppelin Airport Rhine-Main near Frankfort o.M. in the case of trip **No. 9 by exception during the night from Monday to Tuesday.** In the case of trips **No. 7—8 and No. 10—22 during the night from Wednesday to Thursday.** On the day of embarkation passengers assemble at the Hotel Frankfurter Hof in Frankfort: Hof in Frankfort after 5 P. M., in the case of trip No. 11 at the kurgarten-Hotel at Friedrichshafen a. B.

Intermediate landings at Seville will only be made when necessary, i. e. if at least 4 passengers have been booked for Seville.

Fares

Frankfort Recife (Pernambuco) RM 1400.— , Frankfort — Rio de Janeiro RM 1500.—

for the Zeppelin Service (including meals and tips)
Recife (Pernambuco) RM 1400.— , Frankfort — Rio de Janeiro RM 1500.—

Airplane Connections maintained by Syndicato Condor Ltda.
Rio de Janeiro — Montevideo ..... RM 330.—
Rio de Janeiro — Buenos Aires ..... RM 350.—
Passengers using this connecting service stop overnight at Porto Alegre. Hotel expenses and transportation between airport and hotel are included in passenger fares.
Subject to change without notice.

Airplane Connections to the West Coast
Rio de Janeiro — Santiago RM 375.— plus $100.—
(at prevailing rate of exchange), including hotel expenses in Porto Alegre and Buenos Aires.
From Buenos Aires to Santiago by regular air service, starting from Buenos Aires on Wednesday, returning from Santiago to Buenos Aires on Sunday.

Subject to change without notice.

Airplane Connections in Europe: To and from Frankfort o. M. (Airplane and Zeppelin Airport) and Friedrichshafen by the regular services operated by the Deutsche Lufthansa.

Round-Trip Fares: 20% reduction on return fare of round-trip tickets when purchased in advance. Round-trip tickets good for 12 months. This also applies to airplane connections.

Children's Rates: Children, if ordinary berth is not required, up to 6 years pay one-quarter fare; up to 12 years half fare.

Baggage: 120 kilos (264 pounds) of baggage will be carried free on any ticket. 20 kilos (44 pounds) of this baggage allowance may be carried by the airship and the balance of 100 kilos by a German steamship.

Air Mail and Air Express: Use the fast and reliable Zeppelin service for your urgent letters, printed matter and parcels post. Inquire at any post office. For Air Express rates and information ask for our special folder.

For special Zeppelin Trips to the United States see last page.

1937 Special Sailings of the Deutsche Zeppelin-Reederei to the United States

Europe–North America

Airplane connections from all points in Europe are maintained by the regular services of the Deutsche Lufthansa and other European air-lines. Passengers from principal European cities arrive in Frankfort in time by starting their air journey on the day of airship sailing.

Subject to change

Service of the Deutsche Zeppelin-Reederei

Voyage No.:	1	2	3	4	5	6	7	8	9	10	11	12	13	14	15	16	17	18
Airship:	Hinden-burg	Hinden-burg	Hinden-burg	Hinden-burg	Hinden-burg	Hinden-burg	Hinden-burg	Hinden-burg	Hinden-burg	Hinden-burg	Hinden-burg	Hinden-burg	Hinden-burg	Hinden-burg	Hinden-burg	Hinden-burg	Hinden-burg	Hinden-burg
Leave Frankfort for New York (westbound) [For embarkation see last page.]	Monday/Tuesday 3/4 May	Tuesday/Wednes-day 11/12 May	Tuesday/Wednes-day 22/23 May	Saturday/Sunday 2/3 June	Saturday/Sunday 12/13 June	Tuesday/Wednes-day 22/23 June	Saturday/Sunday 3/4 July	Sunday/Monday 11/12 July	Wednes-day/Thursday	Friday/Saturday 20/21 Aug.	Friday/Saturday 27/28 Aug.	Friday/Saturday 3/4 Sept.	Friday/Saturday 13/14 Sept.	Friday/Saturday 17/18 Sept.	Tuesday/Wednes-day 28/29 Sept.	Friday/Saturday 8/9 Oct.	Tuesday/Wednes-day 19/20 Oct.	Saturday/Sunday 30/31 Oct.
Arrive New York (Lakehurst)	Thursday/Friday 6/7 May	Friday/Saturday 14/15 May	Tuesday/Wednes-day 25/26 May	Saturday/Sunday 5/6 June	Tuesday/Wednes-day 15/16 June	Friday/Saturday 25/26 June	Tuesday/Wednes-day 6/7 July	Wednes-day/Thursday 14/15 July		Monday/Tuesday 23/24 Aug.	Monday/Tuesday 30/31 Aug.	Monday/Tuesday 6/7 Sept.	Monday/Tuesday 13/14 Sept.	Friday/Saturday 20/21 Sept.	Friday/Saturday 1/2 Oct.	Monday/Tuesday 11/12 Oct.	Friday/Saturday 22/23 Oct.	Tuesday/Wednes-day 2/3 Nov.

Preliminary schedule, subject to change without notice. (columns 13–18)

Service of the Deutsche Zeppelin-Reederei — North America–Europe

Voyage No.:	1	2	3	4	5	6	7	8	9	10	11	12	13	14	15	16	17	18
Leave New York (Lakehurst) for Frankfort (eastbound)	Thurs-day/Friday 6/7 May	Friday/Saturday 14/15 May	Tuesday/Wednes-day 25/26 May	Saturday/Sunday 5/6 June	Friday/Saturday 15/16 June	Tuesday/Wednes-day 25/26 June	Tuesday/Wednes-day 6/7 July	Saturday/Sunday 14/15 July	Friday/Saturday 17/18 July	Monday/Tuesday 23/24 Aug.	Monday/Tuesday 30/31 Aug.	Monday/Tuesday 6/7 Sept.	Monday/Tuesday 13/14 Sept.	Monday/Tuesday 16/17 Sept.	Friday/Saturday 1/2 Oct.	Monday/Tuesday 11/12 Oct.	Monday/Tuesday 22/23 Oct.	Tuesday/Wednes-day 2/3 Nov.
Arrive Frankfort	Sunday/Monday 9/10 May	Monday/Tuesday 17/18 May	Friday/Saturday 28/29 May	Tuesday/Wednes-day 8/9 June	Monday/Tuesday 18/19 June	Friday/Saturday 28/29 June	Friday/Saturday 9/10 July	Saturday/Sunday 17/18 July	Thurs-day/Friday	Thurs-day/Friday 26/27 Aug.	Thurs-day/Friday 2/3 Sept.	Thurs-day/Friday	Thurs-day/Friday 16/17 Sept.	Thurs-day/Friday 20/21 Sept.	Monday/Tuesday 4/5 Oct.	Thurs-day/Friday 14/15 Oct.	Friday/Saturday 25/26 Oct.	Friday/Saturday 5/6 Nov.

Fares (including meals and tips) Frankfort–Lakehurst: Westward voyages No 1–8, No 15–18 and eastward voyages No 9–18 RM 1000.—, single cabins RM 1700.—; westward voyages No 9–14, and eastward voyages No 1–9 RM 1125.—, single cabins RM 1875.—, (season rates). The free baggage allowance for 1937 has been increased to 30 kg (66 pounds) per person. For further details regarding fares, reductions, etc. see last page.

Special airplanes of the American Air Lines are maintaining the fastest connection between the Lakehurst Airship Port and Newark, the airport of New York, in about 20 minutes flying time. The fare is $ 6.— or RM. 15.— per person, including baggage and automobile conveyance from Newark to New York City.

1937 Schedule for South American Service of the Deutsche Zeppelin-Reederei

Europe–South America

Airplane connections from all points in Europe are maintained by the regular services of the Deutsche Lufthansa and other European air-lines. Passengers from principal European cities arrive in Frankfort in time by starting their air journey on the day of airship sailing.

Service of the Deutsche Zeppelin-Reederei

Voyage No.:	1	2	3	4	5	6	7	8	9	10	11	12	13	14	15
Airship:	Hinden-burg	Graf Zeppelin	Graf Zeppelin	Graf Zeppelin	Graf Zeppelin	Graf Zeppelin	Graf Zeppelin	Graf Zeppelin	Graf Zeppelin	Graf Zeppelin	Graf Zeppelin	Graf Zeppelin	Graf Zeppelin	Graf Zeppelin	Graf Zeppelin
Leave Frankfort	Tuesday evening 16 March														
Leave Friedrichshafen on Lake Constance		Tuesday evening 13 April	27 April	11 May	25 May	8 June	22 June	6 July	19 July Monday	3 Aug.	17 Aug.	31 Aug.	14 Sept.	28 Sept.	12 Oct.
Arrive and Leave Recife (Pernambuco)		Friday 16 April	30 April	14 May	28 May	11 June	25 June	9 July	*Provisional special trip of the airship between Rio de Janeiro and Buenos Aires	6 Aug.	20 Aug.	3 Sept.	17 Sept.	1 Oct.	15 Oct.
Arrive Rio de Janeiro	Satur-day 20 March	17 April	1 May	15 May	29 May	12 June	26 June	10 July	23 July Friday	7 Aug.	21 Aug.	4 Sept.	18 Sept.	2 Oct.	16 Oct.

Fares (including meals and tips) Frankfort-Recife RM 1600.—, single cabins RM 1600.—; Frankfort-Rio de Janeiro RM 1500.—, single cabins RM 2200.—;
For further details regarding fares, reductions, etc. see last page.

Direct Airplane Connections maintained by Syndicato Condor Ltda.

Porto Alegre / Montevideo / Buenos Aires		Sunday 21 March	18 April	2 May	16 May	30 May	13 June	27 June	11 July	'25 July	8 Aug.	22 Aug.	5 Sept.	19 Sept.	3 Oct.	17 Okt.
Santiago de Chile		Monday 22 March	19 April	3 May	17 May	31 May	14 June	28 June	12 July	26 July	9 Aug.	23 Aug.	6 Sept.	20 Sept.	4 Oct.	18 Oct.

South America–Europe

Service of the Deutsche Zeppelin-Reederei

Voyage No.:	1	2	3	4	5	6	7	8	9	10	11	12	13	14	15
Santiago de Chile		Sunday 21 March	18 April	2 May	16 May	30 May	13 June	27 June	11 July	'Satur-day 24 July	8 Aug.	22 Aug.	5 Sept.	19 Sept.	3 Okt.	17 Okt.
Buenos Aires / Montevideo / Porto Alegre		Monday 22 March	19 April	3 May	17 May	31 May	14 June	28 June	12 July	26 July	9 Aug.	23 Aug.	6 Sept.	20 Sept.	4 Oct.	18 Oct.
Leave Rio de Janeiro	Monday 22 March	19 April	3 May	17 May	31 May	14 June	28 June	12 July	27 July Tuesday	9 Aug.	23 Aug.	6 Sept.	20 Sept.	4 Oct.	18 Oct.
Arrive and Leave Recife (Pernambuco)	Tuesday 20 April	4 May	18 May	22/23 May	15 June	29 June	13 July	28 July	10 Aug.	24 Aug.	7 Sept.	21 Sept.	5 Oct.	19 Oct.	
Arrive Friedrichshafen on Lake Constance	Satur-day/Sunday 24/25 April	8/9 May	22/23 May	5/6 June	19/20 June	3/4 July	17/18 July			25/26 Sept.	9/10 Oct.				
Arrive Frankfort	Satur-day/Sunday 27/28 March								1/2 Aug. Sunday/Monday	28/29 Aug.	11/12 Sept.	23/24 Oct.	9/10 Oct.		

The free baggage allowance for 1937 has been increased to 50 kg (44 pou nds) per person.   For details regarding fares, reductions, etc see last page.

Upon arrival at Friedrichshafen a special airplane is operated from Friedrichshafen via Frankfort to Berlin. From Frankfort o. M. (Airplane and Zeppelin Airport Rhine-Main) airplane connections are maintained by the regular services of the Deutsche Lufthansa and other European air-lines. Inquire for the fastest air services. Special fare reductions are granted to round-trip passengers.

From Frankfort (Airplane and Zeppelin Airport Rhine-Main) airplane connections are maintained by regular services of the Deutsche Lufthansa and other European air-lines. Inquire for the fastest air services from Frankfort to Berlin and other points in Europe. Special fare reductions are granted to round-trip passengers.

Bibliography

Airships

Abbot, P *Airship*: Bath, 1973

Airship Guarantee Co. *Airship R100*: Howden, c.1928

Allen, H *The Story of the Airship*: Akron, 1932

— *The Story of the Airship (non-rigid)*: Akron, 1942

American Society of Naval Engineers, Vol XXXVIII, No.3, *Technical Aspects of the loss of the USS Shenendoah*, August, 1926

Amundsen, R and Ellsworth, L *The First Flight across the Polar Sea*: London, c.1927

Arneson, O *The Polar Adventure*: London, 1929

Bauer, M *Luftschiffhallen in Friedrichshafen*: Friedrichshafen, 1985

Beaubois, H *Airships*: London, 1974

Brandenfels, T von Buttlar, *Zeppelins over England*: London, 1931

Brigole, A *Santos Dumont*: Rio de Janeiro, 1943

Brooks, P W *Historic Airships*: London, 1973

Brossard, de *Lachez Tout*: Paris, 1956

Chamberlain, G *Airships – Cardington*: Lavenham, 1984

Clarke, B *The History of Airships*: London, 1961

Collier, B *The Airship*: London, 1974

Cooke, D C *Dirigibles that made History*: New York, 1962

Countryman, B *R100 in Canada*: Erin, 1982

Davy, M J B *Aeronautics: Lighter-than-Air Craft*: London, 1934

Dean, C (Ed) *Housing the Airship*: London, 1989

De Forge, L and Sazerac, Capt. *La Conquête de l'Air en Dirigeable*: Paris, 1910

Dene, S *Trail Blazing in the Skies*: Akron, 1943

Dick, H G, with Robinson, D H *Graf Zeppelin and Hindenburg*: Washington DC, 1985

D'Orcy, L *Airship Manual*: New York, 1917

Dudley, E *Monsters of the Purple Twilight*: London, 1960

Dumont, A Santos *My Airships*: London, 1904

Dürr, L *Zeppelin-Luftschiffbau*: Berlin, 1924

Eckener, H *Count Zeppelin*: London, 1938

— *My Zeppelins*: London, 1958

Ege, L *Balloons and Airships*: London, 1973

Engberding, Marine-Baurat *Luftschiff und Luftschiffahrt*: Berlin, 1926

Giudici, D *The Tragedy of the Italia*: London, 1928

Glines, C V *Lighter-than-Air Flight*: New York, 1965

Goldsmith, M *Zeppelin*: New York, 1931

Goodyear *Aerial Ambassadors*: Akron, 1967

Grieder, K *Zeppeline: Giganten der Lufte*: Zürich, 1971

Guttery, T E *Zeppelin: An Illustrated Life*: Aylesbury, 1973

Hansen, Z *The Goodyear Airships*: Bloomington, 1977

Hartcup, G *The Achievement of the Airship*: Newton Abbot, 1974

Hearne, R P *Airships in Peace and War*: London, 1910, 1916

Heiss, F *Das Zeppelin Buch*: Berlin, 1936

Higham, R *The British Rigid Airship, 1903–31*: London, 1961

Hildebrandt, A *Airships, Past and Present*: London, 1908

Hood, J F *The Story of Airships*: London, 1968

Hook, T *Shenandoah Saga*: Annapolis, 1973

— *Sky Ship, The Akron Era*: Baltimore, 1976

Jackson, R *Airships: In Peace and War*: London, 1971

Joux, E *Un Dirigeable Militaire*: Paris, 1931

Keller, C L *USS Shenandoah*: West Roxburg, Mass, 1965

Kinsey, G *Pulham Pigs*: Lavenham, 1988

Knight, R W *The Hindenburg Accident*: Washington DC, 1937, 1971

Leasor, J *The Millionth Chance*: London, 1957

Lehmann, E *Zeppelin*: London, 1937

— and Mingos, H *The Zeppelins*: London, 1927

Lewitt, E H *The Rigid Airship*: London, 1925

Litchfield, P W and Allen, H *Why has America no Rigid Airships?*: Riverside, 1976

Luschnath, H *Zeppelin-Weltfahrten*: Dresden, 1933

Maitland, E M *The Log of H.M.A.R34*: London, 1920

Marben, R *Zeppelin Adventures*: London, 1931

Masefield, Sir Peter *To Ride the Storm*: London, 1982

McKee, A *Disaster in the Arctic: Ice Crash*: St Albans, 1979

McKinty, A *The Father of British Airships*: London, 1972

McPhee, J *The Deltoid Pumpkin Seed*: New York, 1973

Meager, G F *Leaves from my Logbook*: Akron, 1961

— *My Airship Flights*: London, 1970

Meyer, P *Luftschiffe*: Koblenz, 1980

Mooney, M *The Hindenburg*: St Albans, 1974

Morison, F *War on Great Cities*: London, 1937

Morpurgo, J E *Barnes Wallis: A Biography*: London, 1972

Nielson, T *The Zeppelin Story*: London, 1955

Nobile, U *With the Italia to the North Pole*: London, 1930

— *My Polar Flights*: London, 1961

Norway, N S *Slide Rule: The Autobiography of an Engineer*: London, 1954

Pesci, G *The Italian Airships*: Modena, 1983

Poirier, J *Les Bombardements de Paris, 1914–18*: Paris, 1930

Polman, K *Zeppelins over England*: London, 1960

Pratt, H B *Commercial Airships*: London, 1920

Provan, J *Count Zeppelin, a System Builder*: Hellaheim, 1988

Rimell, R L *Zeppelin*: London, 1984

Robinson, D H *Giants in the Sky*: Henley-on-Thames, 1973

— *LZ129 Hindenburg*: Dallas, 1964

— *The Zeppelin in Combat 1912–18*: London, 1962

— and Keller, C L *Up Ship*: Annapolis, 1982

Role, M *L'Étrange Histoire des Zeppelins*: Paris, 1972

Rosendahl, C E *Up Ship!*: New York, 1931

— *What About the Airship?*: New York, 1938

Schiller, H von *Zeppelin*: Bad Godesberg, 1966

Schütte, J *Der Luftschiffbau, Schütte-Lanz, 1909–1925*: Munich, 1926

Sinclair, J A *Airships in Peace and War*: London, 1934

— *Famous Airships of the World*: London, 1959

Smith, R K *The Airships Akron and Macon*: Annapolis, 1965

Spanner, E F *About Airships*: London, 1929

— *Gentlemen Prefer Aeroplanes!*: London, 1928

— *The Tragedy of R101; Vols 1 and 2*: London, 1931

— *This Airship Business*: London, 1927

Sprigg, C *The Airship*: London, c.1931

Sumner, P H *The Science of Flight, Vol 1, Airship and Kite Balloons*: London, 1926

Tapper, O *Armstrong Whitworth Aircraft since 1913*: London, 1973

Tittel, L *Die Fahrten des LZ4, 1908*: Friedrichshafen, 1983

— *Graf Zeppelin – Leben und Werke*: Friedrichshafen, 1986

— *LZ129 Hindenburg*: Friedrichshafen, 1987

Toland, J *Ships in the Sky*: London, 1957

U.S. Navy Gas Engine School *Aircraft of Belligerents: 1914 Airships*: New York, 1914

Veeth, J G *Graf Zeppelin*: London, 1959

Ventry, Lord and Kolesnik, E M *Airship Development*: Huddersfield, 1976

— *Airship Saga*: Poole, 1982

Vissering, H *Zeppelin: The Story of a Great Achievement*: Chicago, 1922

Von Langsdorff, Dr Ing W *LZ127 Graf Zeppelin*: Frankfurt, 1928

Voyer, H *Les Ballons Dirigeables*: Paris

Whale, G *British Airships, Past, Present and Future*: London, 1919

Whitehouse, A *The Zeppelin Fighters*: London, 1966

Williams, T B *Airship Pilot No.28*: London, 1974

Wykeham, P *Santos Dumont*: London, 1962

Zeppelin *Zeppelin-Metallwerken GmbH*: Friedrichshafen, 1964

Balloons

Alexander, J *The Conquest of the Air*: London, 1902

Bacon, G *By Land and Sea*: London, 1900

— *The Dominion of the Air*: London, 1904

— *Balloons, Airships and Flying Machines*: London, c.1904

— *The Record of an Aeronaut*: London, 1907

— *All About Flying*: London, 1925

— *Memories of Land and Sky*: London, 1928

Baker, J A and Pritchard, N A *Balloons & Ballooning*: Princes Risborough, 1986

Bethrys, G *Les Aérostiers Militaires*: Paris, 1889

Butler, F H *5,000 Miles in a Balloon*: London, 1907

Broke-Smith, P W L *History of Early British Military Aeronautics*: Bath, 1968

Clément, P L *Montgolfières (Hot-Air Balloons)*: Paris, 1982

Cornish III, J J *The Air Arm of the Confederacy*: Richmond, Va, 1963

Coxwell, H *My Life and Balloon Experience: 1st and 2nd series*: London, 1889

Crouch, T D *The Eagle Aloft*: Washington DC, 1983

Dollfus, C *Balloons*: London, 1962

— *En Ballon*: Paris, 1962

Duhem, J *Histoire des Idées Aéronautiques avant Montgolfier*: Paris

— *Histoire de l'Arme Aérienne avant le Moteur*: Paris, 1964

— *Musée Aéronautiques avant Montgolfier*: Paris

Eiloart, A and Elstob, P *The Flight of the Small World*: London, 1959

Fisher, J *Airlift, 1870*: London, 1965

Gardiner, L *Man in the Clouds*: Edinburgh, 1963

Gibbs-Smith, C H *Ballooning*: London, 1948

— *Balloons*: London, 1956

Gillespie, G C *The Montgolfier Brothers and the Invention of Aviation*: Princeton, 1983

Glaisher, J *Travels in the Air*: London, 1871

Grover, G E and Beaumont, F *Military Ballooning, 1862*: Chatham, 1863

Haining, P *The Dream Machines*: London, 1972

Hardy, Sir Alister *Weekend with Willows*: Gloucester, 1986

Hodgson, J E *The First English Aeronaut*: London, 1928

Hoehling, M *Thaddeus Lowe: America's One-man Air Corps*: New York, 1958

Jackson, D D *The Aeronauts*: Alexandria, 1981

Jobe, J *The Romance of Ballooning*: London, 1971

Lachambre, H and Machuron, A *Andrée and his Balloon*: London, 1898

Lowe, T *America's One-Man Air Corps*: New York, 1958

Lunardi, V *Account of the First Aerial Voyage in England*: London, 1784

Marion, F *Wonderful Balloon Ascents*: London, c.1875

Norgaard, E *The Book of Balloons*: New York, 1970

Reynaud, M H *Les Frères Montgolfier*: Vals-les-Bains, 1982

Rolt, L T C *The Aeronauts*: London, 1966

Sims, L *Thaddeus Lowe*: New York, 1964

Smith, A *Throw Out Two Hands*: London, 1963

— *The Dangerous Sort*: London, 1979

Sundman, P O *The Flight of the Eagle*: New York, 1970

Swedish Society of Anthropology and Geography *Andrée's Story*: New York, 1930

— *Andrée Diaries*: Stockholm, 1931

Turnbull, C *Hot Air Ballooning*: London, 1970

Turnor, Hatton *Astra Castra*: London, 1865

Upson, R H and de Frost-Chandler, C *Free and Captive Balloons*: 1926

Watson, C M *Military Ballooning in the British Army, 1862–1902*: Aldershot, 1902

Yeatman, J *Daffodil and Golden Eagle*: St Albans, 1974

General Aeronautical History

Barnes, C H *Shorts Aircraft since 1909*: London, 1967

Berget, A *The Conquest of the Air*: London, 1909

Bonomo, O *L'Aviation Commerciale*: Paris, 1926

Brooks, P W *A History of Technology: Ch. 7, Aeronautics; Ch. 33, Aircraft and their Operation*: Oxford, 1954, 1978

Burden, W A M *The Struggle for Airways in Latin America*: New York, 1943

Chambe, R *Histoire de l'Aviation*: Paris, 1948

Cole, Christopher and Cheesman, E F *The Air Defence of Britain, 1914–1918*: London, 1984

Collinson, C and McDermott, F *Through Atlantic Clouds*: London, 1934

Commission Interalliée de Contrôle Aéronautique en Allemagne *Deuxième Partie: Raport Technique*: Chalais-Meudon, c.1921

Cuneo, J R *Winged Mars, Vols 1 and 2*: Harrisburg, PA, 1942

Davy, M J B *An Interpretive History of Flight*: London, 1937

Dollfus, C and Bouché, H *Histoire de l'Aéronautique*: Paris, 1932, 1942

Dollfus, C, Beaubois, H and Rougeron, C *L'Homme, l'Air et l'Espace*: Paris, 1965

Dwiggins, D *The Complete Book of Airships, Blimps and Hot Air Balloons*: Blue Ridge Summit, 1980

Encyclopedie par l'Image *L'Aviation*: Paris, 1929

Gamble, C F Snowden *The Story of a North Sea Air Station*: London, 1928

Gibbs-Smith, C H *A History of Flying*: London, 1953

— *Aviation: An Historical Survey from its Origins to the End of World War II*: London, 1970

— *Sir George Cayley*: London, 1968

Gibbs-Smith, C H, Lacey, G W B, Tuck, W J and O'Shea, W J *Aeronautics*: London, 1966

Gillies, J D and Wood, J L *Aviation in Scotland*: Glasgow, 1966

Grey, C G *History of the Air Ministry*: London, 1940

Grierson, J *Challenge to the Poles*: London, 1964

Hammerton, J *War in the Air*: London, 1936

Hart, C *The Dream of Flight*: London, 1972

— *The Prehistory of Flight*: Berkeley, 1985

Hodgins, E and Magoun, F A *Sky High*: Boston, 1929

Hodgson, J E *The History of Aeronautics in Great Britain*: London, 1924

Hogg, I V *Anti-Aircraft: A History of Air Defence*: London, 1978

Hoorebeeck, A van *La Conquête de l'Air, Vols 1 and 2*: Verviers, 1967

Jackson, G G *The World's Aeroplanes and Airships*: London, c.1929

Jones, N *The Origins of Strategic Bombing*: London, 1973

Joubert, Sir Philip *Birds and Fishes*: London, 1960

Lecornu, J *La Navigation Aérienne*: Paris, 1913

Loughead, V *Vehicles of the Air*: London, 1909

Merin, P *Conquest of the Skies*: London, 1938

Middleton, E *The Great War in the Air, Vols 1–4*: London, 1920

Morris, J *The German Air Raids on Great Britain, 1914–18*: London, 1920

'Neon' (Bernard Acworth) *The Great Delusion*: London, 1927

Neumann, G P *The German Air Force in the Great War*: London, 1920

Penrose, H *British Aviation*: London, 1967–80

Raleigh, Sir Walter and Jones, H A *The War in the Air, Vols 1–6*: London, 1922

Rawlinson, A *The Defence of London, 1915–18*: London, 1923

Roskill, S W *The Naval Air Service Vol 1, 1908–18*: London, 1969

Salt, A E W *Imperial Air Routes*: London, 1930

Saunders, H St G *Per Ardua: The Rise of British Air Power, 1911–39*: London, 1944

Saville-Sneath, R A *British Aircraft, Vol 2*: Harmondsworth, 1944

— *Aircraft of the US, Vol 2*: Harmondsworth, 1946

Sueter, M F *Airmen or Noahs*: London, 1928

Talbot, F A *The Aeroplanes and Dirigibles of War*: London, 1915

Taylor, J W R *A History of Aerial Warfare*: London, 1974

— *History of Aviation*: London, 1972

Thomson of Cardington, Lord *Air Facts and Problems*: London, 1927

Turner, C C *The Old Flying Days*: London, 1927

— *The Struggle in the Air, 1914–18*: London, 1919

Valentine, E S and Tomlinson, F L *Travels in Space*: London, 1902

Vivian, E C and Lockwood Marsh, W A *A History of Aeronautics*: London, 1921

Walker, P B *Early Aviation at Farnborough, Vol 1*: London, 1971

Ward, G H *Flight: Year – The Annual Picture History*: Los Angeles, 1953

Warner, E P *Aerostatics*: New York, 1926

Winchester, C *Wonders of World Aviation*: London, c.1937

Periodicals and Yearbooks

Aeronautical Journal, Journal of the Royal Aeronautical Society from 1897

Aeronautics, 1907–09

Flight, from 1909

The Aero, 1909–14

Aerocraft, 1909–10

The Airship, April–June 1934 to winter 1948–9

Buoyant Flight (formerly *Journal of the Wingfoot LTA Society*), from 1953

Journal of the American Aviation Historical Society, from 1956

Icare, No.46, summer–autumn 1968

— No.56, winter–spring 1971

Inside the Control Car Issue 29, September 1979

Jane, F T *All the World's Airships*, 1909: London

– *All the World's Aircraft*, from 1910: London

Index

The Index refers entirely to the text, the illustrations and the notes – not to the Appendices nor to the tables of data which appear at the end of each chapter and are largely self-indexing.
(Page numbers in italics indicate illustrations)